Dedicated to
Donald Nicholas "Mike" Nau, and Jim, Mick,
Amos, Miles, and Frances,
without whom, there is no adventure at all

THE LAST CADILLAC

a memoir

NANCY NAU SULLIVAN

Walrus Publishing | St. Louis, MO

Walrus Publishing
Saint Louis, MO 63110
Copyright © 2016 Nancy Nau Sullivan
All rights reserved.

For information, contact:
Walrus Publishing
An imprint of Amphorae Publishing Group
4168 Hartford Street, Saint Louis, MO 63116

Publisher's Note: This memoir is a work of imagination and truth.

Manufactured in the United States of America
Set in Adobe Garamond Pro
Interior designed by Kristina Blank Makansi
Cover Design by Kristina Blank Makansi

Library of Congress Control Number: 2016935414
ISBN-13: 978-1940442129

THE LAST CADILLAC

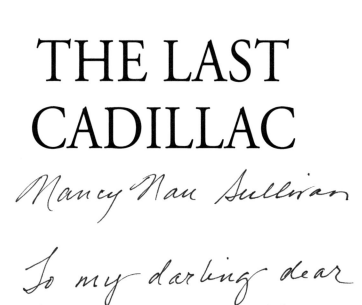

Nancy Nau Sullivan

*To my darling dear
Adventurer, Miles,
all my love,
Mom
5-5-16*

"To thine own self be true…"
– Shakespeare, and my mother, Pat Nau

1

OMG

My father reached for another cigarette, his fingernails scrabbling over the glass-top table. I lit his cigarette and then my own. We both took deep drags as I leaned over and brushed the ashes off the front of his jacket. We sat there on the patio of the condo under the grey Indiana sky. Silent. Smoking.

Time didn't seem to have an edge to it anymore; it just flowed out around me like dark water. I needed to breathe, so I smoked. It was a bad thing, sitting there smoking with my father, but bad felt normal. Everything was different now. My mind raced. My mother is dead. My marriage is dead. What am I going to do, Dad? What are *we* going to do?

My mother had only been gone a week. Her apricot roses withered in vases all over the condo, and I couldn't bring myself to throw them out. I cleaned around them, attacking piles of laundry and bills, getting rid of health-care equipment, pills, and crusty aluminum pans. But it didn't matter. I could not wash it all away. I kept reliving disaster. Along with losing my mother and facing my distraught father, my marriage was kaput. I had become: a divorced woman.

I had to get out of there, go somewhere—maybe back to Florida. Now.

The kids called it "The Adventure," and they kept after me about it everywhere I went.

"When are we going?" they demanded. "When?"

I told them, "Soon."

But that was not entirely true. "Soon" was stretching it. I had a to-do list, and Dad was right there at the top.

I lit another cigarette, then got up and flipped the soggy cushion on my chair. I sat back down. I was exhausted. All I wanted to do was sit there. Next to the cool, green golf course, one foot resting on a pot of ivy and petunias. The condo was dark, no one hurrying around, and finally, no more emergencies. The phone had stopped ringing. The front door locked everything out. It was quiet for now, but I didn't want to go back in there. Back inside, where all the memories, painful, again took over.

The chill did not drive us inside. As I remember that misty afternoon, it was like an Irish day, and I welcomed that. We all loved Ireland. The good memories.... I zipped my jacket to the neck and tucked my wet hair back behind my ears. Dad was snug in his khaki jacket and tweed hat decorated with the pins from Dublin and Killarney. The hat I gave him. Sometimes he was confused since the stroke, but never about whose hat it was and where he put it, along with the whereabouts of his coat and shoes. He was always ready to go, and it was usually me who took him there.

I wrapped my fingers around his and squeezed, but he was off in another world. I left him there. It wouldn't do any good to bring him into mine where I began to feel the stirrings of dread. I let go of Dad's hand and slumped in my chair. My siblings were coming over for "a family meeting." My brother, Jack, a tennis-playing, leather-wearing young millionaire; my sister, Julia, a meddling, nurse-Poppins who had a pill for everything; my sister, Lucy, a svelte, suit-wearing restaurateur who was five-star at getting the latest boy toy. I couldn't wait to see them and find out what sort of trouble we could get into this time. If there was one thing consistent about our relationship, it's that we disagreed on family matters. Sometimes we laughed. But mostly we disagreed, especially on any business having to do with Dad.

Even so, I was determined to work out some comfortable arrangement for Dad. We should talk calmly and productively, I told myself. Besides, I was the eldest, and I was responsible. They had to listen to me, and I should listen to them, which was like sticking needles in my eyeballs.

I laughed, but it sounded like a cross between hacking and choking.

Dad smiled. "What is it?"

"Nothing, Dad."

He patted my hand. "Well, it's good to hear you laugh."

Everything will be all right. No. Nothing will be all right. Nothing is right.

Florida. Yes. The more I thought about it, the more I wanted—and needed—to go back.

To the cottage. I dreamed of getting back to the cottage where we went every winter. The annual trip had always been the most glorious part of growing up, and I never grew out of it. I was like a migrating bird.

But if things didn't work out in Florida—and I could think of a number of reasons why they wouldn't, Dad's situation being number one—we'd be right back in Northwest Indiana. I hoped that wouldn't happen, because I liked sunshine and the beach and the idea of getting away from the Ex. So, until I found our own place, I'd take the kids to Anna Maria Island. To the family cottage.

For the time being, I was stuck in Indiana, juggling a part-time newswriting job, Dad, and the kids. Between the news assignments and feature stories about Russian baseball players and chili recipes, I took care of the bills and medical forms. The accountant and the lawyer helped, but someone needed to be there all the time with Dad.

I was torn. I should probably stay up north, but the idea was killing me.

The mist shifted to a cool drizzle, reducing the cigarette butts in the ashtray to a pile of dead brown minnows. I poked at them idly with a burnt match.

"What are you thinking, Dad?" I'd grown up on his common sense, and now was as good a time as any to hear some of it.

As soon as the words came out, it struck me that I'd hardly asked him how he felt during all the confusion since Mom got sick. I'd coddled him, and, frightfully, he had teetered along on that cane. But I didn't really talk with him. None of us did. Not during the whole year of misery. For a family that talked so much, we certainly didn't communicate very well.

"Dad."

"I'm ruminating." His short, straight eyelashes were wet with rain, or tears. I couldn't tell.

"Tell me, Dad."

"My Patsy, my Patsy. More than fifty years we had together. I never believed it would kill her."

"Dad, no one believed it."

"I had faith in the doctors … that they could cure it. But then she went so fast."

His shoulders began quaking up and down as he rumbled

along to the end of his sentence. I put my arm around him and rocked him a little. Sometimes I could get him back on track. Like jiggling a reluctant old machine. But it didn't work this time. He kept sobbing.

My father, the Navy commander. He shouldn't be crying.

"It's all right, all right," I said.

He covered his face with a handkerchief and held on to me. His grip was strong, but I was losing him, too. My parents. I could not hold onto either of them.

I straightened up, then promptly fell back into my chair, hit hard with memories of that day. The day my mother called.

"Gall bladder cancer!" she said.

I'd gripped the phone so hard my fingers cramped while she went on like she was talking about bad weather. "The technician was doing an ultrasound, and, out of the blue, he gasped. I suppose he shouldn't have done that!" Then, of all things, she laughed. "Gall bladder cancer! It sounds so unfashionable!"

I almost dropped the phone. I didn't laugh, but at the same time, I didn't think gall bladder cancer could be all that bad—certainly not terminal. Who needs a gall bladder?

"Mom! This is crazy!"

"I'd say so."

"Why don't they just take it out?"

"They can't," she said. "There's nothing they can do. I could go to the moon."

But we both knew, there was nowhere she could go. Nothing she could do. Nothing anyone could do. She died fourteen months later.

Until she was gone, though, she died little by little, in unexpected steps. One day, or even for a week, she seemed fine. Then she'd take another step down. After she died, I'd have dreams that the wake was inside a dark mahogany room filled with elaborate flowers and many people, but she just got up and walked out. Like nothing ever happened—like she was leaving a cocktail party at the country club. For a long time, when I was not dreaming, I still expected to see her come around the corner. She couldn't be dead. She was too alive. But then, no one knew what to expect when she came up with gall bladder cancer, least of all the doctors. They'd given her six to eighteen months. They just couldn't be "sure."

At first, I was so busy watching Mom, I didn't notice Dad's steadily deteriorating condition. It all happened so fast. Jack said Dad needed therapy, and maybe a pill or two. He insisted Dad had "stuck blood," which meant Dad had to be massaged and coaxed to get up out of his chair. Without physical activity, Jack was afraid we'd have a statue of a dad. Julia agreed with Jack, especially about the pills. The two of them never lost an opportunity to push pills on our parents. Julia shoved horse-size, orange pills on Mom (I still don't know what was in them). Fortunately, Mom couldn't swallow them. Jack even ordered shark cartilage and fruit extracts from Mexico.

Their pill pushing had become a creeping disease of its own. And even though I was alarmed, Julia and Jack wouldn't listen to me. It probably didn't help that I sounded like a cross between a harpy and a shrew.

Lucy, my sister the restaurant manager, on the other hand, didn't weigh in on the pill-taking. Most days, she was on duty at the Ritz, decked out in her suit and heels and pearls—one such day, stealthily watching Mel Gibson and his brother drink beer in the Atrium.

All the while, Mom was dying, Dad was going down hill, and my siblings and I were floundering in disagreement.

Except for one thing. I did agree with Jack about the exercise—one of the few things we all agreed on. Dad needed something, just not another pill.

Certainly no pill could cure Mom, and no pill would cure Dad, who was stricken with sadness at seeing his wife slowly die of cancer. With my father's brain in the condition it was, he needed a miracle, not another pill. Besides, his reaction to the drugs was exactly the opposite of the intended effect, which was to relieve anxiety, enable sleep, and increase appetite—in other words, to find a healthy "normal." Only, normal didn't exist. I couldn't find normal anywhere, and there was no sense in trying to induce it through pills.

As the days ticked on, I became more frustrated, trying to save Dad from my brother and sister, and the pills. Amitriptyline (according to the label), stated, "use in elderly is associated with increased risk, and safer alternatives may be available." That one added to Dad's confusion—and mine. The next pill, Prozac, didn't work. Yet, the doctor put him back on it. Paxil was another loser. It made him more restless than ever. But Melaril was the star of them all. Dad seemed worse than ever on that one.

In desperation, I called my cousin, Chuck, the pharmacist, when I found out Julia had steered Dad to that pill.

"My God, Nancy, why are they giving him Melaril? Is it that bad? That's what they give them at the end when they want them to sit there and be vegetables."

The drug made him fall down and wet himself, and he didn't know his children—except for me, whom he called "the old bitch." He called me that under the influence of the pills I hated, because I kept after him to remember things and go to the bathroom, and to try. Try, Dad. Try, try, try. I was the cheerleader of my dad. I believed he could do better if he tried harder. I did manage to get him off that pill, for starters, and I forced him to remember things, quizzed him, encouraged him daily.

One day I cornered Julia in the kitchen where she was arranging her mini-pharmacy in a cabinet next to the fridge. She shuffled a frightening array of pills in all colors. Then and there, I wondered, Does baby blue make you feel better than happy yellow?

"You know, Julia, the medication just doesn't do it for Dad." I tried to speak evenly, but it was a stretch.

"You don't know what you're talking about," she said. "There are wonderful things being done in research and development ..."

"I don't care what they're doing in research and development, damn it!" So much for nonchalance. "Dad's not a mouse in a laboratory."

She shut the cabinet with a click. Everything she did had that definite, soft click to it. Her remarks. Her kitten heels. Her clipped bureaucratic speech, which was incomprehensible half the time. She huffed away, which had become our way ending every conversation. At one time, we had almost been friends, but the death of our mother was hard on us in all ways, and there were losses at every turn.

I nosed around in the kitchen pharmacy for a clue about the pill experiment, but it all looked like Greek to me—except for the disturbing side effects that were written in English. For some reason, every person who had the remotest connection to the health care industry advised taking a pill, especially when a hint of depression entered the picture.

Dad wasn't depressed. He was grieving! The pills—those tiny little dots that represented control of Dad—moved around between my sister and me. In my own mind, I was convinced I could get a saner, happier, still-funny Dad without pills. I wanted to find some of the old Dad left in there, but the pills were anesthetizing him out of his mind.

I started weaning him off pills with a flush of the toilet, along with the help of the doctor, whom I finagled to see alone about the pill problem. Fortunately, Julia had a full-time job in Minneapolis, so I had days on end without her starting Dad on yet another pill.

Eventually, Dad seemed clearer, and better physically, in part, because of the new prescription: a regular diet, less medication, and more exercise, thanks to Stan, the therapist. But I had to face the fact that all of my efforts might fall apart while I went off on "The Adventure." The thought squashed my excitement for a new start, flat.

Dad had come to rely on me. Sometimes we didn't even talk. I brought him a coffee, or, fixed the remote for the television, or steered him off to the bathroom, or to a nap. When we were together, we were like two wheels going forward on automatic, and it was becoming clear that it would be difficult to leave him alone up in Indiana.

Besides the worrisome pill-taking, I wondered who would cook for him? Drive him around? Hug him on a regular basis? If left alone, he wouldn't open a can of soup. The only thing I ever saw him make was oatmeal, and the last time that happened I was about twelve. I asked myself how he could go on living in the condo, near the golf course he could no longer use, while the rain and snow brought on one gloomy day after another? Here it was late June, and it was just as gloomy and grey as February.

To top all, Dad and I were smoking. I looked over at him. He had a large cigarette burn in his jacket near the zipper. His clothes were beginning to look as ventilated as a Swiss cheese, and I wasn't helping any by bringing him the cigarettes. We had lapsed into this miserable habit together, especially when Mom got sicker and sicker. It was temporary relief, but it made no sense at all. The smoking had to stop. Change was certainly in order.

I crumpled the empty pack of Marlboro Lights into a wet ball. It was about time to go in and dry off. I resigned myself to the family meeting. *Que será.* But first I needed fortification, perhaps a vodka tonic, or something of that nature. I checked my watch to see if it was five o'clock. The time, however, was of minor consideration. While I had problems with certain aspects of medication, my self-medication with vodka didn't bother me at all.

I tried once more. "Dad, talk to me."

Nothing seemed forthcoming.

I waited. We each grew damper and damper. We couldn't sit out there much longer. The dampness was actually becoming a health hazard.

"Dad, what do you want to do ... you know ... now that Mom's gone? We have to talk about it, Dad, and they will all be over here soon."

"I don't know. My heart is broken." His shoulders shook a little, and he slouched into his chair.

"Yes, I know." Really, I had no idea what he was going through, as close as we were. In my own marriage, I hadn't even made it to the halfway mark of his fifty-two years with Mom.

"I'll just go away," he said. "Yes. I think I'll just go away."

"Go away?"

"What?" He looked as far away as the next planet.

"Where are you going? Dad! What are you talking about?"

The rain started up again, and this time it was relentless—a cold, hard soaker. It made me shiver with a new shade of cold. I was afraid he wanted to lie down and die now that Mom was gone. But that wasn't it at all.

"I'm going with you." His voice was strong. "I'm going to Florida with my Nancy." He sat up straight in his chair and reached for my hand again.

Then, just as quick as lightening, I knew what he'd been ruminating about. His face lit up like the sun on the beach.

I was stunned.

Now what?

2

THE CASE OF
THE SIMMERING SIBS

"What?" Jack said.

"You're going where?!" said Julia. "DAD?"

Lucy stood at the dining room table with her arms folded across her chest. One painted nail tapped an elbow, but she didn't say a word. Her mouth was screwed into a remark that seemed stuck and wouldn't come out.

"I said—I'm going to Florida with Nancy and the kids."

"Well, that's just ridiculous," said Jack. "No way in hell that's going to happen." He threw his coat on the dining room chair. I rolled my eyes. A new Burberry.

Jack stomped into the kitchen and opened the refrigerator. I could see him across the counter that divided off the dining room. His face broke into angry lines as he bent forward and pushed cans and bottles noisily around the shelves. He pulled out a Bud, popped it open, and took a swig, nearly draining the can.

"Great," I called after him. "That's real helpful, Jack."

He turned around and glowered at me, then slammed the fridge door. He finished the beer and kept looking at me like I'd kicked him. I stood up, hands planted on the table. Like a feral cat, I felt like springing at him. But that wouldn't take the look off his face. At this point, nothing I could do would change that. So, I yelled. "What the hell did I do to you? This was not my idea, you know."

He looked stunned. They all did. Even Dad, whose eyes got round, then crinkled at the corners. He reached for my hand. No one said a word, for once.

Dad's announcement had totally shocked me, too. Like my siblings, I needed time to sort this out. Clearly, we were all absorbing the news in different ways. My insides clenched. No one asked me how I felt about the prospect of taking Dad to Florida, which was a good thing, given that I probably couldn't have come up with a sane comment.

Jack turned away, and I sank back into my vodka tonic. Julia and Lucy leaned over Dad, hovering like parentheses. What did Dad's care mean to them? Of course they cared about Dad. They just weren't there with him as much I was. Julia was in Minneapolis, although she used her invisible umbrella as Nurse Poppins frequently. Lucy was busy chasing juicy, young men all over Chicago. Dad ignored my sisters while Julia plucked at his collar and Lucy kneaded his shoulder. He stole a peek at me. I smiled back at him.

The girls kept at it, ignoring me, all the while I felt Jack's cold stare. Dad removed himself from the situation by concentrating on the ceiling. My father usually had a good sense of timing, but this? You have to pick the moment, he'd say. He had certainly done that.

I decided to let my siblings flap awhile until they ran down, even though that probably wasn't going to happen.

Finally, I said, "You're poking him."

"We're not poking," said Lucy. "Right, Dad?" My sister had big teeth that gave her an uncharacteristic savagery when she was excited. I had the feeling she was mad at me, too; that Dad's announcement was my wrongdoing. I pressed my hands to my face. I felt defensive—which was not good. I knew myself too well. It would only make me drink more. It would only make me angrier.

Jack walked across the dining room with another beer. "Crap. Florida." He sat down at the table and slammed the Bud on the table, causing a plop of foam to shoot from the can and make a puddle.

"Are you going to clean that up?" I said, somewhat peevishly.

"You clean it up," he said. "You're the one making a mess."

I set my teeth on edge and tried to control my irritation. Our little family conference was clearly off to an unproductive start, but I suddenly felt this burst to make some headway, despite my anger smothering anything productive that might grow out of this.

"Jack, you know how much he likes Florida. You shouldn't be so surprised," I said, feeling very surprised myself. "Maybe he should go."

Jack looked right through me. How did it happen that he had such a short memory? Or, did he just remember what he wanted to remember? He loved Florida, too. They all loved Florida. I know they did, because I was there with them when they did.

Then, suddenly, Julia exploded. "You can't do this!" Her neck glowed with red splotches, a sure sign she was upset. That hadn't changed in the forty-odd years she'd been my little sister.

"Me?" I tried to be level, but outrage kept bubbling up. Modulate, I told myself. Breathe deeply and try not to leave the room, never to return. We all had certain buried feelings, and now, unfortunately, they were unburied, like zombies shooting out of their graves. We hardly looked like the loving group we'd been when we grew up together, when our parents encouraged us to "love one another." But with the death of our mother, half of that very influential glue was gone.

"He's not going to Florida with you," Jack said.

Julia was nodding like a bobblehead.

"It's settled," he added, as his eyes darted from face to face.

For the moment, quiet was the only thing that settled in the room. We all sipped our drinks, inebriation being part of solving our problems.

Jack was used to giving orders, and, he was used to getting his way. And, as always, he was consistent. If things didn't run smoothly for him, the result was instant crankiness. He didn't like to quibble over the annoying inconveniences of life. Instead, his focus was on the tennis game ahead.

"No, Jack, nothing is settled," I said, finally, choking on the air that hung in the room. "I didn't say that Dad is not going with me. He just told me not ten minutes ago that he wants to go to Florida with me. I have to think about it. I guess we should all think about it, don't you? Or do you ever think, Jack?"

He didn't seem to hear me. He abruptly turned away, the chair skidding across the tile, and his head was in the refrigerator again.

I glanced at Lucy. She'd been fairly silent, but now she moved closer to Dad and shook his arm gently. He paid little attention. He tapped his cane up and down and occasionally reached for me. I wanted to hold onto him, and at the same time, I wanted to get out of there.

We often argued, but this was something new. I was unprepared for their "over" reactions, but I realized that it didn't matter. This family did little preparation of any sort. We just fell into the next drama and let it take over. Lucy's face contorted into an expression I hadn't seen since high school when she played Myrtle opposite Harvey, the invisible rabbit.

"Dad, we just lost our mom," she said. "Now we're going to lose our dad?"

He patted Lucy's hand and sipped his "special" martini. It was mostly ice, water, and lemon, upon which I floated a quarter ounce of vodka. Today I'd added an extra capful to make it just a bit stronger than usual.

"Lucy, you are not losing me. I'm not about to be put into the ground. Not yet anyway."

"But if you go to Florida, when will we ever see you?"

Dad kept patting Lucy. He worked his way up her arm to her head while she still peered into his face. "You come and visit me sometime in Florida. That would be nice."

I wondered about that. With all of our jobs and kids, the year had been a struggle to keep up with our parents. Florida might be a dream, not just for me and my kids, but for everyone. Jack loved tennis, particularly the courts in Mexico and Hawaii. There were plenty in Florida, dozens in Sarasota County where he had reciprocity with the country clubs. The idea of taking Dad with me started to make some sense. Maybe the attraction would nudge Jack into visiting his father; Poppins could employ her umbrella; and Lucy could bring along one of her beach-boy toys.

But Jack was having none of it. "Dad, why do you want to leave your family and friends and move hundreds of miles away to Florida? Your roots are in the Midwest. You were born here, and your business and family are here. Dad, your wife died and is buried here!"

Scowling, I checked Dad for tears, but instead he appeared to be annoyed.

"My Patsy! Don't bring her into this," Dad said. "She's in a much better place than Florida."

Jack clenched his jaw. "Dad, you just can't go to Florida."

"What the devil are you talking about?" Dad picked up his glass and then clapped it on the table. "Florida's full of people who have come to their senses. They left the cold and the snow up here, didn't they?"

"Well, why not?" I chimed in, as much as for Dad as for myself that Florida was a glorious place to be. "It would be a lot easier on him down there. And, you know he's always loved the cottage and the sunshine."

"Will you stop?" Jack's face turned the color of his wine-red Brooks Brothers tie.

Julia suddenly re-appeared from a trip to the liquor cabinet where she'd collected herself and calmed down. "Come on. If you can't say something nice, then don't say anything at all." She was holding a Waterford old-fashioned glass, full of ice and vodka, which took me eerily back to Mom and her penchant for liquor as medicine. The awful year washed over me for an instant. We were all our mother's daughters. I took another sip, but it did nothing to calm me down. All it did was turn up my volume.

"Really. Enough!" I yelled. "And Jack, you stop already!"

"Well!" said Julia. "We really should try to be more pleasant."

Jack stepped back, and Lucy was still leaning over Dad. She looked oblivious; Dad perplexed.

"Julia, you sound like Sister Mary Fides," I said. "And we are not getting anything settled here."

Jack pounded away. "I'm just saying. Dad, you can't just

get up and leave after spending your whole life here. You even have the key to the city."

"Oh spare me," I muttered.

Jack walked around next to Dad and put his hand on his shoulder.

"Another thing, Jack," I said. "If he did stay here, who is going to come over here and take care of him? Are you going to cook, watch television with him, drive him to the doctors? You're never in your own house, so I can't expect you'd be over here taking care of Dad."

"We can get a nice Polish lady to come and clean." He took his hand off Dad's shoulder.

I'd reached my limit. The pipsqueak. I changed your diapers!

"Polish lady? Are you serious, Jack? Getting a maid while you're in Maui? You don't have any idea. What's a nice Polish lady have that I haven't got?"

"She's here, and you'll be in Florida."

"One other thing, while we're on the subject of tennis …" I said.

"No, you're on the subject of tennis," he said.

"Well, I guess I am. How would you like to sit here and stare at this gloom all winter?" I pointed vaguely beyond the dining room through the sunroom to the patio and the nine-hole golf course and tennis courts beyond. In so doing, I spilled the rest of my drink. "He can't get out much anymore. He can hardly walk. He wants to sit in the sun and listen to the seagulls."

Confusion vanished from Dad's face, and the sun came out again. He smiled; I smiled. He looked at me. We were both thinking about the same thing: the cottage, the beach at Anna Maria, the sound of the waves and birds, the warmth of that great, old burning ball rising and setting over the Gulf of Mexico.

So, I went for it. My siblings had backed me into a corner, forcing my conviction. Why not? The whole year had been crazy, so why not keep it up? It probably couldn't get any crazier.

"Look," I said, "this is beginning to make some sense, I think. I can take care of Dad. I'm, sort of, between jobs." What I meant was that I was between my elderly father and my kids, between my sporadic journalism career with its ups and downs through the years and all those moves during the marriage—and God-knows-what else. I was stuck in a sandwich of sorts, but I could do this. I could give it a go with the Lord Almighty's help.

My siblings turned away from me. Together, like they'd timed it.

Julia plopped herself down next to Dad. "What about Minneapolis?" she said, leaning on his arm. Her voice changed to a light singsong that declared Minneapolis to be a splendiferous destination. She pulled her chair closer to Dad, edging Lucy out, who gave up and went off to the kitchen.

"I'm not going to Minneapolis," said Dad. "That's that." Julia looked like she'd been slapped.

"I just meant, Dad, we have lovely retirement facilities for ambulatory clients there."

"Julia. Do you mean a nursing home? A place for old people who can still walk around? I'm not going to a nursing home in Minneapolis." He toned his voice down a notch, took her hand, and smiled at her. "I really want to go to Florida. With my Nancy."

And there it was. The Rub. He preferred to go to Florida

with me, his eldest, his bridge partner, the "matriarch of the family," as he called me. The accident of my birth order had everything to do with Dad and me being close, and nothing to do with the worth of my siblings as caretakers. But who was thinking about that? The whole thing was one big, old accident.

Dad and I were always close—closer than my mother and I were. I adored my father, and I was definitely Daddy's girl. My mother may have resented it, but maybe she was just tired. There were four of us by the time I was six. Growing up, I had a never-ending assortment of chores that were meted out ... to control? To punish me? Who knows. I just had a lot of them, especially dusting and vacuuming, which I saw no purpose in doing, since the mess my family made instantly replaced my daily cleaning efforts. None of my siblings was exactly domestic—Julia left the bathroom un-inhabitable, and on a regular basis, Jack nearly burned down the house making a pyre out of the garbage cans. Lucy had an uncanny talent for disappearing at the sight of a dust rag or dirty dishes, which were mostly left to me. I hated it. At the end of the school day (after a cherry coke and fries, and a couple of Kent's on the bus with my friends), I just wanted to be left alone. I ran home to watch American Bandstand. My mother found me there at four o'clock in front of the black-and-white television with Arlene and Ken, and Justine and Bob, my feet propped up on the woodwork, drinking a Diet-Rite (as punishment for the fries). I could tell Mom was fresh from her nap because her eyes were puffy. Why didn't she do the dusting?

"Here," she said, handing over the Pledge and a list of other chores. It irritated me, and we never settled the slight tug of war between us, which—in part—had to do with

Dad. It was like we were at a department-store sale, waltzing carefully around a rack of clothes we both wanted to buy.

He deferred to me; she did not. I was the child, not my father's confidant, and so she discouraged my involvement in decision making. To be fair, my fiercely independent parents didn't involve any of us much—and that was part of the problem. We could never sit down and work things out together because we had no practice in it.

But, from the beginning, I was my father's daughter. I became a pleaser. I began to take on responsibilities. I babysat from age nine for a quarter an hour; I was often a cleaner, helper, driver, cook. Through the years, Dad and I sort of grew on each other. He depended on me and told me early on "to set an example." I usually did. Except for a few minor detours when I was in high school and threw a party in my parents' absence, during which about a hundred of my hooligan friends showed up and drank all the booze, wrecked the furniture, and took the car on a joy ride—after which, the police came.

I recovered from sophomore year, got straight A's ("See, I told you you could do it," Dad said), earned some scholarships and a double major, and then went on to a successful, albeit short, career as an assistant editor for a decorating magazine in New York. The career ended abruptly when I fell for a West Point cadet, and he for me. We got married right after his graduation and flew off to Germany, Georgia, and Alabama, during which time he anesthetized himself at the Officer's Club with his newfound buddies returning from Vietnam. He had not served in the war because of his low class standing—711 out of 749 cadets. He was lucky, but he didn't think so. He tried to forget his lost opportunity by drowning himself in bourbon.

His loss, oddly enough, was an opportunity. We ended up at Fort Benning, Georgia, where I got a job as a feature writer at the *Columbus Enquirer*, and he was happily jumping out of helicopters. While he didn't come home, I stayed up all night with Tolstoy, Godden, Hemingway, Roth, Dreiser, Bellow, McCarthy, Buck, Steinbeck, Updike, Caldwell, Hardy, and London. They were my friends, and I wallowed in my friends, not wanting to leave the comfort of my pillows and covers pulled up to my chin, turning the pages into an eternity of writing. I had a reading slump through high school and college, but now I was thirsty and couldn't put the books down.

My career sputtered with all of our moving around, but then, along with the reading, I started writing more. I would not let it die. I kept notes and wrote away the hours, in notebooks and steno pads and scraps of paper galore. Nothing could stop the flow of words I put into journals, and into my head from the books I read. I was always writing from the time I was in high school, when I had a column in the newspaper called "Nau's Notions," which mostly touched on prom fashions, or the activities of the football and basketball players. In college, I was a page editor and columnist. I wrote deep, thoughtful editorials about the existential experience— which, to me, was *Waiting for Godot* meets my exceptionally handsome philosophy professor, Mr. Walter Toby.

My father was anything but existential, believing in platonic ideals of love and courage floating out there somewhere in the clouds. He even believed in Richard Nixon because he was a "president," and, he believed in any Catholic priest or nun, and, of course, the pope, because of "the office" they held. We argued politics often. Except for that, I was my father's daughter. I drew on his strength of conviction and his loudness, and I loved his humor and magnanimity over and above his politics and religion.

But in those early years, we argued about everything. He didn't know what to do with me, so he yelled a lot. We yelled a lot together. When I hit puberty like a bomb, we had screaming fights.

"No drive-ins, no beach parties, no tattooed men," he growled.

It ended when I stomped to my room and slammed the door, only to break a succession of mirrors clipped flimsily to the back of the door. I can still remember that slight wobble and rattle before the mirror came crashing down in an exclamation of teenage rage. After I broke the third one, Lucy looked up from her bed where she was sprawled, reading *Seventeen*.

"You can punctuate a sentence better than anyone, Nancy. You sure don't need a course in self-assertion." Then Lucy pointed out, regularly, "Mom will just replace the mirror again, but think of all the bad luck you're stacking up."

Lucy could make me stop in my tracks, but she also had a sense about when to back off. Confrontation was not a part of her makeup. She had a way of getting out of fights and confusion, which I admired greatly. I had no practice in the art. Lucy just didn't want to engage in unpleasant talk if she could dance around it. But she found she couldn't always do what she wanted—something she was not entirely happy about. It was evident in the way she ended her marriage. If there was one thing Lucy learned about being married, it wasn't always good to avoid conflict. At least I had conflict well practiced, especially after twenty-three years with Hubby. On the other hand, Lucy had few fights during her eleven years with Adorable Couch Potato. The worst thing about the end of her marriage, Lucy said, was that they didn't talk about the split. They never even yelled. They simply walked away from each other, leaving edges frayed and issues unresolved.

Lucy taught me a lot by just being Lucy, and about the concept of conflict, which I kept practicing on everyone around me, and continually nurtured in myself. It fed me and pushed me, right on up to the edge until I was nearly, but not quite, ready to fall into a large hole of nothingness. Somehow, I always pulled myself up and got away. I was learning, in part, thanks to Lucy.

Now, Lucy was determined to avoid the fight over Dad. I could read it in her expression, the slow sipping, the nonchalance, the waning of the tapping fingernails. She knew Dad might just go to Florida with me, and she had no intention of spouting off like Julia and Jack. It was not her style. I hoped, with time at least ... that maybe, just maybe, I could get some support from her, that we could put our heads together and come up with a suitable situation, whatever happened with Dad.

Lucy sighed and finished off her vodka tonic, while Jack and Julia gathered their resources to carry on the campaign to save Dad from Florida. And from me. They huddled around Dad and appeared to be advancing.

"Stop. All of you," said Dad. "Look-it. I want to go to Florida. It's cold here, and it's warm there. I want to be warm." His grip remained firm. "I want to be warm, and I'm going with Nancy."

"Dad," said Julia. She folded her arms. "Just look at this lovely little house that Mom put together so nicely for you."

"I don't like the dollhouse," he said flatly.

"Come to think of it, he didn't have a thing to do with this place," I said.

Their eyes, as one, burned into me then for my sacrilegious remark. Mom had poured the last of her strength into decorating the dollhouse—with the help of a pompous decorator who ran between the Chicago Merchandise Mart and my mother with every sample she could carry, huffing and puffing with chintzes and wallpaper. My mother loved the flattery and the shopping and writing checks. But Dad didn't know a *toile* from a teapot. Everybody kept saying what Dad liked and didn't like. Except Dad.

"That's just not true. Dad had a lot to do with this place," Jack said. "Dad loves it here."

"No, I don't. But she did," said Dad, and with that, his shoulders shook in a burst of weeping.

"It was all Mom," I said. "I was glad she was picking out chairs and rugs and distracting herself from thinking about cancer. But why didn't we talk about the important stuff, especially about how this would all end? Why didn't we talk about Dad, and what to do when she was gone? Why didn't she say something? Did she ever ask Dad about any of this?"

They looked away, but Dad straightened up, the loss changing his expression. He nodded at me.

Lucy spoke up. "Come on. They were a team. They did everything together."

"Well, they didn't do this together," I said. "We should have talked about it. All of us. Together."

The last year had been heart breaking, listening to Mom yell at Dad in the middle of the night. He got up and walked around, confused as a result of pills and grief, and Mom couldn't get any sleep while dying. Balancing the present with the inevitable future had unfortunately tipped in favor of providing comfort, at all cost, to the present.

I gave Dad a hug and walked around the table. We'd been

talking for more than an hour, and we still hadn't resolved a thing.

The air around me was rare, like the suction in the middle of a tornado. I dropped into a chair, facing Dad.

With finality, Julia said, "We can get a maid."

"Not that again," I said. "Polish, Spanish, Irish, French? You're in this with Jack?"

"Well, yes, we've talked, and I think it would be a great idea," said Julia. "And she could do it better than you could in Florida."

"What's that supposed to mean? A maid would be better at caring for him than his own daughter?"

"You know what I mean."

"No, I do not."

"He has so much more support here," said Julia.

"Whatever are you talking about now, Julia? None of you are here."

"Stop, I tell ya. That's all," yelled Dad. "I'm going to Florida." He squeezed my hand.

I squeezed back and looked him in the eye. "OK, Dad." Not knowing what I was talking about, I said, "We'll go." I was certainly not thinking about the future, only about getting away from my siblings.

So, the issue was settled. Sort of.

3

THE CLEAN GOODBYE

The kids went to camp that summer and then occasionally to their father's house, which was actually his new wife's. I stayed at the dollhouse and contemplated a checklist for our move. We were going to give this adventure a try, together. I was happy for the kids' resilience and their laughter, but I never thought further than my nose about what all this divorcing, dying, and moving around was doing to them. I had too much to do that day, and the next, and the next. I would think about the consequences later.

When my daughter, Little Sunshine, was at the dollhouse, she liked to curl up in the window seat of the spare bedroom with the pillows and her doll, Suzie Frugnut. I found her there one afternoon reading a chapter book to Suzie. My daughter was proud of herself that at the age of nine, she was working her way through the Laura Ingalls Wilder series. She was deep into *Little House in the Big Woods*. She looked up at me when I walked into the bedroom, and her blue-gray eyes followed me around the room.

"This is my favorite book."

"Why?

"Because they're all happy and they get maple syrup out of the trees and make quilts and stuff."

That sounded very un-Florida-like to me.

"That's one way to be happy," I said. I sat down and squeezed her foot in the red sock with black polka dots. She had red bows in her braids, and wisps fell on her forehead. She blew them out of her eyes. "Suzy looks happy," I said. I couldn't bring myself to ask her if she was happy, afraid of the answer.

Little Sunshine patted the doll and looked out the window. She stuck out her lower lip, and I had a terrible feeling she wasn't a baby anymore, that she was drifting off to a place I couldn't quite reach. I wanted more than anything for her to be happy, always and ever. I hoped I was doing the right thing for all of them. And Suzy Frugnut.

I grabbed both my daughter's feet and clapped her polka dots together. "We're going on an adventure! You know that? Want to know something else? I think Gampers might come and stay with us in Florida!"

Her eyes opened wide. "Really?"

"Would you like that?"

"I'd love it," she said. "I think I can really help Gampers a lot."

I kissed the top of her big toe and then hugged her. "I know you can."

Post-divorce, number one on the checklist had been to pack up my old house. Even if I'd wanted to stay in the lovely brick-and-timber Tudor house in Hammond, Indiana, I couldn't afford to keep it up at $900 a month for gas and electric in the winter. Northern Indiana Public Service

Company—an odd name for people who were averse to "service"—had loved us. We shoveled money at them. The seventy-year-old house was nearly impossible to insulate in summer, or in winter.

It all had to go, inside and out, and I was in charge of the disposal, because it was all mine in the divorce. I put up most of the furniture for auction, but before it was all gone, I went into each room and picked out one piece that I would keep—the new eight-drawer walnut chest with brass fittings from the bedroom. The eight-foot oak trestle table from the family room. The white pine bookcase with glass doors purchased from an antique shop in Gay, Georgia. The Sheraton sofa with the down cushion, and the two chairs that matched—upholstered in crewel. I kept several Moroccan rugs my mother gave me, and my grandfather's cedar chest. These were my treasures, and these would follow me out of storage and take up residence, I hoped, in a little dream house in Florida someday.

While I walked slowly from room to room, marking this for storage, that for auction, Little Sunshine was stuck to me like Velcro.

"What about my stuff, Mom?" she said. "Do I have to throw everything away?"

I'd almost forgotten she was there, she was such a natural attachment. "No, of course not!" I said, knowing full well we were getting rid of almost everything. I smoothed the top of her head and tugged lightly at one of her braids, where a hair ribbon was missing.

She shrugged away and put her hands on her hips. "Well, I don't need that, or that." She pointed to the pink Barbie playhouse and tiny set of table and chairs. "I'm big now."

"We can take whatever you want." I looked around the

bedroom. She had her own bathroom, and the leaded glass windows in her room looked out on pine trees, lilac bushes, and a wide sloping lawn on the corner lot. I sat on the edge of her mahogany four-poster bed that had a pink and green chintz duvet, with curtains to match. This will go real well in Florida. Oh, what were we getting ourselves into? What was I getting myself into?

Little Sunshine put one finger firmly in her cheek. "No, I don't think we'll take that big bed. But Tigger, Pooh, Eyore, and Peter Rabbit are all going to Florida." She threw herself in the corner of some twenty furry creatures and nearly disappeared. I made a mental note to remind myself once again—it was never enough—that this was not just my move. It was also theirs—Dad, Little Sunshine, and Tick.

Tick, my son, was traveling light. He'd already moved his special pile—a pillowcase full of Legos, and his Axis and Allies game—to the condo to wait out the transition.

"Mom, this is how I roll," he said.

Wherever did he get such minimalist ideas? I was just glad, because he certainly was growing up in a family with baggage of all sorts.

The auction house hauled off the Welsh sideboard and the buffet. Out went all the wedding gifts and things that reminded me of the marriage, including the Wedgwood with strawberries and vines, the federal-patterned sterling, all the crystal, china, ceramic mugs and pitchers from Germany, the paintings and the twelve-by-fourteen oriental rug that covered the parquet in the dining room. I got thousands for all of it, and it went into the bank for my move to Florida. I think I got ripped off, but I didn't care. I just wanted to get on with it.

Hubby didn't get—nor did he ask for—the house or

anything in it. The only items I returned to him were tied into a dirty sock—all the jewelry he'd given me: two diamond rings, aquamarines and amethysts, gold and silver, rings and chains and stuff I never wanted to see again, because all of it was payment for the pain he'd inflicted. I was especially glad to part with an amethyst and diamond ring that reminded me of a black eye. Mine.

I didn't care a whit about any of it, not even to this day—swear on a stack of bibles and on my grandmother's grave. It was time to start over, clean.

4

SAIL ON

I stood guard in front of the bottles of pills on the medicine shelf in the kitchen and made sure Julia didn't try a fast one. She hadn't gone to the doctor for more pills, and I was keeping Dad off medication for the time being, much to Julia's professional consternation. The further Dad got from Amytriptiline and Melaril, the Prozac and the Paxil, the better off he seemed to be. After a clean spell off the pills and on a good diet, he was sleeping better. I didn't know if it was the lack of medication, or the fact that he wasn't staring at my dying mother all night in that hospital bed. It was hard to tell, and I didn't ask because I didn't want to upset him. He was content. That was all I cared about for now. We were still only weeks from her death, but I could see the regimen taking effect. His color was brighter, and we were all clearly looking forward to The Adventure.

Except for my siblings. Lucy, Julia, and Jack still came up with ideas to keep Dad from going with me. They looked into assisted living communities—there was only one decent one in the area, and the waiting list was a year long. They wanted him to take turns living with each of them. Jack was still looking for a Polish maid—to replace me. I let the idea of taking Dad to Florida simmer for a week or two. They never did ask me if I was happy about the idea of taking Dad to Florida, and I'm glad they didn't, because I truly had mixed feelings. I was not going to bring it up, either, which only would start another row.

I thought of explaining to Dad how difficult the adjustment would be, for all of us. But the thought paralyzed me. If I did that, it would sound like a straight-out rejection of my father after losing my mother. After all he'd gone through, it seemed that he should do what he wanted at the age of seventy-seven. I really felt I had to help him. The long-term consequences of our plan were furthest from my thoughts—how would it affect the family, all of us, and especially my kids, to have their grandfather living with us? He would be there when they came home every day. My father would be there for dinner, when they did their homework, invited their friends over. I'd be spending time driving him around and caring for him during the day, and during the night. How was this going to work out? I had no way of knowing until I tried, and I was willing to try.

Dad and I talked. It would have helped if we'd all tried—and learned—to talk about it together. But we didn't. We couldn't, because we didn't know how.

Dad sat in the dining room waiting for Stan the therapist. Dad wore three layers of clothes, like his Irish mother, from whom he'd inherited poor circulation. As a consequence, he liked to bundle up, whatever the weather. He simply would not be talked out of it. Humidity went right to his bones, and Florida was going to be damp, hot or cold.

I made another attempt to test him, while I was also testing myself.

"Dad, it's ninety-eight degrees in Tampa today, and it's going to stay that way for at least three months. It's hot and uncomfortable, and it's humid down there."

"Good, I like hot weather; the hotter the better. What's the temperature here?"

"Well, it's in the eighties, I guess."

"We could stand it a little warmer."

I decided to take a different tack with him. "Dad, don't you think if you go to Florida that it should be a family decision? Shouldn't we talk some more about this?"

"Look-it. I've never consulted them before, and I'm not going to start now."

"You think this is a good thing, so soon after Mom's death?"

"I'm going with you."

"I know you love Florida."

"I love Florida," he said. "And I love you. Whither thou goest, I go. We're going to the cottage."

Yes, the cottage. The thought of it made me feel fine. I woke up from a dream and remembered in the night seeing my mother's silhouette—and that of the Ex—both of them communing on the white beach under a blue-black sky full of stars in front of the cottage.

"I want it all, and I want it now," she yelled at the crashing waves.

"And you have it," said the Ex.

She loved the Ex, loved manipulating him to do things for her that he didn't mind doing in the first place, and then they laughed about it. They got a huge kick out of beating Dad and me at bridge, which they did regularly because

Dad was an outrageous gambler who thought he could make no-trump with twenty points after all, with just those two aces. He never listened to his own mother, my grandmother, "No-Trump Liz," who said the cards have no home. Dad and I didn't win often, but we loved the game.

My mother played by the book, as did the Ex—at least at bridge. He was a sad person, my mother told me, and insecure, like she was. She understood him, while I did not. That was the implication. I resented that, and, that she compared herself to him with affection. I resented that he left me and her as well.

Now they were both gone, and everything had changed. Running around all day, I could forget, but not when the dreams came. It was different then.

In my dream, at least my mother was there again, and she was healthy and full of life. Things were as they once had been. Her laugh was a gift, and her relentless zest was just like always. That's what I missed, never seeing that again, never turning to ask her something that I just had to know. She'd know. And now, I could never do that again. The loss was unbearable after the dream, where she threw her arms wide over her head, her white curls shining in the moonlight, the wind billowing her skirt against the waves. I'd only ever see her there.

She wanted me to go on an adventure.

Sail on …

I could hear it clearly, like the snapping of a sail under the moon.

Like in a song I used to love.

5

THE DOLLHOUSE

Julia began announcing to friends and family that I was "kidnapping Dad!" What an unpleasant surprise! I seethed, and, at once, the disappointment over the continual sniping and lack of support from the family nibbled away at me.

I explained to anyone who would listen that it was not my plan to kidnap Dad. Where did Julia get such ideas? I wondered. I had to bite my tongue and bide my time, because I was on the verge of confronting her, and it wouldn't be pretty. She'd called me a kidnapper. That's a felony. All the while, Jack's objections to "Dad running off to Florida" dwindled and reappeared with annoying regularity. The idea of him running anywhere was ridiculous enough. Dad just smiled and didn't join the argument. He remained adamant about going. "How can I stay here? My Patsy's not here," he said. It was as simple as that. My heart broke.

I didn't try to talk him out of it, and I avoided discussion with my siblings, because there was no such thing as discussion, just yelling. I was determined not to argue with them, taking a clue from Lucy's non-conflict approach.

I made up my mind. Unless something earth-shaking

happened to change everything, Dad and I and the kids were all off to Florida at the end of August.

I finally told Little Sunshine and Tick. "I have some incredible news, kids. Gampy is going on The Adventure with us! He's coming to live in Florida! We're going to stay at the cottage." I winked at Little Sunshine. It had been our secret. She clapped her hands over her mouth, then danced around the table and off the patio on to the grass. There she collapsed in a heap of pink ruffles.

"Yeah! It's really happening!" she yelled.

Tick looked at his sister and tipped his chair back. We were sitting on wrought iron outside at the dollhouse, so I didn't have to correct him for unhinging the furniture. "Cool," said Tick. A smile broke slowly across his face, as the plan dawned on him. "You're not kidding, Mom?" And then the chair tipped forward with a clatter. "Really? That is awesome."

My daughter sprang up and danced around the yard. "The Sunshine!" she said. "Oh, how fun!" She called her grandfather Sunshine, but when he was grumpy, she called him Storm Cloud. He named her Little Sunshine.

Dad and Tick got on well, too. When they were together, they rumbled and laughed together—a peculiar mix of young and old voices. Dad came up with "Tick." When Tick could hardly walk, he liked to stick to Dad's leg and ride around on his shoe. Dad would laugh and pick up his grandson and sweep him into the air with one hand, holding him up high until he squealed. I didn't think of my baby son as a fat bug, but the name stuck.

We were definitely headed in a new direction, this family of my elderly father and young children—and me in the middle.

"Gamps can have my room," said Tick.

"That's very generous of you," I said.

"Or we could build an addition to the cottage."

"Where?"

"We can finish off the storage room. We'll set up a little club in there and jam and stuff. Gamps likes MTV."

That was puzzling, and true. The stroke had left him with some odd interests, including MTV. The music and dancing were as foreign as another planet to him, but maybe that's where he wanted to be—totally removed from his present surroundings. He fixed on Sinead O'Connor, mesmerized by the Irish woman's bald head and plaintive voice. Then he sang to me, "Nothing compares to you," which was flattering and confusing.

Tick said, "Mom, I mean it. He can have my room."

"We'll think of something," I said. "I just want you to know that things will be different."

"Mom. Everything's different every day all the time around here," said Tick. "I'm talkin' really different."

This was also true. The kids had gone from their beautiful house with mom and dad at home, to camp in the woods, to "the museum" where their dad lived with The Mop, to the dollhouse where their grandmother died and their grandfather and aunts and uncles were driving everyone to distraction—all within about a year's time. The thought of it was dizzying.

The kids were cheerful and excited—and in the moment. I charged ahead, packing and planning for the great Adventure. I, too, was in the moment, just happy to be getting out of this one and into a happier one in Florida.

I didn't think about the turmoil that could come of this. There weren't enough moments in the day for that.

Dad and I met his accountant, his lawyer, and his banker. Joe Glotzbach, the accountant, told Dad he didn't need two houses. He owned the dollhouse and also part of the Florida cottage with his two sisters. He didn't need the dollhouse with the antiques, condo fees, and utility bills.

Joe's office had the atmosphere of a funeral parlor and a country club bar all at once. The comfy maroon leather arm chairs on metal ball feet moved around easily, and the mahogany walls meant serious business.

"Sell it," Dad said. "Sell the dollhouse."

I looked at Joe, who was chuckling, but I felt a wave of panic.

"Wait," I said. "What if you all of a sudden, you know, decide you want to come back?"

"I'm not coming back. My home is with you."

Joe raised his eyebrows and smiled. "He's always known what he wants."

I clung to the idea that we were all making the right choice, building this new life, all of us together. Swept along in the rush of it, I felt I had little choice. And Dad wanted to come along. He had his good and bad moments, and I was always looking for the father I knew, the strong man, the funny one. It was energizing to hear the lucid Dad. If we were in this together, how could things go wrong?

I was emptying a drawer when Margie Everett, one of Mom's best friends, knocked on the front door, her bubble head, wavy through the leaded glass. Margie had a small motor in her brain that kept her mouth in perpetual motion. She was dear, but I wished she'd go away.

"Great," I mumbled to myself. It was a frantic morning,

with the realtor, the kitten Tick found in the parking lot of the 7-Eleven, and a to-do list of sorting, retrieving, cancelling, cleaning, and calling. This was a time in which I rose to new levels of multi-tasking. If I could have used my feet to dial and hold the phone, I would have.

Dear, sweet Margie. I didn't have time to chat, but, at once, I was compelled to put a good face on it. My appearance was another consideration altogether. I had not even brushed my teeth, and I wore an old robe that had a hole and a coffee stain plopped among the faded daisies.

"Oh, dear, I hope I'm not disturbing you," said Margie.

"No, no," I lied, knowing perfectly well I looked mighty disturbing.

Margie was dressed in a fine navy-blue St. John knit suit, her signature look. She pointed one slim, spanking-new Ferragamo over the doorstep, while I stepped back into the dim foyer. She handed me a white box from Butterfingers, our favorite bakery. I could smell its sweet goodness through the cardboard, reminding me that I hadn't eaten anything since yesterday.

I found an uncluttered area at the dining room table for us to sit, and I brought coffee and the cups. I opened the box and took out the crescents, putting them on a plate, and offering her the first. My mouth watered for something flaky, delicious, pleasing, satisfying—anything but arguing, yelling, correcting, coaxing, whining, and mewing.

"I know this is none of my business, and I probably shouldn't be saying this," she said.

The crescent halted above my plate midway to my mouth. My bullshit-o-meter started to go off.

"You know how I love you and your family," she said.

I studied the flakiness of the crescent and took a big bite.

Margie Everett was a very nice person, but I didn't love her, and I wasn't going to say I did.

"And I know how difficult it is for you and the family," she said, "but do you really think it's such a good idea to take your father away from his family and friends? Just now? So quickly, you know, with Patsy's passing." Margie dabbed a corner of one eye, delicately.

The mouthful of crescent began to taste like paper, and I put my coffee cup down carefully. "Margie, I am not taking my father away. This is not my idea. It's his. He is taking himself away, and I happen to agree with him."

There, I said it, and I didn't care what she thought of it.

"But he's so vulnerable now."

"We all are, Margie."

"Well, yes, I suppose so. I can see how you'd say that."

She tilted her head, and her eyebrows wiggled up and down. I tried to keep a straight face with all that wiggling going on.

"I know you're the apple of his eye. I know you'll take good care of him," she said. Then her tone changed slightly, and in a blink, she was on to topic number two. "And what about this lovely condominium?"

She looked around the dining room full of moving boxes, papers, and clutter and into the adjoining sunroom that over-looked the golf course. It was a rainy day, and no sun entered the floor-to-ceiling windows to light up the oriental carpet and floral chintz loveseats, the brass and china, and Dad's leather chair and ottoman. It really was beautiful and comfy, and I felt a slight tug of regret, but not much. This was where my mother spent her last days, on the loveseat with a mohair blanket over her knees and a small satin pillow at the crook of her neck. I could still hear the depressing, soft *clap-clap* of the oxygen machine that gave her some relief from the cancer that was eating away in her middle.

I had to get out of there. We all did.

I looked back at Margie, who tilted her head at me for an answer. "The condo, yes. What about it?" I said.

"I hear it's on the market, after all your mother did to make it so special, so uniquely her own style. I just love the built-in bookcases, and what she did with the guest room! Who would have thought to use so many shades of blue! But it really works, don't you think?"

Margie would leave me that morning, and go directly to the country club for lunch and tell every person she knew, and she knew a considerable number, about her conversation with me. It was sure to be a frightening version of the facts. It would do no good to antagonize her. I needed to win her over. I stood, tucked my robe around me, and straightened up, hoping posture would make up for looking like a slob.

"This packing and cleaning," I said, mindful of an even tone. "It's so tedious, such a never-ending job of sorting and wrapping, and then all this scrubbing." I hoped she didn't look too closely at the kitchen floor, which had several layers of pizza sauce, Sprite, and one melted banana popsicle in the corner.

"Dear, I wish I could help." Her face registered sympathy.

"Oh, thanks. That's so sweet, but we're just about finished," I said. "The kids are so excited, and Dad is, too." I stretched a bit, awkwardly, and then sat down. We went back to thoughtful chewing of the crescents, sipping our coffee tentatively. Margie, clearly, however, was not through with me. I had tried to gently end the discussion, and failed. She waited expectantly for me to continue, and I bit.

"Margie," I said, "my father really doesn't need two houses."

"Oh, you're right about that."

"He says he wants to go to Florida with me. That would make him happy. I think my mother would have liked that. Don't you?"

"Yes, oh, yes. Definitely," she said. "You're so right about that."

"Thanks."

"But it's all happening so fast."

"Yes."

"Well, you have our love, love, love."

"The condo, I guess, won't sell overnight," I said, standing up again. I began to inch away from the table with a peek at the clock. It was nearly noon, and my stomach dropped at the thought of all I had to do. I sidled in the direction of the front door. "Wish us luck on our adventure!"

"Adventure! Oh, that's darling," she said. "We'll see then, won't we?"

She got to her Ferragamo-ed feet. Margie checked her watch, pecked me on the cheek, and was off to lunch. I stared at the door that clicked softly behind her. With all of her fluff and meddling, Margie was concerned. She did, in fact, give me something to chew on besides the crescents.

I didn't believe for one minute that Dad would come back to Indiana. I hoped The Adventure worked, because if Dad were to return, I was afraid he'd die in no time. I had that much blind faith in myself to believe I could keep Dad happy down there in the good ol' Florida sun. Yes, I could do it. I did not accept the fact that I was dispensable. However, the Ex had made it perfectly clear that I was entirely dispensable by divorcing me after twenty-some-years and settling down with the adoring, flannel-mouthed church lady on our street—after dropping the trailer-trash girl friend from southern Indiana.

I had to put it past me. The kids needed me, I was sure of that, and Dad needed me, or he would sink into deep sadness and listlessness—with a strange, Polish maid taking care of him in the dollhouse. I could just see Dad trying to get used to this stranger, while she explained a Julia-inspired, new-found miracle pill, and how to work the remote on the television, and get his teeth in and out, and put one foot in front of the other, and get him all around town to five or six doctors, all in Polish, which was Jack's dream. It made me frantic. In that case, he might as well be in Poland, or Paris, or in *Star Wars*.

I looked down at the squashed crescent in my fist, dropped it in the cardboard box, and went back to the mess. The crescents somehow ended up in Florida, packed up with butter in the butter dish, and an ashtray full of cigarette butts.

The dollhouse drew an offer nearly overnight, which made me frantic to finish the tasks. A mystery person, probably someone around the age of ten, broke the leaded glass in the front door. A toilet got plugged, and the realtor found what appeared to be a leak in the basement, which I traced to the piddling stowaway kitten. Tick had hidden the cat downstairs at the dollhouse, because he couldn't keep it at "the museum."

"It looks like a story out of Edgar Allen Poe over there, Mom. The cat will get nightmares."

"I thought they had cats."

"They do, but they're all scared, and weird."

The to-do list before our move kept growing. And then there was Jack. I was going to prevail upon him to babysit the cat until further arrangements could be made. Maybe the cat would like Florida, some day. I kept saying "the cat" because it had so many names, including Pansy, Kitty, Blackie, Wart, and Puny, which is what Tick called it. Puny seemed to stick.

Jack appeared one evening as I was taking lasagna out of the oven. I'd been thinking about Puny, and I was just about to bring up the warm and fuzzy subject of finding a temporary home for the cat with Jack. A smile came over me. Here he was, taking the time to sit down with his father and his big sister and have dinner.

But he wasn't there for Italian, or to talk about the cat. The expression on his face was anything but warm and fuzzy. He was there to give me instructions.

"I want to see the checkbook and all the receipts," he said.

"For what?" I was stunned, yet again, especially since Jack knew the accountant and banker were involved in financial decisions for Dad.

"What do you mean, for what? For your purchases, with Dad's credit card."

The blood rose to my head. I was sure it would spurt out my ears. His cold tone filled every space in the kitchen as he stood there, with his hands in his pockets. He didn't even sit down. He just stood there, watching me, irritating me.

"Are you serious? May I ask why?" I wanted to drop the lasagna on his new Cole Haan loafers.

"I need to know."

"Once again, why?"

"We need an accounting of everything you spend."

"Joe Glotzbach is getting a detailed accounting of every check I write and every charge I make."

He deflated like I'd stuck a pin in him.

"I can't believe what I am hearing." I muttered the last

and shoved the lasagna to the back of the stovetop. Tomato sauce leaped out on to my blouse.

"Don't take it the wrong way."

"Really? How should I take it when my little brother demands that I give him an accounting of the expenses for taking care of our Dad? How should I take it?"

"Julia wants to know, too. I haven't gotten hold of Lucy yet."

He didn't move, or change his frigid tone.

"Why don't you ask Dad?" I said, and immediately thought better of it. "No, call Joe. He does Dad's taxes. I'm sure he'll be happy to oblige you."

I was dumbfounded. Jack had his own business, and Jack was insisting that I give him an accounting of the American Express bill. His insinuation that I didn't know what I was doing, and that I was profligate, was doubly insulting.

"I think this conversation is over." I felt ill. I felt confused. I did have to use Dad's credit card for a number of expenses, not the least of which was running the dollhouse. Last I checked, I hadn't been to Saks for a new outfit, although I certainly could have used one.

I left Jack standing in the kitchen with his fists stuck in his pockets and a self-righteous look on his face. There was absolutely no love lost at the prospect of getting the hell out of there as fast as I could and getting down to Florida, using Dad's American Express Card.

6

HUBBY COMES AGAIN

I cleaned up the lasagna. And the next day I had another mess on my hands. The Ex appeared at the front door. I opened it, and we stood practically nose-to-nose. It was a shock. I still had trouble looking him in the eye, but I had no other choice. It was that, or look at my shoes. His hair, more grey than I remembered, was clipped very short, military style, and his cheeks were smooth and scrubbed pink like he'd taken a wire brush to himself. He was a strong, trim man, but he wasn't happy about his short legs, which placed him among the short people of the world. He hated Randy Newman's song about short people who have no reason to live—which Lucy, in one of her devilish moments, sang to him. But he was short, and standing a step down at the front door, he was even shorter. It never mattered to me. He'd been adorable, a sort of Paul Newman straight out of Hud. Once we'd nearly seen eye-to-eye, all the better to get along nicely. We'd made mad love in the Indiana dunes, the West Point library, and every place in between; we'd sworn "everything forever," and believe me, it finally came down to that: a world of joy and hurt and regret. Except there was never any regret about those kids. We were ever so blessed with the kids. That blessing, however central to the marriage, did not hold us together, and now we stood, on opposite sides of the brick threshold of my parents' condo. We might as well have faced each other across the Grand Canyon.

"Who let you in?" I said.

"What's that supposed to mean?" he said.

"This is a gated community." I sounded snobbish. It came out the wrong way.

"Yes, I know." He stood squarely, almost like he was at attention. I had the urge to say, "At ease," but I didn't care if he were ever at ease again.

"They didn't call from the guardhouse and warn me you were coming."

"Sorry. I guess I should have called you." He spoke like a courteous stranger, this person I'd been married to for more than twenty years. For some reason, the distance between us felt good.

"That's all right. I'm not doing anything, except about a million things. How did you get in here?"

"I'm a member of the country club. The guard let me in. It's on my sticker."

"We should all come with warning stickers."

He looked at me blankly, and patiently, which was unusual for him. He was making me nervous.

Finally, I said, "You're a member of the country club? I thought you didn't like country clubs, too elitist and all that."

"I've changed." He didn't say that his new wife was a member of the country club, and that was the reason he was a member. He didn't bring that up, or that he'd moved into her house, mortgage paid, with all the dark, gloomy furniture of a museum, and the heavy draperies and other frippery to keep him warm and cozy, and secure, the shithead.

"You've changed. That's nice." I didn't ask him in. He seemed pleasant and subdued enough—but he was stiff and poised, sort of like a snake, before it strikes.

Then, he struck.

"She threw me out." His face went from pink to pale, and he shifted to his other foot.

My mouth dropped open, but nothing came out.

"Then she threw every piece of paper and clothing I own down the stairs and out the door. Except for the computer, which I guess was too heavy." He trailed off on the last detail.

"Crazy," I said. I'm surrounded by crazy people, and it's making me nuts. He'd married the woman before the ink had dried on the divorce, and I should feel sorry for him? But I did feel sorry for him. God help me, I did. What could I say? I was glad that the father of my children was on the street? What exactly was I supposed to do with this bit of news?

"Want to go to lunch?" he said.

We sat in a brown, sticky plastic booth at Wing Loh Fat's Chinese restaurant on Indianapolis Boulevard, which ironically is US 41, and a direct, if ponderous, route to Florida. How far away from Florida I felt, looking at oriental glazed broccoli and beef, shiny pineapple-candied chicken and fried rice, and the face of a stranger, my ex-husband, in a restaurant not fifteen minutes away from the gross steel mills of Gary. I cracked open the cookie and wondered what my fortune would say. "You will meet a tall stranger." Boy, that was wrong, too.

We hardly said a word, but I noticed some things had not changed. His appetite had not dimmed; he shoveled large forkfuls here and there, with nauseating speed and a lack of discrimination about the food itself. I either had to keep up or lose my appetite, which was quickly happening. His smooth jowls bulged in and out like a squirrel, a creature he had a lot in common with. They both ate with abandon and on the run, except that the squirrel sat in the tree. Hubby, on the other hand, often reminisced fondly about the "field" of his old Army days when he ate a variety of C-rations dumped into a helmet and cooked over an open fire. He was the type of person who needed to consume all those, and everything, around him. He once stuck an entire Big Mac into his mouth in two bites, and given the assortment of Chinese in front of us, he was about to eat the whole table in five minutes.

His cell phone rang and he answered it, lowering his face almost into his rice. His wife's screams came through the tiny black holes of the phone into the large hole in his head. I could hear the hollow echo of her voice and imagine the tiny impotent woman trapped inside that phone, and trapped in a life with him. She had taken him, and she could have him, if she could get him back.

Suddenly, I pushed away my plate. In the place of an appetite for Chinese, I felt a sense of possession, of a future without him and a time of possibilities. Yes, she could have him. I was good, very good, with that. It came to me like a door opening in my head, and I felt better than I had for a long time. I was free of him. Really free. There was no knot of dread anymore for the fits he would spring on me; I could just walk away, or hang up, or do whatever it took to get away from him.

He flipped his wife closed, back into the tiny black holes from which she emerged to scream at him, and he put her in his pocket. He gave me a sheepish look. I knew that look. He was embarrassed, and he knew that vulnerability often won me over.

"I love you," he said.

"Oh, please. It's a little late for that."

"I've always loved you. You're my girl, my woman."

He reached for my hand and turned it over. The pleading. This was truly incredible—he actually thought I would go back to him, like I'd done many times. I pulled my hand away.

"I'm tired," I said. "I want to go home."

"You know I love you. Say you still love me."

"I can't say that. I won't say that. You're married."

"So?"

"What do you mean 'so?' You left."

"You were going to leave me. You said you were."

"I said that after you went to see a divorce lawyer, while you were diddling with that trash from southern Indiana, and God only knows how many others, and finally that fuzz ball you're married to now."

"You're my wife," he said. "She's just my spouse."

"Are you planning to leave your spouse?"

"Will you come back to me?"

So, that was it. He wanted a commitment from me before he pulled the plug on his latest marriage. I almost choked on the nonsense he was making up as he went along. In fact, I would choke before I told him that I would go back to him. I'd jump off a bridge before I'd break up their happy little duo.

He had just called me up one night and simply said, "I'm filing on Tuesday." I remember that night. He'd been gone a lot around the time of that miserable Christmas, trysting away, moving his computers, going on "business" trips. And he was the one who was "filing." I'd felt very cold at the sound of Hubby's voice over the phone—so cold and impersonal. That night, I only said, "Good-bye." That was it. After all the years, he was filing on Tuesday, and to this day, I'm sorry I didn't see his face when he said it. But I knew what I'd see there. Nothing. Just the empty cold look of the needy.

My family didn't say much about the divorce, except to keep reminding me that I'd known Hubby for years before I married him. But Dad was finally resigned. "You're a strong one," he said. "You'll be fine, whatever you decide." Dad was the only one who gave me a vote of confidence, and maybe Lucy. But I didn't feel fine, not until that moment over spicy beef and broccoli and glazed chicken with fried rice.

I slid out of the booth and walked toward the door. I hoped he would follow me out of the restaurant, because I didn't want to walk three miles back to the dollhouse on a hot, August afternoon, but I would gladly do it to get away from him.

He still had the same sad, pleading question on his face.

"No," I said.

Later that day, mopping the floor, which usually rattled some sense into my brain, it occurred to me—he still hadn't said a word about the kids and our move to Florida. I'd filed the paperwork with the lawyer, who served Hubby the notice. Then I waited. Nothing. What a strange man. And I thought I knew him, but actually it showed me I didn't know all that much about the person I'd married. Why on all of this good green earth did I ever think I knew the man I married?

7

PLAYING WITH MATCHES, BURNING IT DOWN

I splashed the mop around and whacked into the walls. It felt good, but I couldn't help remembering, and wondering, why he would even think to try and come back to me. He had the most convenient memory of any person I'd ever known.

It might have been different for us—even with the misery that preceded the divorce. We'd had our arguments and broken furniture. But I always held that very small glimmer of hope that things would change for the better. Such is the goodness of hope; it doesn't die easy.

Then it did. Everything changed in one day's time. I'd known him for so long, and all it took to end it—definitively—was the space between 3:00 and 4:00 a.m., on a dark, cold morning. I can say that for sure now—with the hindsight of the lucky, and my sanity relatively intact. That one time hit me like a rock hits water. After that morning, the events rippled out and enclosed us in larger and larger circles until we were all floating in the warp with no way out of what we fell into: the divorce, the family fights, the fleeing to Florida.

It was very early that day when I heard the annoying rattle of the garage door going up. It woke me up instantly; but that was easy. All those mirthless nights, I slept on the edge of disaster, ready to jump to God-only-knows-where. The clock said 3:09 a.m., and I was alone in the bed again. The garage door was disturbing; but it was not just the clackety-clack that made me sit up in the dark. Something was different, even though this had been his routine for many weeks. He left in the night, and he was still gone in the morning when I woke up to get the kids off to school. He told me he had to work at odd hours because the office was moving to another building. He and his staff needed the time to relocate computers when business was shut down.

"That's a great idea," I said. It was a new business for him, after leaving the army behind. We both wanted it to work. He'd gone into a partnership, and his plan was to buy out the retiring owner. I wanted it to work out, not only for financial reasons, but for us, too, with all the moving around and his efforts to give up drinking behind us. Some days, I even thought it might be possible. I wanted to believe it because I had once loved him, and besides, he came with a military guarantee: Duty, Honor, Country. He would never lie or cheat.

I sat in the dark, listening to his car fade away, at an hour before birds chirped, when the traffic began to hum at the burst of day, and then I remembered an address: 1776 Fairview.

It grabbed me. It was easy to remember—our American Independence, and a familiar street. And it was written on the inside of a matchbook cover. I'd picked it up the day before among the Kleenex, wallet, and keys dumped on to the bureau, an odd thing to carry since he didn't smoke anymore. I fiddled with the cover, reading it again and thinking about the address, while he shaved and scrubbed himself in the bathroom. He always emerged looking blister-clean and smelling of Irish Spring.

I remembered that piece of cardboard with an ad for an upscale local Italian restaurant on one side and an address on the inside. The matches—lined up like red-capped soldiers guarding an address.

That cold early morning, it hit me all at once. After everything, it would come down to a matchbook cover.

I flew straight out of bed, down the stairs past the hallway mirror. My hair was wild, the result of another failed permanent, my eyes were dark holes in my white face. I didn't even bother to stop for shoes. I needed to get this done. I ran. Afraid.

It was still dark when I put the key in the ignition, and for an instant I thought it would be better to go back to bed, put my head into my comforter, and stay in the dark and not know and not care. It was not too late to drop the whole thing. I should be calm and sensible and look at the big picture of all the years together. I should let the affair pass, if there was such a thing, and I wasn't even sure there was. Call it a bad cold. Sleep it off. But the thought of not finding out flew right out of my head, because I had to know.

I mercilessly ground the gearshift into reverse, narrowly missing the lawnmower, and the car spun out of the garage. In less than ten minutes, I was driving past the snug brick bungalow at 1776 Fairview where the windows burned yellow in the dark. They were the only lights visible down the length of identical houses on the block, but I wasn't looking for the lights. I drove along looking for his car. It wasn't parked anywhere on the block. What did I expect, that he would be standing next to it, or that I would see him in her doorway waving at me? Hear I am, honey. How are you?

I pulled to the curb in a slump. I was tired and I didn't want to deal with this. I'd been so sure, waking up, remembering the address and pieces of past conversations. The things he'd said: "Oh, I saw Pammie. You know, Pammie. She's moved back up here from Kokomo. . . ?" Pammie? It had to be a Pammie? Not a Mathilda or a Mary or a Martha? Pammie on Fairview. I couldn't even remember her last name.

Maybe I was wrong.

I relaxed my grip on the steering wheel and decided to go home and curl up in bed for what was left of the morning. I turned the corner at the end of the street to head home, and— one more time—I glanced in the direction of 1776 Fairview.

I wonder what would have become of me—of us—if I hadn't taken that one last look?

But I did. The alley opened up like it was shouting at me. And there, stuck out at an angle about halfway down the gravel stretch behind the back fences, his red Pontiac. He'd parked it out of the way of traffic, out of view.

At once, it was a triumphant moment. I had been right. But then, anger rushed through me, made me blind with fury. I yanked at the wheel and shot down the alley. I wanted to believe it was true—and at the same time, I didn't. There had to be more than one red Pontiac in the suburban Chicago area.

The tires bit the gravel and spit rock against fence rails and garbage cans and garage doors. I pulled up and hit the brakes just behind his car, and there it was: license plate ELG321. I had the presence of mind to check the numbers again. They were still the same; they belonged to him. I slammed my fist onto the horn and blasted it again and again, stopping just long enough to let each blast seep into the quiet houses of the surrounding neighborhood.

Rage is selfish. I wanted everyone around me to be as disturbed as I was, to have their lives deprived of their peace. Feel my anger. Feel the betrayal.

With the continual shriek of the horn, lights, one after another, blinked on in the other houses. But nothing changed at 1776 Fairview.

Then a shadow passed over the light inside. The door cracked open. I wanted to see his face, but darkness interfered. I imagined his confusion, and surprise, and then, the nonchalance of someone who always had his own unimpeachable reasons for everything he did. Then she came to the door. The two of them stood together, his foot propping the screen open, just a silhouette at first. He was wearing a T-shirt and unbelted pants, and she, her head like a growth sprouting from his back, peered over his shoulder. They didn't move, and all the while, I sat in the Taurus in the alley, my fury exploding. I kept up the wild assault on the horn even though it wouldn't do any good. He wouldn't answer a screeching horn. Besides, there was no answer for this.

I glared at him across the back yard of her house, over the garbage cans. I squinted through my anger; I wanted to see his face, but I couldn't make it out. All I saw was an outline of the two of them. Then, she withered away from his shoulder, and he pushed the screen door all the way open. In response, I leaned out of the car window and screamed at him, my face rock-hard, words I don't even remember. It was as effective as the horn. Up and down the alley, more lights came on, and doors opened. I didn't care. I think I yelled that I never wanted to see his face again. At least that was true. After that night, I could hardly look at him.

He stood there and listened to me scream, until finally, he stepped back into the house. The door slapped shut. The lights went out, and by then, all the doors had closed up and down Fairview.

He let me finish my screaming, and that was the last of it. At least he gave me that. But it didn't feel good. Nor do any good. Although I sat there for minutes, or maybe an hour, I don't really remember, he didn't come back out. I didn't expect him to. I didn't want him to. I couldn't move, sitting there, clutching the steering wheel, my motor running like crazy. I didn't know where to go or what to do, but one thing I didn't do—then, or ever—I didn't cry. It just wasn't in me. I was far too angry for that.

I sat in the car in the middle of the alley. It was near sunrise, and most of the world was still. I didn't hear a bird or a garbage truck, but thoughts ricocheted through my brain. The road ahead had rolled up that morning. And now I had to figure out what direction to take to get out of this mess of a marriage. It was broken; beyond fixing. Lucy's words from one hellish Christmas past came back. "You can't go on." I had agreed with her then, although, at the time, I was not thoroughly convinced. Now I was.

What the hell. I wanted to believe this tearing away would make me stronger. I would make myself believe it. Whatever happened next would be on me—all my own doing. No matter what, I had to make the best of it.

That day was the last day of "us" together, as a couple. But it wasn't the last and only time he was a cheat. It no longer mattered; I was finished, and I guess, he was, too, because he beat me to the finish line. In a phone call, not long after that morning, he told me, "I'm filing. On Tuesday."

8

HEAVY LITTLE KEYS

I sorted Dad's clothes. I packed boxes to ship later. I threw out fifteen garbage bags full of stuff that my parents had moved into the condo that I was not going to move again—except to the curb. The furniture had been appraised, and with Dad giving us the go ahead, we decided to divide it up among us. Fortunately, that was something we could all agree on.

In the blur of activity, however, I forgot about the Cadillac. But Dad didn't.

"The Cadillac," he said abruptly. "We need the car down there." He was sitting at the breakfast table, halfway into his favorite sandwich, a grilled peanut butter and ham sandwich—the treat he and Mom had shared during their college years at Purdue a lifetime ago.

I looked up from packing the soup tureen and bowls and linen placemats, and other stuff no one needed.

"OK," I said, layering a box of knives on top of a boom box and a carton of light bulbs.

Focus.

I hadn't thought about the Cadillac. But I took out the

to-do list that propelled me through the remaining weeks in the North, and in that moment, the Cadillac went right to the top. Of course, we were going to take the Cadillac.

How are we going to do that?

His last Cadillac sat in the driveway of the condo. He couldn't drive it anymore. Age had left him too slow and uncoordinated to drive, although it hadn't done much to dim his sense of humor and love of a good story, especially the one about the black Cadillac convertible he owned in the '80s—a doozey—with white leather interior and wire wheels. A thief stole the fancy wheels off the car, and later, he tried to sell them back to Dad, as they sat side by side, in their respective cars, during a one-minute stop at a red light. No deal. Dad got a kick out of that one. He found the value of a good laugh more important than owning anything fancy. After that, he kept his wheels plain and simple.

Dad's Cadillacs rolled along in the stories: of trips and football games, of dinners, and christenings, and weddings— even parades through town—of all the places those cars took my parents after Dad's business picked up and he could afford to buy his first Cadillac in the early '60s. Now, this one, the last of Dad's Cadillacs would have a story all its own.

Dad got up from the table and hobbled over to his walker. "Come with me," he said.

I closed the flap on the cardboard box I'd just filled and followed him. "What are you doing? Do you want some help?"

"I'll say."

He headed to the front door, and I was right behind him. "Dad, where are you going?" But he didn't stop.

We reached the door and I opened it, hoping he didn't trip on the raised threshold.

"We don't have time to go anywhere today, Dad." Impatience intruded, but I scurried along behind him.

He stepped down onto the front walk and pointed at the Cadillac. As he fumbled in the pocket of his khaki jacket, I had the urge to tell him to stand up straight. Here I was, in the middle of another role reversal, and another childhood memory hounded me: Stand up straight. Don't fidget. Eat your carrots.

Then, to my surprise, he pulled out a set of keys.

I thought I knew everything about Dad. His favorite sandwich. His regularly scheduled television programs. Every tie and sock and pair of pants I'd washed and packed. But, seeing him produce those keys, I was reminded—again— that I would never know everything about anybody. I hadn't even known my husband. And now, for the life of me, I didn't know how my father had come up with those keys. Unmistakably, they were to a car. Dad's Cadillac.

He handed them to me.

"Here. I want you to have these," he said, extending the keys in a curled palm. His nails were getting long again. He needed a haircut, too. As usual, I was easily distracted.

"What's this?" I'd driven his car every now and again, to the doctor's or grocery store. But we really hadn't cruised around town in the Caddy. There'd been no time.

"The keys to the Cadillac," he said. "My last Cadillac." His shoulders hunched up and down, and then he stifled the weeping, looking at me with teary, smiling eyes.

"Dad, you old sweetheart." I hugged him awkwardly as he leaned on his walker, and I stood in my bare feet, in my bathrobe, in the driveway, in the heat. "Thanks, Dad."

I turned the keys in my hand. He was proud of that special set of keys hanging on a ring with the familiar Naval crest.

Holding them, bouncing them in my open palm, I felt the weight of them. The responsibility. The heavy responsibility.

"You don't get it," he said.

"Yes, I get it."

"Take the keys; take the Cadillac. I want you to drive now. You're in charge." He straightened up, his eyes clear and blue.

"Thanks, Dad. I'll try."

"Don't take any guff." Then he turned to go back inside.

"What's that supposed to mean?"

"Just keep your eye on the ball. You'll be fine."

I dropped the keys into my pocket. Such a small thing, and so heavy. I patted them, then looped my arm through Dad's. "I hope I know what I'm doing, what we're doing," I mumbled, as I steered him back into the house.

"Well, damn it, I hope so, too," he said, shaking his head. He put his weight on my arm. "You can handle it. I know you will."

His walker rattled back to the table, and he sat down again with his sandwich. He took a large bite. Then he smiled up at me. "When do we blow this pop stand?"

Later that afternoon, when Dad was napping, I went out to the driveway of the dollhouse and looked at the 1994 Mocha Deville. I didn't get the "Mocha" part, because the car was definitely a mix of silver and purple and hadn't a thing to do with any shade of coffee brown. The leather interior matched the exterior, and the whole job looked like a large, shiny boat.

I climbed in, scorching the back of my legs on the wide seat. Since I hadn't driven it much, it would take some getting used to. I adjusted the seat forward and back, floating smoothly with each automatic surge. This would certainly be better than driving my seven-year-old Taurus—"The Shark," the kids' nickname for it—which was on its second transmission, thanks to my brainy idea to use it to pull a U-Haul full of our belongings. The car had certainly lived up to its name for its ability to eat every last dollar in my checking account. I loved The Shark (eventually my godson Peter ended up with it), but I much preferred Dad's last Cadillac.

I slid out of the car and shut the door crisply.

"Well, dearie," I said to the Caddy, "we're going to Florida. I don't know how, but we're going."

"We be stylin'," Tick said. I hadn't heard him come up behind me.

I turned around, grinned at him. "Don't get any ideas."

Suddenly, I remembered Lucy and me, and all the times in high school—and even before high school—when we took turns sneaking out with the family car. One Saturday afternoon when our parents were away, I talked Lucy into going for a drive in our enormous, grey Ford station wagon. I was just shy of a bold thirteenth year. We ended up crashing into a gas pump in downtown Lansing, and somehow, miraculously, the impact didn't do any damage (and, thankfully, police were not involved). That was a time they knew how to build cars—childproof cars with steel parts, not plastic. Lucy wouldn't go out with me after that, but the trip had been worth it. The thrill of driving that car, the thought of getting caught, knowing I had crashed it, and the fear of that excursion ending my secret rides were truly among my fondest, crazed, childhood memories. Didn't Dad know that we knew about the extra set of keys in the pitcher on his nightstand? If he did, he never let on. We finally told him years later what we did, and he even chuckled. I guess with relief that we hadn't killed ourselves or someone else.

Tick and I stood in the driveway, musing at the Cadillac, each for different reasons. He put his arm around my shoulder, and I reached for his strong hand. I stole a look at him, tanned and smiling. He was such an easy-going kid, almost a teen, and growing fast, with none of that impossible, withdrawn, sullen angst teens are so famous for. I couldn't figure out where he got his quality—to rise above it—except for, maybe, a gene from his beloved deceased grandmother. His irreverent teasing, however, was another thing.

"Nice, Mom," he said. "Are you going to let me pimp the Caddy?"

I poked him in the armpit. "I don't know what you're talking about, and if I hear you use that kind of language again, I'll give you a good one. And don't even think about taking the car out."

"Oooooooooo."

"Don't be smart."

"OK, sorry, Mom. I'll be dumb."

"You're being smart."

Tick was a long way from a driver's license, but he was dreaming of the day. I saw it in his eyes—I could see me in his eyes.

"Someday you'll drive it," I said, reluctantly. Time flew very fast, and, in a blink, he, too, would be driving his first Cadillac. When he ran for president of the United States.

Next on my to-do list was to find a way to get the Cadillac to Florida. Our realtor recommended Mr. Karr of Karr City, who transported her car to Florida every winter. "Sure," he said, "no problem. I'll get it down there in fine shape for $550."

The day finally came when I drove the Cadillac to K-Mart and met Mr. Karr in the parking lot. I handed him the keys and watched as he pulled the Cadillac up into a berth on the car-hauling trailer for the trip south. A silver-purple ship ready for launch.

"It'll be all right there?" I said.

"Haven't lost one yet," he said.

Let this not be your first, I thought, watching Dad's last Cadillac bounce one more time, and then settle down for the trip.

"Meet you safe and sound in Florida," he said.

9

WONDERFULAND

The first time I left for Florida was on a January morning in 1952 when I was six years old. My grandparents invited me to drive south with them in their new hunter green Cadillac, the early '50s bulbous version with pokey little fins. They spent half the year up North, next door to us on Bernice Road in Lansing, and the other half down in Bradenton near Anna Maria Island. Out of the dozen or so grandchildren, it was my turn that year to go with them to Florida.

That morning, dressed up in a new, maroon coat with a fur collar, direct from Little Bramson's in Chicago, I walked over to my grandparents' house with Dad, our feet crunching on the frozen grass and cracking the thin ice in the dip between our houses. The sun was just reaching over the trees, shining on the leafless, ice-covered poplars and housetops. It was a wonderland. A frosty, candy-coated morning. And I was on my way to Florida.

I was glad to be leaving home. Mom was expecting another baby, and that was a lot of babies in less than six years. It was chaotic and messy. Every morning, a baby was standing in the crib crying and wet with a runny nose. I already knew how to change a diaper and give the baby a bottle. At first, it was thrilling, but the thrill wore off—fast.

Even though I was glad to be going, I didn't want to leave my dad. He sang Irish songs and tickled us. He stood on his head, and we raced around to pick up the coins that fell out of his pockets. I loved that he had wavy black hair and was tall and handsome, with the distinction that he had a nose all over his face because he'd been a Golden Gloves boxing champ.

He picked me up and hugged me, then looked me in the eye. "I know you'll be a fine girl."

"I will."

"I'll miss you."

"Me, too."

"Who's the strongest man in the world?"

"You are. My dad is."

The seats in my grandfather's new Cadillac were plush, grey-striped, and scratchy. And the back seat where I spent four days was big as a couch. By the time we arrived in Florida, I'd thrown up many times on that seat, but my grandparents didn't say a word about the mess.

Grandma only said, "Poor sweetie, are you better now?" And my grandpa said, "Give her some of that magnesia." That night, my grandmother chased me around the motel room with a nasty, chalky liquid in a blue bottle.

I stayed with my grandparents for three months in Florida. That is when Grandma found the cottage. My grandfather, of course, went along with her wishes to buy it. They both had a nose for real estate of all sorts.

One afternoon on the porch, my grandmother was reading *The Bradenton Herald*, crinkling up the want ads, while my grandfather watched *The Secret Storm*, his cigar smoke mixing with the scent of gardenias that wafted through the screened door. He growled at me for racing back and forth off of the porch and into the yard among the orange and grapefruit trees. I flew across the spongy Zoysia grass, bouncing along with Punky, the cocker spaniel, his blond ears flopping, like we were running across a wide, green bed.

Later, I sat sweating on the porch, drinking a Seven-Up. My grandmother tapped the crumpled pages of the newspaper with a pencil and smiled at me. "Ha! Let's go out there and have a look." I didn't know what she was talking about, but I was excited, and, in my six-year-old brain, I knew this had to be something special. "Out there" meant the beach.

We drove just a few miles west to Anna Maria Island. My bathing suit was wadded up under the front seat, just in case. Off we went. My grandfather with the cigar in his mouth, and my grandmother with a frill of white hair blowing in the humidity. We clacked over the wooden drawbridge, past the tall, spindly palms and the mangroves, the Brazilian berries and the Australian pines, out to the white beach and turquoise water. Small, stucco, ranch houses were popping up, but in those days, the narrow, seven-mile-long island was still a tropical paradise of overgrown sables and palmetto.

The cottage stood on stilts, slightly crooked on the white sand, at the edge of the Gulf of Mexico. It was built of enormous cypress logs that were interspersed with wide swaths of stucco; it was a striped house, the black logs alternating with the white stucco. A rusty-red shingled roof topped it off, and the white-framed windows on either side of the faded green door were like two great eyes that peered right into my happy soul.

My grandfather was laughing when we pulled up to it. "Liz, the Gulf is almost at the door!" But that didn't seem to bother her. She was falling in love, and I was, too, the two of us standing next to one another looking out at the water, my hand holding her silky fingers. I squinted up at the sun. There, all around, yellow, soft, golden sun. The Gulf sparkled with diamonds of sunshine, and from that minute on, the turquoise water dazzled me.

My grandfather came around right then and there, chomping the cigar and looking up into the palms that lined the short street of crushed shell to Gulf Drive. Grinning, he nodded at my grandmother. She raised the edge of her floral housedress and waded into the foamy surf. (She went to her grave saying the salt water was good for her bunions.) I immediately flopped into the waves beside her, bathing suit forgotten.

My grandmother had saved for just this place. She kept "egg money" tucked in her rubber stocking, and it was from those savings she was able to make a down payment on the cottage. She was always frugal, washing and saving tin foil, making gooseberry and grape preserves from the arbor—she watched me pour the hot wax over the jelly to seal the jars. She was the first person I ever knew to clip coupons. As reluctant as she was to spend money, my aunts made a point of dragging her to Goldblatt's in downtown Hammond for a new outfit at least once a year. Sometimes I went along, and even then, we had to go directly to the bargain basement.

My grandmother bought the cottage and the surrounding lots—most all of it under water—for approximately $7,000. The seller was glad to get rid of it.

Over the years, when we were growing up, we left freezing Northwest Indiana and drove down to the cottage. The trip usually started on cold, dark winter mornings when my Dad woke us up, but I was always dressed under the covers, ready to go, a book and a bag of penny candy under my pillow. In the early days, we piled into the maroon Chevy station wagon with wood on the sides, someone always throwing up in the backseat, one lucky one standing up in the front seat between Dad and Mom. One time we flew down, the propellers of the airplane making me deaf for days afterward, which only added to the totally mind-altering experience.

The beach changed, receding and advancing, until finally we ended up with a football-size playground of sand like white sugar. We hid in the sea oats and then ran out in shrieks of laughter; we buried each other up to our necks, dug for coquinas, and made horrible soup with the tiny shellfish (with a recipe from an Old Cortez fisherman). We scoured the beach for sand dollars, periwinkles, and olive shells. We watched for dolphins, and fed lettuce to the manatees, and stale cereal to the seagulls.

To me, the cottage was paradise. We brought our school-books every winter and never opened them. All day we were on the beach, and at night, I watched the white edge of the Gulf in the darkness from my window when Lucy and I settled down in our small bedroom. The wind creaked and sang through the cracks between the logs. I went to sleep soundly, listening to the waves that rolled in beyond our window. Some nights, the Gulf rose up and the waves lapped against the cottage. Lucy was terrified, but a splash thrilled me. My grandfather told me the pilings under the cottage went seventeen feet into the sand. We were safe in the best place on earth.

One year, though, we couldn't go to the cottage, the year I was nine. My parents talked all the time about austerity and recession, words that I didn't understand, but my mother and father were obsessed with the financial situation. They whispered about it to each other. They never talked to us about finances, except in nebulous terms. The "situation" went right into that category of other unmentionable topics, which included certain illnesses. Finally, Dad announced that we couldn't go to the cottage because of the "situation with the business." What damn business, I wanted to know—repeating damn, damn, damn over and over again to myself in my bedroom, after slamming the door and locking it. It didn't make any sense.

I was inconsolable, chewing on the ends of my braids and crying into the cracks between the piano keys, when I should have been practicing the malaguena for Sister Loretto's recital. My mother shushed me, and, once again, I felt the gloom take over. I pouted.

"Don't pout," my mother said. "Your face will freeze that way."

"It wouldn't freeze if I was in Florida."

"Don't talk back to your mother," my father said. He snapped his *Chicago Daily News* open, hiding behind those pages as big as a tent, and took another sip of his martini.

We rarely missed a year at the cottage. We went back almost every winter until I was grown and out of college, and then we took our own kids down there. It was magic, day and night, winter after winter, and into March for St. Patrick's Day and dad's birthday. We jumped in the fierce winter waves and rolled in the sand until we were sugar cookies. We grew up on that beach, in the sun and under the moon, and the party went on and on. Until it stopped.

Now, that time is gone, but still, I hold on to it. It's there when I smell musty logs and the sea, or when I hear a seagull. I go back there instantly from wherever I am. It will always be there, the cottage that held us together in one laughing bunch with the waves rolling onto the white beach—as long as there is memory, no matter what.

We drove out to the cottage many times. In the '50s, we clattered over the wooden drawbridge, which made a frightening sound as the boards rose up under the weight of the wheels. We watched the eagles swoop out of the tall narrow pines on the causeway between the mainland and the island.

Burning pitch wafted from the fireplaces in the new neighborhoods—Key Royale, Sand Dollar Lane, Coquina Corners. The salty air was crisp in the winter, and even on cold sunny days, we went swimming and jumped in the high waves and walked on the beach.

My grandfather and I "stepped out" together to the Cortez fishing village, where he bought me a Chinese hat, and we watched the fishermen unload grouper and red snapper from their day's catch. Grandma and I baked cakes and made donuts. I wrote long letters to Lucy that consisted of wavy lines. My grandmother sent them anyway. I ran around and pressed gardenias to the dog's wet nose, thinking he would love the flowers, too, but he sneezed and ran off in circles. It was heaven.

My mother said, "I definitely left you down there too long."

10

JUST GO ALREADY

One blurry day, well before my mother's death, I had decided to move to Florida. That day had begun like any other abnormal day. I was going to interview a Buddhist priest for the newspaper. I hoped to get some tips about living the calm, unobstructed life as my marriage crumbled into a heap of dust. I didn't think I'd have any luck, but I was going to try. I was planning to get the secret of life and the story written by 8:00 p.m.

The kids and I were still in our big old house with the divorce close at hand. Sometimes they spent the night at their father's temporary digs, an apartment over a paint store in Lansing. This was before he moved in with The Mop. He was going through some strange creative phase, making furniture out of plywood and PVC pipe. Tick said his table wobbled and fell down. He was planning a spring wedding, and I told him the kids couldn't go. The ink wouldn't even be dry on the divorce papers.

I took a trip to the garbage cans, dumped the trash, and lugged the cans out to the back curb. At that moment, my next-door neighbor hobbled out of her front door. She shuffled, but at a fast pace that I knew would allow her to catch up to me. I was about to be ensnared in one of her question and answer sessions, but I would be forceful. I had many tasks on my to-do list.

"Hellllooooo, I didn't know you and the mister had patched things up. I see him come and go, and I hear him playing that pi-anny so loud, right-cheer in the middle of the day," said Mrs. Krantz. "Such a lucky thing for you, you poor dear thing, with those children and all."

"Oh, OK, thanks, Mrs. Krantz," I said, teeth set on edge. I shook the garbage cans fiercely and retreated.

I fumed. I could not even look him in the face. Now he's sneaking in to play the pi-anny. In my house. Which he left.

I slammed the door behind me and mulled this one over in my usual spot at the kitchen sink, finishing the dregs of old coffee and looking out at the garden that didn't grow. My neighbor was the local gossip to end all, and she pumped me at every opportunity for details of my disastrous decline into singlehood. The talk of the neighborhood, she called it, with the Ex carrying on with the other woman just down the street and all. I did not like being the Talk of the Neighborhood, but the good part was that it felt less and less like a disaster. I was glad he was gone.

But he is still coming back, I thought, as I pushed off the sink. When I'm at a town hall meeting, or running after a feature story, or visiting my parents, he is here, in my house.

I went to my comfortable, old butcher-block countertop and began slamming, chopping, and beating the components of a tuna casserole into a combination of ingredients that ended up more like tuna soup. I was spending far too much time in the slamming and beating stage of life. But I admired Mrs. Krantz for one thing: She was a pretty good reporter of everyone's comings and goings. Come to think of it, I had seen his unmistakable markings, like a cockroach leaves his trail. The bathroom rug was moved to the front of my toilet, a comfortable arrangement he enjoyed for hours on end upon the throne. I thought Tick had picked up the habit. But it wasn't Tick. It seemed the Ex continued the dumping even when he moved out, leaving a coffee cup and the daily newspaper ragged and defiled on the bathroom floor.

Later that same day—with the interview completed and a new lease on life—temporary though it was—I stared out the kitchen window, contemplating my two matching, lovely Japanese maples, when a very loud voice boomed from the front yard and through the house.

"ATSAPEPPER ATTABOY ATTAWAYTOGO."

I walked across the kitchen and down the hall, annoyed at myself for tiptoeing through the rooms of my own house. I peeked out the front window.

There he stood, feet planted like a general, so that all the neighbors could see and hear what a good dad he was. He was playing catch with Tick. I should have been pleased that he tossed the ball around with our son, when a lot of dads didn't bother, but I couldn't stand the sight of him since he'd moved out, and had at last taken up with the quiet, venomous Babsy—the name stuck in my teeth like old meat. That simpering adoring hypocrite, the one who taught Sunday school, all the while she was screwing my then-husband. That was some feat, since he claimed he was only fixing her tire.

The Ex showed up nearly every afternoon, and his baseball talk and his bravado woke up the squirrels, scared the dogs and cats, and thoroughly pissed me off. Today, he wore a new pinstripe suit, gold-stripe tie loosened. He bent over and wound up for a pitch, making a show of it, with his wing tips dug in the grass next to the For-Sale sign that stuck like a dagger into my yard. I still hated seeing that realty sign and knowing I would have to give up my house with its lovely, large rooms, parquet floor and winding staircase, and the wallpaper it took me weeks to pick out—an enormous blue and red Victorian trellis design on cream. But, the house would eventually have to go, and so did I. As I looked out at the Ex, I knew that sooner would be better than later. His shouts of encouragement, all the fake cheers, hurling the fact before the neighbors' ears, that dad was home, when, in fact, he was not, wore on me until I went to the back of the house and stayed in the kitchen, which, for all the irony, I realized that is exactly where he always preferred me to be.

I took the tuna casserole out of the oven carefully, set the bubbling concoction on the stovetop, and screamed.

I hadn't spoken to the Ex since his lawyer, who had trouble fitting into the leather armchair at his grand conference table, sat the two of us down during the divorce proceedings and said to me, "Before things get too far out of hand," it was up to me—as the "defendant" in the case—to rethink the topic of "maintenance" (like I was a car), and that I was asking too much of his client. And further, that I wasn't even entitled to any such support in the state of Indiana (or Texas, for that matter, the attorney added, somewhat unnecessarily). I should "be less negative about the whole thing anyway, and look for a real job," he said. "Get out there and earn a good buck."

I wanted to punch him in the face. The meeting ended when I got up and tipped the chair over, tangling my purse and tripping over myself.

"Why are you causing all this trouble?" the soon-to-be Ex said, half rising out of his chair. He put one hand out, then slapped it on the table. His face grew white and hard. For a second, I couldn't believe what I was hearing, and I was unsure whether he was going to help me or kick me out the door, but such is the confusion of divorce proceedings. It's all about getting out the door. And I couldn't get out of there fast enough.

We somehow settled the whole mess, but the Ex was still making himself at home in the front yard, every evening, just about dinnertime—and apparently, as my neighbor told me, at other times as well.

At six, with the tuna casserole still quaking from my screams, I opened the front door, and called, "Dinner's ready, Tick. Come and eat."

But the words froze in little shapeless forms and shattered when the Ex swung the mitt over his shoulder, grabbed his baseball buddy by the shoulder and said, "Naw, we're going for cookies and cream at Sloop's. Right, Pup?"

Tick shifted from one foot to the other and didn't look at me. He was almost as tall as his father, and he was growing up alarmingly fast, I realized suddenly, with a wiry strength that set him off as a fine athlete. He loved to play ball, and I was loathe to take the moment away from him. Still, he had to eat, and not ice cream. I stood my ground.

"Gotta go, Dad," Tick said, after taking a quick check of both parents who hadn't moved a hair in a full minute. "See ya." Tick bounded across the lawn and grinned at me as he flew toward the kitchen.

I glared at the pin-stripe body. It wasn't the first time he'd pulled this one, but I swore it would be the last.

The plan to move to Florida began to form. The idea hung around like an ever-shifting cloud, until the land of liquid sunshine seemed more appealing than ever.

After the papers were signed and the divorce was final, I had the foresight to tell my lawyer I needed to relocate.

"Do you have a job down there?" my attorney asked, in one $75, fifteen-minute phone call. "You should have some good reason to go down there."

He made down there sound like hell. I pointed out that up here was hell.

"How about, I'm going to go insane if I stay up here much longer and I may kill my Ex who lives in the same neighborhood with that phony witch and comes and goes with or without the kids anytime he pleases. I'm not free up here. I'm not divorced up here."

"Those are not very good reasons," he said. "Let's be serious. You are divorced."

Getting serious with my lawyer meant paying him more money. He talked of settling and not causing hassles, and he cautioned me about the hurdles of court costs and decision-making. I would be better off to agree to the Ex's demands and be done with it, he said. Of course, he always managed to point this out in billable increments—phone calls and meetings at $300 an hour. He told me during one perturbing $650 session that he was "worth it." As for leaving town, he said, I had to petition the court and notify the Ex that my intention was to move the kids more than fifty miles away (and to earn a "good buck"), however temporary or permanent the move might be.

"Go ahead. Do it," I said.

"That will be approximately $750, with court costs," he said.

"All right. I don't have much choice."

"You'll need to wait about six weeks for the paper work and the response, and if he objects there will be further recourse."

"ALL RIGHT."

The papers were prepared and delivered expediently. An answer never came from the Ex, not in a month, six weeks, or ever. When it was finally time to go some harrowing months later, I packed with a fury and looked forward to a new start in Florida. For all of us.

11

LEAVING THE DAMN KNOT BEHIND

Soon after Dad's decision to go to Florida, the dollhouse went up for sale, and we promptly had an offer. Every day was a step closer to getting out of there. We'd pretty much cleaned out the place—with Dad's blessing and moderate kibitzing.

Finally, the day of departure arrived, and I hired a limousine to take us to the airport. Dad climbed into the back and promptly banged his cane up and down. "Let's go, let's go, let's go," he said. He hated to be late for a flight, but we were four hours from takeoff. It was only a one-hour ride to the airport.

Tick was in the front seat with the driver, Tony, and Little Sunshine lounged in the middle seat, taking up enough room for four adults. They said their goodbyes and began waving. Jack, Julia, and Lucy stood in the driveway with their arms crossed and lips clamped. Julia was crying.

"Why does it have to be like this?" I said. I stood next to the car, the last to leave, hoping for a last-minute happy farewell.

I got no answer, except for a shifting of feet and a lot of

sighing. I had an awful feeling—that damn knot—in the pit of my stomach. I wanted to leave it in the driveway of the condo, because I was sick of carrying it around with me.

"Wish us luck?" I said, opening my arms for a hug. But none was forthcoming, and I didn't wait around for further rejection. I scooted in beside Dad.

"Bye," I said.

I looked back, but they didn't even wait until we turned the corner. They were gone. The knot was gone, too.

I opened a split of champagne for me and Dad, which was a bad idea. It gave me a headache, and Dad was incontinent. I hadn't thought of that. He was wearing diapers, but he still found ways to leak around them and get "damp pants," as he called them. He didn't complain, so I hoped he would be comfortable. We had a long day ahead.

Tick and Tony the Driver seemed far away from where I sat. Tick was enthralled with the workings of the limousine. Tony regaled Tick with stories about his adventures with Chicago's rock bands.

"I picked up the Rotten Turnips early that summer and drove them around Chicago to their gigs, and they trashed my limo." I closed my ear to the details, but Tick was glued to the drama.

"I'll bet we're a real relief after all that," said Tick.

"Oh, yous guys are golden. Golden, I tell ya," said Tony. "I'd rather have a hunnert of yous from here to the Yukon and back, than take those jackrabbits and all dem speakers and pear-fer-nalia around the corner."

I drank a second split, hoping it would drown the headache. Dad held on tight to the door handle and stared ahead. He'd been anxious to get on the road, and now that he was actually going, it made him even more anxious to be driven, flown, or shipped anywhere. He hadn't said a word since leaving the dollhouse. His last home, and the last place he saw his wife. What must he be thinking? He'd had the first stroke almost eight years earlier, and since then, the decline was obvious. Before the stroke, he was a man firmly in control. After, he was skittish about losing control. He didn't trust the world to go on by itself. Something would come crashing down, as he knew it would. The stroke happened in seconds, without warning, and he was changed forever. My mother lamented that sort of death in my Dad until the day she died.

I dozed off and on until we arrived at the airport. My daughter played with the knobs on the television, but gave up because it didn't seem to work. She started teasing her grandfather. She wasn't getting anywhere with that either, so she took a different tack.

"Sunshine, what's wrong?" she said.

"Oh, nothing," Dad said. "Really."

"You know, it's a miracle that your brain works." I opened one eye and was about to correct her for being a smart aleck, but I was slow. I saw the look of concern on her face.

"You had such a horrible stroke," she said. "But don't you worry about a thing. You just keep on being your little sunshine self."

Still holding tightly to the door handle, he leaned forward and chuckled, and with that, the anxiety of leaving was broken. He looked at Little Sunshine. "I'll try. I have good days."

"That awful stroke," she said. "What does it feel like?"

"Like you're not there at all. Floating somewhere," he said. "Then the doctor comes and he doesn't help much. They don't know a lot about the brain."

"But what does it really feel like? Does it hurt?"

"Well, yes, but I don't remember too well. You get a headache, and it's messy. I threw up all the time. It's not nice."

"I throw up, too."

"Well, don't do it now!" He tapped his cane up and down, and Little Sunshine laughed.

"Oh, I'll give you warning," she said.

I grimaced. I knew it wouldn't be much.

"When you were in the hospital, did you get ice cream?" she said.

"Why?"

"My friend Ally told me that people in the hospital get ice cream all the time."

"What kind?"

"I don't know. But you have to get something good out of all that bad stuff that happens to you."

"Yes, you do," he said. "I have you."

"Oh, Sunshine," she said.

I sat up and looked at the two of them. She wiggled in between us, and Dad relaxed. We were almost to the airport, and it looked like we were off to a fine start.

My dad enjoyed the bustle at the airport and the skycaps fussing over him, tipping their hats and moving him around gingerly and expertly. It always appeared to me that they liked their job, with the jokes and camaraderie that went on and on, and Dad acted like he was one of the guys. They produced the wheelchair crisply, tagged the luggage, and whisked it away, even before I realized the tickets were in the big blue bag on the cart.

I rolled Dad through the airport and he waved at people. On other trips in earlier years—Dad, with his white hair, ruddy complexion, and big nose, intrigued some travelers who asked if he was Tip O'Neill, the great Speaker of the House. Right off, they wanted to know what dad thought of Jack Kennedy. He was always willing to give his opinion of Kennedy, whom he described as Saint Jack, but then Dad would admit that he was not the Speaker and had never run for office, so that ended the celebrity interview. Soon, however, it would start again.

"Next one, I'll tell them I'm Tip."

"Dad, Tip O'Neill is dead."

"Oh, that's right. Who should I tell them I am?"

"The strongest man in the world."

"That's what I told you when you were little."

"I'm still little, sort of. And you're still the strongest man in the world."

He started crying then. As a result of the stroke, he cried often—especially when someone mentioned the Navy, or when he watched *Lassie* and *Loretta Young*, and *The Sound of Music*. He was just one big, old, sweet softie.

The airline staff wheeled Dad to the front of the line, and we followed. (If I were hard pressed to come up with something good about getting old, being whisked to the head of the line would be one thing.) When they strapped him to a carrier and put him in a tiny elevator, panic spiked briefly in his eyes. I quickly climbed aboard the cage and put a hand on his shoulder. The whole procedure—from the curb to the plane—was easier than getting him out of bed, into the shower, and dressed for breakfast.

Once he was in his seat on the plane, he couldn't wait for a rum and Coke. The drink, he said, reminded him of Trinidad and his days in the Navy. I was afraid he would get teary again and I'd have to explain the tears to the woman next to me, as well as to the flight attendant, but he settled down. I breathed a sigh of relief. I'd learned to take them one at a time, when they came.

Tick and Little Sunshine sat behind us with the headphones on, already lost in the world of music. They could have been on the school bus, or a train to Timbuktu. It didn't seem to matter to them. But during takeoff, Dad became anxious again. So, I took his hand and held it, like he'd done with mother. Anytime a plane was taking off, he stared ahead, just like he was doing now. He didn't like any talking and activity going on around him; he didn't think it was appropriate. He was praying.

"Dad, are you all right?"

"Oh, yes, I like to fly." When we landed at the airport in St. Petersburg, Dad told the pilot what a good job he'd done and that he ought to keep his job. The pilot thanked him in that hale-and-hearty way we have once we are grateful to be out of the air and on the ground.

Once we stepped out of baggage claim and into the sunny breeze and humid air, I immediately began to unwind.

Florida has a way of doing that.

It wasn't a long drive to the cottage, less than an hour. Once we were all loaded into the taxi, we were silent, tired. But when we rounded the curve on Gulf Drive and the cottage came into view, Tick whooped and Dad laughed out loud. Little Sunshine, though, was curled up on my sweater, like a cat; the excitement had finally knocked her out.

Our little home on the beach, the waves beating music

against the shoreline, opened welcoming arms. Sunset was approaching. Rain drops glistened on the sea grape and queen palms at the cottage door. As I pushed the door open, a flood of memories washed over me. It was hot inside the cottage. I strode through the living area to the porch and stared out at the Gulf of Mexico, letting the warmth wrap around me like a blanket. It was all just as I'd left it, the white wicker with faded cushions, arranged in a chatty corner of the porch, the rusting lamp on the table. I turned and threw the back door open.

We're here. We made it.

Seconds later, Tick was racing along the edge of the water toward the jettie.

Dad, Little Sunshine, and I followed Tick out to the beach. We sat in white plastic chairs and dug our feet into the sugary sand. The sun lowered quickly, spreading a gold path across the water, and soon the sky was filled with pearly pink-and-blue ribbons. To Dad, sunsets meant the end, but for me, this was a beginning. Our new beginning. Together, the four of us, perched on the edge of The Adventure.

12

WATER IT AND IT WILL GROW

The languid, hot August days induced complacency, but there was no time for it. The height of hurricane season was upon us, and soon enough the weather reminded us of this with a jolt.

It all began with one long, endless cycle of torrential rain, night after night. The water rose up out of the Gulf into the clouds, and then dumped its cache onto the roof. It sounded like we were holding out inside a hollowed-out drum. Thankfully, the roof and windows held tight. The mornings, though, sparkled clean and humid, and in the midst of it all, the kids started school. In the afternoons they ran around the island with their new friends like a pack of cats. But at night, again, the rains came.

One of those nights, in a deep sleep, I awoke to the strange sound of gigantic bubbles bursting in slow, lazy belches. I imagined I was inside my stomach after a huge Italian dinner, but slowly, the spooky sound launched me out of a drifting sleep. I lay there listening to the continuous *baloop, baloop, baloop*. Then I knew.

Fresh hell, because there was never enough of it. I sat

up slowly, swung my legs off the bed, and landed in water ankle-deep. Not thinking or caring about the possibility of zapping myself, I snapped on the light. In the dim glow, water bubbled up from under the baseboard along the wall. The floor shimmered with rainwater. A small rug drifted by and bobbed gently, like it was about to take off. With all the thunder and lightning, the kids surely would be frightened out of their minds. And now this.

Dad slept soundly. Holding up my pants legs, I splashed my way over to the kids. Shoes, socks, shorts, and tops were all on the move. An open paperback floated by. Nothing on the floor was anchored, except the beds. At that point, though, nothing would have surprised me. I began to get a dreadful feeling in the pit of my stomach, and it wasn't Italian.

Tick woke up and looked at me and at the floor with a sleepy eye, and then turned over and snuggled down into his covers. My girl sat up—a little angel floating in a white boat.

"Mom, is this part of The Adventure?" She rubbed her eyes and watched the waves ripple around her bed. The free-floating contents of the room bobbed and wandered, which gave a new perspective to my demands that they pick up their clothes. I tried to smile.

"It's really kind of cool," she said. "We could get a raft and float around in here."

"OK," I said, then sloshed over to her and tucked her in. She sank groggily into her Lion King quilt.

That's when I had a moment of terror at what I had done. I had brought a hurricane of sorts to my family, hadn't I? What have I done? I peered out the kitchen window and stared into the dark, impenetrable curtain of rain. We were a long way from Northwest Indiana, and family and friends. We were alone. No … I am alone. Maybe it was the dark, but the newness of The Adventure was beginning to dawn on me. I needed the sun. Not this incessant, unforgiving rain.

It was almost four in the morning. The rain continued to pelt the roof without cease. I don't know how long I sat on that kitchen bar stool, absently watching the hallucinogenic patterns on the kitchen floor, searching for solutions, considering my options in my divorced, jobless, frustrated, and now flooded state.

Suddenly, of all things, I remembered Kurt Nimmergut and a sunny afternoon and our airplane ride. It was a week after my college graduation when I went flying with Kurt, my college roommate's brother, a handsome, dark-haired hippy. I had no business taking off with him in that two-seater from an airstrip outside Alta Loma, California. But I did. We got up pretty high, and he handed the controls over to me.

"No way!" I said.

"Way," he said.

So I flew.

"Don't panic," he told me. "Take each moment—one minute, one hour, one day at a time."

I pulled back on the wheel, then bussed forward and scooped up the sky. That experience grounded me. I never forgot it, nor did I forget his advice. It was not my parents' station wagon or Cadillac. I didn't crash. I didn't lose control. I flew.

No, I would not imagine trouble and worry over stuff I couldn't do a thing about. There was quite enough to deal with. One day, one moment at a time. Now.

At least, I had a temporary solution. I jumped down off the stool and went for the Pinch. My Aunt Marian, who lived in nearby Bradenton, came over with bottle in hand to visit after we moved into the cottage.

"It's there, honey, in the cupboard. For when you need a little boost, or to celebrate."

Of course, I didn't think she'd meant for breakfast, but I would celebrate this new turning point, and Kurt's good advice. This small step in re-ordering my life. I poured a slug of the scotch into a jelly glass and drank it down. It burned with an earth-grounding jolt all the way to my wet pajama bottoms and damp toes. I climbed back up on the stool. Then, like the fingers on a drum giving up, the rain stopped. Still I sat, and although chilled, I remembered Kurt, and it gave me the warmth of new purpose, comforted me. I grabbed a legal pad and listed ideas and plans that came unloosed with the scotch. Pages and pages of them ended up in paper balls all over the bar, but a lot of good notes made it down, and stayed with me.

We needed to get settled—to find a house—maybe one of those little white stucco ranches, one with a barrel-tile roof. I'd have to figure out how to make a four-bedroom home out of one of them. I listed costs, tallied what I had in the bank—close to $90,000, with the sale of the Hammond house, the furniture, and china and such. I jotted down my favorite realtors with Sunday open houses and visualized my furniture fitting in these small, bright living rooms; pictured myself in the tiny backyards with crackling palms and scrubby grass, watching lazy neighbors who scratched away with their rakes to clean up the pine needles.

I wrote. I wrote some more. I drew floor plans and wrote descriptions of what I wanted (spare) and what I kept running into (clutter). I drew spheres that encompassed the cottage, the water, and the birds; the houses, the streets, the landscapes. It was good practice for setting off for The

Adventure—and for future stories, for my story. I let the ideas take over whenever they came and took shape on paper. My life was becoming a Venn diagram of intersecting circles of events and memory and plans. It was a mess, and lot to think about, and do. But I would do it.

Such is the goodness of hope. I will water it and keep it alive.

I had another belt of scotch.

It had seemed like such a fun idea to start over in Florida. And now, I had to make it work. Manufacture a balance in this new little family. That was the priority. The suitcases were hardly unpacked, and we were far from settled. Still, today, I would start.

I stopped to listen to the rain drip off the gutter. It was a mellow hour, but I knew I'd better not get used to scotch for breakfast.

The gulls were cawing at the first hint of sunrise. With a light buzz, I imagined that I saw the tide of water in the living room receding gradually. At least the rug wasn't floating anymore, and the miniature waves had ceased glinting in the overhead light.

I began sweeping out the last of the water, my feet cold and damp, tired all over, but loving the relief from disaster and the plans I'd written down. By eight o'clock, the kids were off to their dry school in flip-flops (with notes to their teachers). The sun was climbing into a blue sky and smiling cheerily, like the nightmare had never happened and the joke was on me.

Later that morning, I gathered the kids' soaked clothing and shoes into garbage bags and a laundry basket. Much could be saved with a good run through the washer, but the papers and books on the floor were ruined. Then, at the foot of Tick's bed, I saw a composition notebook: "Tick's Journal."

I shouldn't, I told myself, and then I sat down on the end of his bed and opened up the damp pages.

Page One:

I'm twelve years old and my name is Tick, because my grandfather named me that. He tells me that I have the intellect and personality of a twenty year old. He's not far off. I told him I was a grown up inside my body, and he believed me. I guess I'm different, considering the way I feel, think, act, and look at things.

Sometimes I think I'm abnormal. I catch myself philosophizing some out-of-whack mathematical problem, or how a machine works, or how it got its name. If you could explore my mind, you would find it a very complex unit. My father and grandfather say I'm special and gifted. They call me a Renaissance man because I like to work with so many things and express everything that my "advanced" mind concocts. That sounds pompous, but I hope not. That's the way it is and if you don't like it you can kiss my ass. Sorry.

I like to write stuff down about my personal experiences and interests, and I like to talk to other kids about theirs. Some kids have the gift of the pen, like Anne Frank. Now there's some story. I'd like to know this girl. I remember that she wrote about her pen and how great it was. She would probably feel the same way I do about this: I like to watch a sunset on the beach. (I've been blessed to see such beauty.) Look at it some time, and you will find its meaning. And if you are lucky enough, you will see a secret to life. You'll see the true beauty, not material beauty (like a model in some magazine), but beauty that is overlooked many times and cannot be marred or measured. It will always be there, and that's one thing you can depend on, one of the few things in life. You can hardly depend on anything else. That's for sure.

13

THE PROSPECTORS

The rain did let up, but barely. We were only into September, with the hurricane season still ahead, technically, until November 30. More reason to look forward to the holidays. I had the exterior of the cottage graded with crushed shell and coarse sand, plus extra drainage tiles, in hopes of averting more disaster. We had the assurance—on the best authorities of the forecasters at channels two, five, seven, and nine—that we were in for a quiet season and wouldn't be floating off into the Gulf anytime soon. Time would tell.

Meanwhile, we enjoyed The Adventure. The cottage was comfortable. It had taken many a hit through fifty years as part of the family, but it was sturdy and outfitted with all the basic needs. My mother, as much as she didn't particularly enjoy staying there, had made it cozy with practical, second-hand furniture and art posters by Gauguin and Lautrec—and my Uncle Louie had always kept the plumbing, air conditioning, and heating in good working order. The fixtures were pretty antiquated, tending mostly to the avocadoes and oranges of the '70s, but I couldn't help but smile when I leaned on that orange Formica bar that separated the kitchen from the dining area. All the sunburned family and friends, and friends of friends, the kids coloring Easter eggs, the beer drinking until dawn—it all came back when I wiped down that counter, served the kids' sandwiches on it, sat there with a cup of coffee in the empty quiet of an early morning by myself. The Pinch, of course, was reserved for special occasions.

Dad was in great spirits and slept until ten every morning; the kids were adjusting well, too. They went off to school, the ice cream store, and baseball practice with their new friends. I could usually grab a few hours during the day to get the chores done and plan what we were going to do next. It wasn't all a fiesta on the beach. Jack and Julia called to nag me about the renters—to remind me that we had to be on our way. The renters were coming.

"No, they're not," I said, during one terse conversation with Jack.

"Yes, they are," he said. "The first group is due to arrive around Thanksgiving."

"Jack, it's September 2nd."

"So?"

Granted, I still needed to get a move on. Sometimes, I stopped in the middle of picking up clothes or washing a pan, and I panicked. But then I made myself think positively, and that wasn't difficult. I was in Florida. The delightful duty of adjusting to sunny days and lapping waves, and the happiness of newness put a smile on my face. In between the meals and household chores, I managed to sneak in a little beach time, too—to catch my breath, read the real estate section, and think about finding that "dream house." Soon.

After my phone call with Jack, I made myself forget about his nagging, so I took my coffee and newspaper out to the beach to sit in front of the cottage. The sun was hot, but the air was cooler near the water, especially before the beach sizzled around noon. The place was nearly deserted, except for the real natives—the pelicans and gulls, sea urchins and sand dollars, the occasional manatee and dolphin that appeared along the shoreline. The powder-sugar sand stretched for about fifty yards from the cottage to the Gulf, where the birds dove for fish and small-shelled creatures. A few elderly shell-seekers—gone by noon and back by four—meandered along the water with their re-used bread bags half full of shells.

High summer was a slow time on the island, but the world of Anna Maria Island changed in winter, at which time Michigan, Canada, and New York moved in, the restaurants clogged up, and residents grudgingly (snowbirds brought cash) looked forward to Easter when they all went back home. I used to be one of those snowbirds clogging up the place, but things were going to be different, as Tick would say.

I pushed my coffee cup into the sand beside my chair and thought of waking up Dad. Plus, I needed to go to the laundromat and then check out some places for sale on the streets around Gladiola Drive. But the water sparkled and the morning still held a fresh breeze, so I sat, did lots of staring and thinking, and very little reading of the real estate section crumpled in my lap. I thought of my grandmother and how she found this spot, and I said, *Thank you.*

There was time. We'd only been at the cottage a couple of weeks, and with two more months of hurricane season, there wasn't a big rush. Even so, the tourists would come soon, looking for rentals, and the cottage was in demand. It belonged to the family, and we needed the rental income to cover the taxes and the roof. I couldn't put off finding our own place any longer. I knew it, and I didn't need Jack's reminders. I dreaded hearing from him or any of them—their negativity dragged me down. I often feigned emergencies in the kitchen so I could hang up. Thankfully, Dad was available, and able to add a bit of humor and equanimity, and end the conversation.

I had to find a house, something with four bedrooms within the budget. Florida had been a dream. Now I had to make it a reality. Prices on the island were beginning to climb. I went to open houses; drove around, and walked over scorched lots with palms and hedges, shell and sand, into cottages, stucco ranches, and birdhouses on stilts. I inspected appliances, sized up floor plans, flushed toilets, and poked into a variety of machinery and infrastructure, like I knew what I was looking for.

I liked the newer houses, but by law, they were on pilings with the living areas commencing at fourteen feet off the ground. Dad couldn't handle that. The more I looked around, the more I decided to stick with the idea of finding an adaptable ranch. I could make the adjustments to suit us, if I found the right one.

I drained my cup of coffee and stood up. Dad needed frosty flakes, the kids needed clean underwear, and we all needed a house. Thank goodness the beach would always be there, waiting. Something I could count on.

That afternoon, I drove down Pelican Avenue and found the perfect house with a promising yard full of crotons and palms, and neat, new windows set in freshly painted stucco.

I called the realtor for a showing, and once inside, I found a decorating scheme straight out of the Adams Family. Dark, furry bedroom walls and a black-and-brown bathroom, like a dungeon, and black lacquered tables and headboards, complete with gilt Japanese trees and teensy figures in kimonos. The owner had carefully matched all the furniture to the wallpaper. The kitchen, bathrooms, and laundry had never been updated; the garage door creaked like the House of Usher; and the windows were so layered with tapestries and sheers and thermals, I couldn't see in or out. If we moved into such a place, I would need an axe and a large Dumpster, to start.

In the following days, I visited many decorating night-mares with possibilities. At night, I went to bed and slept with the floor plans dancing in my head, and by the time I got up next morning, the nightmares had slipped away. Something was always wrong: not only the furry wallpaper and the black bathroom fixtures, but the wiring and other code problems that hadn't been touched in decades. In the light of morning, I faced the facts. I couldn't touch this one or that for all the expensive updating.

I didn't have enough savings to cope. I estimated a budget of $60,000 for a down payment, with some left over for deco-rating. The Ex's lawyer had reminded me how lucky I was to walk away with such a nice chunk. I reminded him, that, in fact, the sum amounted to approximately $3,043.48 a year after twenty-odd years of marriage.

I kept after the real estate agents, and they were getting to know me well. It was a small island, with just so much inven-tory. The agents were chatty and friendly, but soon enough I earned a reputation as a shopper, not a buyer, and they began to tire of me. One realtor I ran into at Tick's baseball game leaned on the fence and said, "You'll never buy a house on the island. You just like to look, and time's running out. Prices are going sky high. But there is that nice little place over on Coconut." His tone was clipped, and irritating, like a dripping faucet or the sound of a bird pecking me out of a pleasant dream.

The kids agreed. It was probably true I wouldn't make the leap. We would have to go on living in the cottage on the beach until we got kicked out—or drowned, Tick suggested.

"Mom, you like shopping," he said. "I don't think you want to give up your hobby."

That's when I met Cynthia. She bubbled over with sales persona. She would get the job done. She was a tigress, but she didn't pounce, and she was the only realtor who called me back more than once. I met her at an open house one Sunday, and after that day, she kept me posted with flyers, prices, and square footages, and indulged my love of poking through various "prospects."

One of her favorite sayings was: "You aren't looking for a 'house'. That's so cold. You are looking at 'Prospects for Progress'."

We became prospectors, Cynthia and I. She picked me up and we drove around to our appointments, and she kept me updated almost daily. If we weren't out on the road together, I saw her at least weekly at church where she stood at the altar and read the epistle. Her short, red-gold hair, depending on the light, gave her a peculiar halo, and when she passed out communion, she smelled of Tabu. I had a healthy mistrust of most salespeople, but Cynthia, despite all, gave off a positive aura.

She was my realtor. She stayed with me, and I decided,

without even thinking about it, that I would be loyal to Cynthia. She was going to collect the commission.

Lucy said that was stupid: "Go with the one who finds you a house, for god sakes."

She had taken to swearing at me on a regular basis now, and thankfully, it was long distance, so I could hang up on her for any number of made-up reasons.

I loved house shopping with Cynthia. She was plump and joyful, looking at me sideways with a glint in her eye like she had a secret, which was usually "the perfect prospect" with my name on it. Before she picked me up for a showing, she made up her eyelashes and pink cheeks and got decked out in a pastel pantsuit, decorated with pins that declared Realtor of the Year, Realtor of the Month, Best Realtor, most popular Realtor, and Chamber of Commerce and Rotary Club member. She drove me around in her large, immaculate white Lincoln, and we lapsed in and out of chitchat. She talked in a low voice, which prefaced serious talk, or in a screeching pitch, which meant she had a good piece of gossip to share. The latest bits were often tame but always interesting: On one trip I heard that Betsy Tibbens, formerly of Marietta, had a son who continually upset the geranium pots at Sun Landscaping. He was on his way to juvie. It made me shudder; where was Tick? This incident surely would appear in the police reports of *The Island Bystander*, but apparently there was more to the story, and Cynthia would fill me in later.

Cynthia, a fountain of knowledge about resources, helped me learn about heat pumps and termites, mold and flood insurance, taxes and code enforcement and overgrown land-scaping, which were the priorities of island ownership. It was nothing like living in Indiana. But she had confidence in me, and exuded the optimism that all things were possible, even the prospect of me finding a suitable house.

She didn't know it (I wasn't too aware of it myself), but she became a sort of therapist to whom I sounded out my plans. The plans were always met with endless enthusiasm.

"Just look at you," she said. "You could do anything, you could go back to news writing, or be a teacher, a public relations consultant, heck, you could have your own private business, maybe in the den of that cute little bungalow I showed you on Tuna."

She rounded off the conversation, as usual, at the bottom line, which meant, it would be difficult to find me a mortgage if I were not gainfully employed. This was a concern, and Cynthia delivered it with all due respect. This was our business at hand, and I'd already worked that one out. Dad was going to co-sign the loan, I was putting my own money down, and Dad was going to be my renter. I would meet the payments with my "renter," my savings, the child support, and "maintenance" I'd receive from my Ex—and the sporadic pieces I was able to send to the *Calumet Times*, and magazines and journals. Eventually, though, I would have to think of steady employment. I'd already looked into teaching English as a Second Language at the local vocational school. That would be my next career leap—into the realm of deciphering the English language for the growing population of Haitians, Latin Americans, and the occasional German and Korean visitor. But for now, I had another agenda. I had to find us a place to live.

Cynthia continued to be a great help. I figured the world needed a couple of million enthusiastic Cynthias to straighten itself out. Part of the reason I'd put off buying a house was that I'd lose Cynthia after the deal went through. But she was patient, worked hard to look for houses for us, and she became a friend. She understood our situation. She kept coming up with possibilities—ground-level houses with three-plus bedrooms—and I held out for that reasonably priced miracle house, because some day, maybe suddenly, Dad would not be there any more. I had to face that awful fact that he would just be plain gone, like Mom.

Dad had announced to the family before we left for Florida that he was going to be my "renter," and that he wanted to help out with the costs of keeping house.

Jack wanted to know, exactly, what that meant.

"Renter?" he said, like he had something distasteful in his mouth. "How much rent is Dad going to pay you?"

"Jack, lighten up," I said. "I don't have any idea how much rent he is going to pay me. It's his idea."

When I was going through the divorce, Dad slipped me some "Grants" and "Franklins," which helped me breathe a bit easier. At a dollar an inch, those feature stories weren't exactly padding my bank account. One time, Dad handed over the green and said, prophetically—"For your dream house. Goodbye chill house." It didn't mean beans to Jack that Dad meant to pay me rent. If I was going to fit us all into that dream house, I needed the help.

Jack called to bug me about it again. I hung up on him—before he hung up on me. The conversations with my siblings were abrupt; we constantly bumped into each other, even with the miles between us. The only problem? We were leaving bruises that might take an awful long time to heal. I prepared, mentally, for many more bumps down the road.

I didn't know where we were going to live, or when. But Jack wanted to know now. Too bad. I wasn't about to tell Jack any of my tentative plans. I was too angry at him, as usual. I was going to buy my own house, and I was thrilled at the prospect. I was also more than happy that Dad was with us. He seemed happy and content, and so were we.

Dad and I started out to the chairs under the windows in front of the cottage one late afternoon—my favorite time of day. The gulls were circling for their dinner before retirement for the evening. Dad picked up his feet carefully along the sand path next to the cottage. He was wearing his Irish hat and khaki jacket; he dug his cane into the sand and held my hand in a firm, bone-breaking grip, but I didn't care. That grip was love, and something I could hold on to.

We made our way slowly over the bumpy, sandy beach. He sat down and looked up at me. "Thanks, my little Sweetie," he said. "This is fine, just fine."

We sat together. The sun was lowering below the horizon in a fluorescent glow, a new one, more riveting and softening than the last. As the birds began circling, I dug my toes into the warm, white sand and held Dad's arm. The gulls frantically squawked and dipped, searching for a last snack. "Having their cocktail hour," Dad said, bending his neck to study them. He took off his hat, and his white hair fluffed like a cloud, like his mother's. Riding in her Cadillac, out to the island, to find the cottage. It took me back, flying up through the hourglass with the sand. I had wanted to go back, and now, we were back. We were a long way from the patio at the dollhouse. We were another step away from bad memories and on the way to make some good ones. I hoped.

14

THE BLUEBIRD OF HAPPINESS

"Cynthia, it's me."

"How are you, and the kids, and Dad?" she said. "I haven't talked to you in, well, days."

"We're OK," I said. "What's going on?"

"Well, a lot. I'm tellin' ya. Everything's going faster than I can list 'em. I had this little two-bedroom on Harkey's Canal, a darlin' fixer-upper, went for nothin' and I wish you coulda seen it, but it was a little small.…"

I loved the house talk. I thought of these places as having personalities, some on the seedy side, and others as quaint, possible friends. A lot of living had come and gone in those two-bedroom houses with yellow kitchens, terrazzo floors, and dusty old ruffled curtains on the windows that looked out on yards full of palm trees and twittering birds.

Cynthia told me about a couple more prospects, and then I broke in.

"Cynthia, you are a doll. You keep me going; you really do," I said. "Fact is, we need to make the move, and soon."

I heard the gears shifting at the other end of the line, and no one shifted gears faster than Cynthia.

"I'll run the list right this minute," she said. I heard her clicking away on the computer, even as we spoke. "You, your dad, and the kids! How did this ever happen?"

"I don't know," I said.

"Well, we'll just see what we can do about it. Something gracious, and spacious."

"Something with enough bedrooms that I can afford."

"Certainly not any of those boxes on sticks. Oh, no. No doubt about that."

"Just something I can paint all white and has enough stretch for the four of us."

The clicking stopped. "You know, I must show you what came up while we were talking. You're gonna love it. It has a barrel-tile roof and it's on a canal. Let me call you right back as soon as I get an appointment from the listing agent. Bye, now."

I'd seen enough white stucco houses with tiled roofs and I was tired of looking, and I bet Cynthia was, too.

Cynthia picked me up and we headed toward Willow Avenue, not five blocks from the beach cottage. We turned off Gulf Drive that divided the island like a spine, with the Gulf of Mexico to the west and Tampa Bay on the east, and right away I liked what I saw. I hadn't been down this road before, and I wondered how I'd missed it, except that vines and fronds shot up so fast on the island that new small jungles seemed to grow up overnight and create their own kind of hideaways. Pine trees, mangos, palmettos, and sea grape made a thicket along the stretch of broken-shell road that ended in a cul-de-sac. It was quiet except for the call of birds and wind in the palms. The Gulf roared faintly in the distance, a reassuring, tumbling sound.

I closed my eyes. Let this be the house.

"Wake up, Sleeping Beauty," Cynthia said. "Wake up and see what that wickedly wonderful old realtor has found for you."

She adjusted her keys, windows, and locks, papers and purse, and rolled out of the car onto the driveway in a flutter of sweaty silk and Tabu. I looked up. A neat stucco house stood proudly about a quarter acre from the road with a tall, silver-sided palm next to the front door—the sort of house I'd seen a thousand times. A row of neatly trimmed hollies ran along the driveway to a one-car, attached carport. The place was quiet as a church.

"Isn't it great?" said Cynthia.

"I think so," I said. "But what's all that?"

Huge shiny boulders—cobalt-blue rocks of glass in varying sizes—dotted the front yard, which was also completely devoid of any vegetation and covered with glittery, white pebbles. The jagged blue rocks looked like pieces of fallen sky on a bright, cloudless day. Some looked knife-sharp and lethal.

How odd, I thought.

"I'm not so sure about these rocks," Cynthia said as she breezed around them, while producing the key in one easy motion. We were inside before I could make anymore comments about the yard from outer space.

There it was—the living room from 1960, and nothing appeared to have changed since the day the house was built. The dining room chairs and table were heavy glass and bamboo, the sort I'd seen in my grandparents' house in Florida years ago. Historical tapestry covered two Early American sofas facing each other, coordinating with the maple touches in all the corners. We walked to the left and found a bedroom done up in gold chenille and red tassels, like Pauline and Ernest's Spanish bedroom in Key West. All I needed was one of Pauline's useless crystal chandeliers.

"Olé," I said.

Beyond the living room, an enclosed porch with brown plastic paneling and dropped ceiling looked out over a deep, wide yard shaded with tall, overgrown oleanders and sabal palms. The thin line of water danced in the sunlit canal, the one bright spot. It cheered me. But throughout the house, sculptured brown carpeting covered every inch of flooring, and unfortunately, it looked almost new and certainly doomed for removal.

"Great house. You really don't need to do a thing to it," Cynthia said. "Maybe a little paint and decorating is all." She raised her arms in a sweeping gesture, taking in every square inch of the place, and then she slapped her hips lightly for emphasis.

I was about to tell her I needed an axe, but she darted off to the kitchen. She turned on the lights, and roaches scurried across the avocado green counter. She quickly turned on the faucet. "See?" she said. The water exploded in a whoosh of brown, which matched the peeling pink and brown linoleum floor.

"At least that works," I said. The water finally calmed down to a nice, clear even flow. Cynthia and I stood there, contemplating the faucet, afraid to look elsewhere. The roaches and unknown creatures, surely, were hiding from us.

Yet somehow, I was already thinking about what I could do with the place, which would be to rip everything out and start over with the shell. After a cursory look at the electric and plumbing, the bare bones of the place appeared to be in pretty good shape. But, best of all, I loved the floor plan.

The front door opened to a living room, and the enclosed porch ran along the back width of the house. Beyond, a real backyard with a view of the canal and hibiscus around a patio thrived.

I walked out to the porch, and surprisingly, found a doorway to an added wing in the back with a bedroom. It was new, all white, with a tile floor, its own bathroom, and fresh paint. At least, I wouldn't have to deal with one room. Sliding glass doors led out to the yard where bougainvillea and oleander adorned the wooden fences. A mango tree as big as a circus tent grew next to the covered patio.

I liked everything I saw. So I looked some more. I opened the door off the porch. I could practically hear the grass growing and the fish jumping in the canal. As if for emphasis, a mango fell from the tree and clunked the corrugated roof of the patio. I could really love this place. Orange and grapefruit trees bunched up at the far end of the yard on either side of the stone path that cut through the grass to the canal. Avocado and kumquat dotted the yard, and suddenly I could see us living in this place. I wanted to sit and listen to the squirrels rustle up the palms, watch the egrets land in the yard, and gulls swoop over the water.

There were two bedrooms and two bathrooms in the main part of the house, but we were still short one bedroom. That stopped me, but for the moment, I put reality aside and enjoyed the view. It might not be big enough, and the plumbing and heating systems were serviceable, which were of minor concern, I decided. The house was solid. And the peace surrounding this place was what I wanted. What I needed. At that very moment, the house was mine.

And what about all those blue rocks? What was all that about? What kind of crazy person puts blue rocks all over the front yard? Maybe the neighborhood was full of goofballs who did stranger things than that. But I didn't care.

"Well, what do you think?" said Cynthia. "I can see that smile on your face."

"I like it, yes, and I'm thinking. It's definitely worth a think or two." We were short one bedroom. I wondered what I'd do with Tick. Later, we talked.

"Tick, sweetie, I'd have to put you in the laundry room."

"Cool. Das cool," he said. "With the washing machine."

"No, not really…. Tick, are you listening to me? Please take that headset off for a minute."

Robert Johnson was entertaining him, and he had no time to talk about the laundry room. He was teaching himself to play blues on the guitar. I could hardly get him to put the music down and get up off the side of his bed and eat, much less talk about moving the washing machine. He finally turned his beautiful hazels on me.

"Wassup?"

"Your room," I said. "I was thinking, we could move the washing machine and dryer into the garage and turn the laundry into a bedroom for you. Put in some built-ins for a desk and drawers. What I mean is, you would have a very small bedroom. What do you think of that?"

"Mom. Dude. I said, das cool! It's less for me to clean up."

"Very practical. And don't call me 'dude.' For someone in an honors English program, you sure talk funny."

"Sorry, Mother Dear. It will be very cool in there, chillin' and livin' large in the laundry room. Really, Mom."

"I'm proud of you."

My Island Boy.

"Cynthia, did you find out what's up with all those blue rocks?"

"Oh, you won't believe it."

"Try me."

"He invented the Bluebird of Happiness."

"Who?"

"The seller. He lives in Arkansas and he makes those darling little blue glass birds you see everywhere, and he makes them out of the very rocks you have all over your very own front yard. Yes! Your very own yard!" she said. "Isn't that something? Isn't that some kind of sign?"

Yes, it had to be a sign. I needed a sign.

I drove over to Willow Avenue, just to have another look, to the end of the cul-de-sac on the canal, past the majo trees and sea grape. I imagined those Bluebirds of Happiness nestled inside of rough jagged rocks, and it struck me as a good omen. If this was the home of the Bluebird of Happiness, I was a fool not to build my nest there.

I drove Dad over to "our prospect" so he could take a look. We sat in the car, pondering the yard.

"The Bluebirds of Happiness," I said. "They come right out of those rocks."

He didn't say anything for a full minute, and then he nodded.

"One time I got a birthday card that said, 'May the bluebird of happiness shit on your birthday cake,'" he said.

"Dad, this is an entirely different kind of bluebird."

"The kind that will stay the hell off my cake, I hope."

15

HELLO, DREAM HOUSE

The deal was settled at $218,000, with a down payment of almost $60,000. The broker insisted that I have a co-signer, because I was not "employed." I was about to argue that I was a caretaker, part-time writer, and a mother, but the words stuck. That wouldn't translate in the real estate world of dollars and sense. So, Dad co-signed the loan, with life tenancy, meaning that when he passed on, the deed was mine. Paperwork seemed so black and white, so stark and in my face. It brought me back to reality and grounded me again. This was only temporary. And down life's path, there were sure to be more changes. Dad wouldn't live forever. The kids would grow and go. And I needed to seriously look ahead to that new career.

Even so, I concentrated on my immediate concern—getting the dream house in shape. I had about $8,000 to $10,000 to budget for repairs and decorating. The inspector said the house was in good condition—old, but good—so, I started looking for a contractor to brighten up the place. This was easier said than done. I coaxed a couple of them away from other jobs. But standing there in my Early American brown living room, they just scratched their chins. They all acted like they were swimming through Jello, which seemed to be the normal island pace. Really, how complicated could it be to take all the old brown stuff out and put in the white? They all needed a good, healthy dose of Cynthia.

I searched the yellow pages and followed up on recommendations, but most were "busy right now." Building new houses, it seemed, was easier and more lucrative than fixing up old ones.

I was running out of time, and all these guys did was puzzle over the nature of the brown plastic paneling on the porch.

"Now, ma'am, you just don't know what you'll find back o' dat," said one contractor. He told me things that had nothing to do with what I wanted—and what the house needed.

"That mango tree there attracts rats. And that there elevation at the canal is an invitation to a flood. That barrel-tile roof, well, it's time is just about up."

Irritated, I was on the verge of telling him I liked mangos and rats, and that in nearly forty years, the water had never come over the bank. Instead, I told him I was late for the library and I had to go, and so did he.

Another contractor told me I had to tear up the concrete floor, re-route pipe around the house, and tie it in to the main sewer at, say, ten dollars a foot for starters. This opinion took most of an afternoon to unfold and, in the end, proved to be entirely not the case.

Finally, Steve Kreider of Horizon Homes came to the rescue. He hired a plumber to hook up the washer and dryer in the garage, and Tick had his bedroom. When I mentioned my all-white decorating scheme to Steve, he offered me ninety-two shades of white from which to choose. Even though it was slow going, he steered me in the right direction. Mermaid Foam for the floor tile. Angel Wing for the kitchen cabinets and counters. And plain old white ceiling fans. One choice was easy: Tomato Bisque for the new French door at the entry. All amazingly within my budget. I just prayed the heat pump didn't give out.

A month later, light streamed into my new, white house; it was truly beatific, a miracle. It was as clean and slick and dazzling as a new egg. A load of Dad's things was due to arrive in a few days. I had other things in storage, which I needed to retrieve, but I'd done this drill many times before—nineteen times in the army with Hubby and the kids.

This new old home—small and spare—was my last stop as far as I was concerned. A place to begin again. I looked out across the backyard. I realized with a stab of nostalgia that my new old Florida house wasn't much different from the very first house Hubby and I had bought together in Columbus, Georgia, many happy years ago. That three-bedroom ranch had small, high windows. It, too, had been dark inside, and was nestled in a stand of tall pine trees with a stream out back that ebbed and flowed with the rain.

There, the Ex gave Tick his first fishing pole. Tick was so small, but the Ex taught him to use the knife, and Tick learned to filet and fry the tiny fish, bones and all, in butter. They were   hardly a bite, but Tick loved the catch and the flavor of being a fisherman.

Then, too, there was a life full of promise, and now, I was trying again. Other than that, nothing really was the same.

Of course, Tick could fish in the canal. Maybe get a small boat. The beach was only two blocks away where Little Sunshine and I could walk to look for sand dollars. The backyard was perfect for enjoying birds and the rain, and

Dad could sit on the patio and ruminate. Feed the herons. Watch Puny chase the gulls. Yes, Puny made it, special delivery with a friend who drove down to Florida.

I walked from room to room, my sandals slapping the new tile. I drew a grid of the house and doodled away. I didn't think past the hazy, October afternoon, except to wonder about yellow walls for the breakfast room, geraniums outside—and inside—year round! Or would it be too hot? What a wonderful dilemma. That afternoon, wandering from one white shell of a room to the next, I knew I needed just a little more time to get the place ready. The moving van wasn't due to arrive for a few days.

That's what I needed—time. There was never enough lately. I walked out to the canal where the sun hovered over the palm trees like an orange balloon. We would move into the house in the next week or two—maybe three, if those kitchen cabinets didn't arrive. Fortunately, we were on schedule to get out of the cottage before the renters descended for the winter.

It would be perfect. But, I had no way of knowing that I had very little time. Not three weeks. Not even two. The move would be upon us before the weekend.

16

WATER IT AGAIN

We did have some warning. But not much.

Soon enough, Josephine hurled herself across the Atlantic and beat a path toward the southern tip of Florida, which was against all predictions. Such is the inexact science of hurricane forecasting. As it was, she was bearing down on Florida with a vengeance.

As Josephine made her way north, my sister Lucy planned to head south for a visit. The renters weren't due until after Thanksgiving, so Lucy wanted to celebrate her birthday at the cottage.

"I'm coming hell or high water," she said. I told her that is exactly what she probably would get for a birthday present. She had already shed her managerial blue suit and packed her black bathing suit, and she was bringing a bunch of friends with her.

I stood on the beach in front of the cottage and looked out at the edge of Josephine in the southwestern sky. The horizon gleamed with a thin layer of silver under towering black clouds. The Gulf beneath was a milky, choppy green. But due north, the sun shone over a bright blue-green expanse of water. Florida weather, like my life, was a mix of lazy, hot and cool, jasmine-filled contrasts. Some stormy days and some smooth days that could likely change with lightning speed. It's what I loved about living there, and also feared.

I ran back to the living room where the kids were glued to the television screen watching the newscasts break into programming with fresh updates. I told them to sit tight and not even think of moving from that spot. Two pairs of eyes stared up at me from the floor in front of the television. My kids were afraid, I could see that. But I would have to trust them to handle The Adventure—again—and to weather this new storm.

"It's all right," I said, hoping they didn't catch the waver in my voice. The two heads turned back to the screen; Tick nodded, his shoulders hunched. Little Sunshine scootched closer to him.

Dad was asleep—he would sleep through a hurricane. The sounds of birds and the waves had done wonders for his mental attitude and sleep pattern. But he had to get up. We had to be ready. And now, in the middle of all this, Lucy was due to arrive. Along with Josephine, who was gathering speed. So far, though, she was only a Category One hurricane, clocking winds of less than eighty miles per hour.

I decided Dad could sleep a bit more. I dashed out to the beach where the wind whipped up the sand into small ghosts, needling my legs. The hurricane was still safely offshore, well to the south, and it was highly unlikely that it would land directly on the island, but the possible outcomes were frightening. Fast-moving hurricanes, packed with high winds, often tore a path straight up the Gulf, blasting into the Panhandle. They didn't normally stop and take an abrupt right turn into the western coast of Florida. Even so, the combination of a passing storm and high tide promised to bring a surge of water onto the shore, especially into the flood zone where the cottage stood. It could be—would be—the perfect storm, when all the parts of nature collide to create havoc.

The water was quickly rising in giant waves. It brought me back to the March 1993 Storm of the Century, when, out of nowhere, the wind ripped off the roof, dumped it in a palm tree down the street, and water flooded five feet deep all around the cottage. That storm cut a narrow swath of destruction, with neatly trimmed edges, directly across Florida, wrecking everything in its path. And March isn't even hurricane season.

I turned back and looked at the low, flat roof, the line of windows behind a dune about thirty yards from the advancing water line. The cottage had withstood decades of storms, but this one promised to be one of the worst. We had to get off the beach.

A bolt of fear shot through me. Lucy and her friends Marque, Ellie, and Bruce were due to arrive later that afternoon.

"I don't give a hoot about the hurricane," she told me the day before, far away in her snug, glass-box Chicago high rise. "What's a little water?"

Swirling around me and riffling through my hair, the ghosts whispered, Water is everything.

When Lucy arrived, she peeked in at Dad, who was stirring, and kissed the kids, who hadn't moved from in front of the television. She shrugged at the forecast. Lucy was well dressed for a hurricane in a fine, merino wool V-neck dress in melon (Saks, no doubt), and polished nails to match.

I was glad to see her, but apprehensive and anxious. First things first, we poured ourselves a quick chardonnay. We both took huge swigs. Then we walked out onto the porch and stared at the Gulf. In the few minutes it took to pour the wine, the waves had pounded closer with alarming speed. A heaving expanse of water, no longer friendly green but menacing grey, rolled toward us. There was still some beach, but it was disappearing. Fast. I took another swig of wine.

Before long, a wave hit the wooden slats under the windows. It was nothing more than a tease, just a gentle splash between the cedar boards.

"Josephine has arrived," I said.

"Who's Josephine?" said Lucy.

I pursed my lips. Lucy's ability to ignore the occasional inconvenience of the world around her astonished me. "Josephine is the hurricane, the devil, the storm. I told you, before you came down here."

"Oh, that," she said. And then she laughed.

I looked at Lucy with alarm.

"What are you laughing at?"

"Oh, remember when we were little and we slept under the windows, and the water did the same thing then? You scared the hell out of me, said we were all going to float away to the Shell World or some such thing. Remember?"

Yes, I remembered. We were seven and eight, and I loved the water slapping the cottage and the dark mysterious storm all around us. Now I was old and afraid.

"You were freaked out. And now you're not?" I said.

"Oh well, people change. Don't they?"

"Yes," I said. Somehow my sister and I had traded places. "I'm freaked out. We have to get out of here, Lucy."

"Why? It's only a little water. Look at that," she said, pointing toward the window with an empty wine glass. "A little trickle."

"But look out there. The beach is disappearing."

"Oh, it'll blow over."

"That's what I'm afraid of. It's going to blow like hell."

As the water began to splash through the cracks with an insistent, unnerving rhythm, we both backed away into the cottage. Now, in place of the wide, glistening white beach, a horrific grey veil of water swayed back and forth outside the windows of the cottage. Wind hissed and whistled in a long melancholy chant. Then something, not so far away cracked. A timber or a branch hit the wall of the cottage behind us. The palm trees at the side door near the Cadillac swooned and bent double in the wind. They could do that. They had amazing agility—so they were at home dancing around in Florida hurricanes. Not so malleable were the non-native Australian pines with shallow roots that towered over the shoreline. Enormous branches crashed into roofs and cars and people.

I stood rooted to the cedar planks of the cottage porch and wracked my brain. We really had to get out of there.

The weather finally created a climate change in Lucy's expression.

She called the Blue Dolphin Motel and started grabbing her things. She was able to catch her friends, who had somehow landed at the airport in the mess of weather and headed them off to dry land on the mainland in Bradenton.

"Are you coming?" Lucy said.

Tick yelled, "MOM, DO YOU SEE HOW CLOSE

THE WAVES ARE GETTING?" He was madly clicking the television remote, scanning the news for fresh reports of disaster. "THEY ARE SAYING WE'RE IN FOR A BIG ONE!" He jumped up and pulled Little Sunshine to her feet. She gripped the back of her brother's T-shirt, her eyes darting from her brother back to me. They both stared at me. "Where's the Gampers? Is he still sleeping?" Tick said. His voice was controlled, his eyes reflected terror, all the while he took his sister's hand. "We better move it," he said.

"Yes." I stood there with my arms stiffly at my sides, deciding what to do next. Trying to make myself move.

"We'd better get him up," Tick said. "It's going to be like pulling a boat to get him out of here, you know that, don't you?"

"Tick, really. We're going."

"Where?" Little Sunshine shrieked.

Yes. Where?

"I'm thinking that today is moving day." I tried to look wise and sound calm.

"Where to?" said Lucy. She was already holding the door open with her back, and having some difficulty, her arms overloaded with magazines and bags. "To that new house of yours? You don't even have beds and stuff. Why don't you come to the motel? There's plenty of room there." She'd had no trouble finding a vacancy, since most tourists stay away during hurricane season, except for Lucy. She let the door bang shut, then hastily scratched down the name and number of the motel and waggled it at me.

I was scurrying around, garbage bags flapping. "Thanks, but I think we'll head over to our new place," I said. "We do have mattresses." My eyes scanned the kitchen and living room for the things I needed to grab.

"That's just great," Lucy said as she turned and dashed for the rental car. I watched her in awe. Backing out of the driveway, she struggled to roll down the window. "Good luck," she yelled. "Call me!" She peeled away, sending bits of shell into the blowing sand and rain. "Happy Birthday to me," she howled.

After her departure, the wind forced the front door of the cottage open and blew it back and forth as I tried to control this large hunk of metal and glass. A final swing in my direction had the impact of knocking some sense into my head.

I ran from the kitchen to the bathroom, throwing pills, peanut butter, diapers, and schoolbooks into a garbage bag. Fortunately, I had a sort of "hurricane kit" already prepared—we had one for the renters, so I decided to borrow it: canned food, flashlight, batteries, bottled water, plastic bags, towels, a deck of cards, and some dice.

"Mom, where are we going?" This time the question came from Little Sunshine and Tick in one loud voice.

I stopped flinging myself from one end of the cottage to the other and dropped the bulging garbage bag. I hugged my daughter and nodded to Tick. His arms were folded and his feet planted, like he was awaiting orders, thank God. "We're moving in. We're going to move into our new house!"

From the look of the roiling Gulf, we probably had less than half an hour to get off the beach. Josephine was not going to land directly, but she was bringing water with her. A lot of water.

Our new house was at a safe elevation, the inspector promised. It was built of cinder block and the canal had never breached the bank and flooded the house—at least not in the last forty years. Then I thought: There is always a first time. But we didn't have a choice. There was no time to get over the bridge with Dad and the kids and all the stuff I had to pack into the Cadillac. We didn't have the beds put together at the house, but we had water—plenty of water—and electricity and mattresses. I kicked myself for not paying closer attention to the weather. I'd wasted time running around picking out colors for the kitchen and the front door, thinking about what flowers to plant in my new urns on the patio, and sketching furniture arrangements for the new family room.

I heard it from Cynthia before I heard it on Channel Five. She called to warn me, but I had not listened. "This one's unusual. It's getting most of its strength in the Gulf!" she said. Tick ran back and forth with pillows and blankets, loading them into the car, along with clothing, books, towels, blankets. He was, as usual, way ahead of me.

"I'm going to get Big Sunshine," my daughter announced. She broke away from Tick and raced up the stairs. I followed her.

Dad was snoring, oblivious to Josephine, or us. I hurried over to the window and slammed it shut, the salt spray blasting me in the face. I'd left it open to let in the cool October air, but now I met a vast, grey humid presence. I peered out of his bedroom window. Josephine engulfed us with no definitive sky or water line. And the beach, as far as I could see, was one heaving expanse of grey and white-capped waves, churning dirty water, restless, like it was being shaken by crazed deep-sea creatures.

"Jesus," I said.

Little Sunshine held a bag of her grandfather's goods while she nudged his shoulder that stuck out of the quilt. He still had his hat on.

"Sunshine, get up," she said. "We have to take another trip."

Dad began to come around, and I helped my daughter sit him up. He was confused. This was not going to be easy. The wind picked up. Irregular, howling gusts rattled the windows. I could hardly hear myself think, even with the windows shut.

"What is it?" he said.

"Dad. Honey. Got to go," I said. I was searching under the bed for his shoes, zipping his windbreaker. Little Sunshine had one of his hands and was stroking the wrinkles smooth. "I mean now, Dad. Let's get these shoes on. Josephine is coming."

"Who?" he said. "I don't know any Josephine."

"It's Josephine … the hurricane, and if we hang around much longer, we will be sorry we met her."

"What the hell are you talking about?" He looked out of the windows, at the sky, full of wild, flying clouds, and I could see him listening. He was still for a moment, and then bent over to slip his foot into a shoe.

"Yes, I see, I see," he said. "Looks like the deck of the *Barnes*."

Dad related more and more to his old Navy days, to the terrifying, heaving days on the ship. Looking out at the water, I felt like I was on the deck of a ship.

Tick hovered in the doorway to the bedroom, waiting for us.

"Take everything, and your sister, and get in the car, Tick," I told him. They both hesitated a second, before bolting for the stairs, but not before Little Sunshine patted Old Sunshine's arm and Tick affixed his grandfather's hat back on his head.

Dad didn't seem concerned about Josephine, no more than Lucy had been. At first. He moved at a snail's pace, carefully running his hands over his jacket and checking his pockets. He picked up a few wads of Kleenex. He put his glasses on. I wanted to hustle him along, but I was afraid of unnerving him—and myself. If I fell apart, it would wreck us all. So, I prodded him carefully down the stairs, all the while he banged the cane on the steps and hung on tight to the railing. I followed with the walker.

When we reached the bottom of the stairs, the water was rushing furiously through the cracks under the window. With maddening predictability, a wave hit the windowpanes, but they resisted. My immediate destination was the car. The beach was gone, and soon the water would be swirling around the cottage and cutting off our escape route. The thought was terrifying. But still, we had time.

I coaxed Dad through the porch and toward the door. Little Sunshine and Tick were already in the Cadillac.

Then, Dad stopped. "I don't want to leave."

"What? Dad, we have to get out of here. Now!"

"This is my mother's house. Elizabeth's house! More water has come and gone here than you can shake a stick at!" He shoved his cane up into the air like an exclamation point.

I was at the point of screaming.

Tick and Little Sunshine peered at us from the back seat of the Cadillac. "Hurry!" Tick yelled, "You can make it. Gamps!"

A wave burst around the corner of the cottage and raced up the front hubcaps of the car. Two plastic chairs and a green-stripe chaise lounge cushion whirled past the cottage door, riding a torrent of water that had washed around from the beach and out to the street.

Dad wouldn't budge. He was a large man, six feet, 235 pounds. I would never get him out of there if he didn't pick up his feet and walk. I could have killed Lucy for leaving me alone, but it was my own damn fault. I had put us all directly in the path of this mess.

Something snapped in my head.

"Dad, if we wait much longer, I can't get you into the car." The words came through clenched teeth. "You'll have to swim. We'll all be swimming up to our asses in alligators."

Little Sunshine leaned out of the car window, waved, and screamed over the wind. "Come on, Sunshine. You can make it. We need a little sunshine."

Dad lifted his head slowly, and then, of all things, he chuckled. Carefully, he stepped over the threshold. I held on to him, all the while the damn walker dangled on my arm, flailing in the wind.

Before I knew it, Tick was out of the car, his hands at his grandfather's back, guiding him. Steady, sure, strong.

I pulled Dad forward against the wind, which he hated, so I had to be ginger, or he'd dig in for sure. Fortunately, Tick was doing most of the work, talking and encouraging his grandfather toward the car. They were like two old fellows going for a walk—oblivious—their heads together, mumbling something I couldn't hear over the wind. As we made our way to the car, a wave broke over my ankles. The force was like a nasty, insistent wall shoving against me, moving me where it wanted me to go. Not the way I chose to go. Dad sloshed through the water, yelling about his shoes. Then with another step, one of them came off and whooshed down the street after the chaise lounge.

Finally at the car, and, God help me, I don't know how, Tick, that young wire of a son of mine, lifted his large unwieldy grandfather into the seat in one piece without any broken bones or other mishaps.

It took all my strength to open the driver's door, but with a gust of wind, courtesy of Josephine, I managed. I climbed in and slammed the door, which skimmed over the top an ebbing wave.

"Jesus Mother of God," I said.

"Yes, pray," said Dad. "And let's put a nickel in it."

Oh, now you're ready.

In the backseat, Tick and Little Sunshine huddled together between stuffed garbage bags, their faces pinched, their eyes wide, as indistinguishable objects flew past the windows.

I grabbed the steering wheel and stared frantically through the windshield where the water fell in wavy, glistening sheets. It gushed deeper and deeper around the side of the cottage, its force worse than the wind, heavy and fierce, and dark. Only yesterday, the water shined blue on the white beach. I backed out of the driveway as the Gulf surged around us and pushed us away from the beach. No one said a word. The wind shrieked. The Cadillac picked up speed. Huge wings of water rose on either side of the car, like some enormous bird lifting us to higher ground and to our new home on Willow Avenue, where we landed sopping, but relieved and tired. And safe. At least for the time being.

The rain thrashed, and buckets from hell dumped from the sky, hurling mangos off the backyard tree onto the roof. I watched from the porch while tree limbs snapped and tore through the yard like hapless arms and legs.

That night we huddled in our new house, each of us settled on mattresses with a scant assortment of bedding we'd dragged from the cottage. In the absence of electricity, I lit candles, and we ate peanut-butter-and-jelly sandwiches and listened to Josephine barrel across the island.

Tick's answer to everything lately was music. I'd bought him a second-hand Martin guitar, and while listening to blues, he carefully picked his way through each tune. He'd done the same with Beethoven on the piano—a gift from father to son, each one with a fine-tuned ear for music. Tick found an old bentwood chair in the garage and placed it in a corner of our mattress-strewn living room, where I hoped to settle Moroccan rugs, and my Sheraton sofa and side chairs one day, if we ever got out of this high and dry.

Tick hunched over his guitar and sang Robert Johnson's "Terraplane Blues," his voice cutting through the terror of the wind. My father lulled, resting his large white head on a stack of pillows. I sat cross-legged with Little Sunshine, arranged amidst an assortment of quilts and pillows in a corner opposite Tick. I was plenty happy—that we were together, that the wind was dying, that we'd made it through the hurricane.

Later that night, curled up under a blanket with my daughter, who finally fell asleep, I listened to the hurricane surge in monstrous gasps over my new old house, and I prayed that the tiles—and the canal—would stay put. Finally giving up, I drifted off. And Josephine whirled away, making a beeline for the Panhandle where, finally, she died.

The next morning, the sun shined bright on the detritus that Josephine left. A scattering of broken trees and leaves littered the roads and yards. The water had risen in the canal over the dock but only splashed onto the curve of lawn where the salt water killed the grass. The storm left us, not only with relief in our hearts, but brooms and plenty of garbage bags for the clean up ahead of us.

17

ONE BEAUTIFUL MESS

My sister Lucy had her fifteen minutes of fame that day, too. She appeared on the front page of the *Sarasota Herald Tribune*, standing on the porch of the cottage, holding her forehead, and grimacing. The caption read: "Owner Distraught Over Loss of Property." But, in fact, Lucy was badly hung over. She and her friends had, after a quick stop at the liquor store, made it to the Blue Dolphin. While they listened to the hurri-train roar through the pine trees overhead, they chugged half a dozen bottles of Murphy-Goode pinot noir and chardonnay.

Standing on the porch of the cottage, I surveyed the damage. Broken chairs, bent window screens, and debris perched atop mounds of sand dotted the beach and created a new landscape. Two walls of the cottage were missing. The rooms upstairs, without support, were cantilevered over the porch. Much of the lost timber, nowhere to be seen, had probably rushed away in the flood, along with the chaise lounge and Dad's one shoe.

Marque stood next to Lucy, wearing the only outfit I'd ever seen him wear—his Speedo. His curls were still tussled but shorter, and he grinned while he sipped a Dos Equis. He looked like a shiny, golden object d'art, something akin to Michelangelo's *David* because he seemed to have no hair except on his head. He continued to be one of Lucy's long-standing *joies de vivre*.

"You have theez hurricanes. Why?" he said.

"God only knows," I said.

"Ah, yes, zee gods. They have made quite a mess here, no?"

"Yes."

Lucy sat down on one of the broken chairs. Ellie and Bruce were out at the water's edge thirty yards away with a case of beer and enough oil to grease their way back to Chicago. They were asleep, or dead, face down on the towels with their feet in the water. The Gulf had again performed. Yesterday she was a grey demon. Today she was a rare jewel. The day was glorious, a perfect specimen of fall in Florida.

They'd had themselves quite a time at the Blue Dolphin, partying through the storm and ending with a very early morning skinny-dip in the motel pool. They made more noise than Josephine, so they got kicked out of their motel rooms. They decided to end the weekend with a sort of camping arrangement in the remnants of the cottage. It was turning out to be an open-air adventure. Most of the northwest corner of the cottage facing the beach, including the door, had blown away. They dared not use the upstairs for fear of crashing into the living room, although Lucy fearlessly crept up there to one of the side bedrooms for towels. The interior was safe and dry enough to survive, so they were reasonably comfortable, which didn't seem to matter, since the whole bunch of them were pretty much anesthetized with various types of liquor.

We studied the picture in the newspaper. We were not in danger of having the cottage come down on our heads because the contractor, my savior, hurried over and propped up the second floor with two-by-fours.

"What a mess," said Lucy. "I hope we don't have to clean this up."

I raised an eyebrow. "When have you ever cleaned anything up?"

She tossed the newspaper in the direction of a sand-clotted plastic chair. Marque plopped down next to her on the new, small dune on the porch floor. Lucy still wore her black bathing suit that clung to her like skin. The front of it plunged to her navel with peek-a-boo silver net coverage. She didn't seem to care what she wore, as long as she could shed it quickly.

"Now, you're giving me another headache. How about we forget this," she said. "Want to go to the Sand Bar for margaritas?" She stuck a fingertip in her cheek and looked to the heavens. "Or piña coladas?"

"Now there's the answer," I said. "Happy birthday."

"Ah, my sweet," said Marque. "I do not try to escape you, but I think I will go have a little nap, down there on the water with those terrible people we came with." He broke into an incredible grin, already flushed with a sunburn to match his deep brown, bloodshot eyes. He was still the most gorgeous thing this side of Antonio Banderas. "You go with your seester." He got up and kissed Lucy on the top of her head and dashed off toward the beach, his backside a display of muscles carved from perfection.

"Nice," I said.

"Yes, nice, and young. I think too young."

"Really, how mature of you."

Lucy shot me a look. One thing she avoided at all costs—from imperfect teeth to grey hair—was maturity. She did not wear it well.

"OK, let's go," she said. "But first, I have to primp, make myself cute as I can." She headed off to the bathroom where the sand was piled up all around the toilet bowl—which, surprisingly, still worked. The electricity worked, too, even with most of the porch gone. Lucy and her entourage would content themselves for the duration of their stay with what was left of the cottage—the kitchen, still functional, and still bedecked with its orange Formica bar—surrounded with new sand dunes.

I'd swept up a bit, but it was pretty useless. The boards had popped up and curled like fruit peels. They would eventually retreat to their once level plane after they dried out, like a dozen times before. The cottage had survived one more storm.

And all the previous and glorious bright spots remained. The sunsets, the beach, washed clean and newly reconfigured, the birds that didn't seem to mind a bit—all reasons why my grandparents chose the island.

"It's a postcard, sent from God Almighty Himself," my grandmother said. "If He had written anything on it, it would be to remind you that life is all about change. Just keep going and nothing will ever get you down."

This was true, even though Josephine tore a hunk off my postcard and took it with her into the Gulf.

"Ready?" Lucy swayed across the porch. She'd wrapped a pareo around her middle in a bow to modesty, but the plunging suit scarcely hid the rest of her. I wore wrinkled shorts and an oxford shirt with the sleeves rolled up, ready for action, which involved working on a Cuervo margarita with a tequila floater, and Shrimp Frances, a deliciously famous dish of shrimp served in hot garlic butter.

"I could use a little respite of margarita. Or piña colada," I said.

We walked off the porch, right through the invisible walls, and across the beach. We checked on Marque, Ellie, and Bruce. They were still passed out and snoring into their towels, so we left them alone. I was glad because I wanted to talk to Lucy alone. I had some things I had to say.

So, we headed to the Sand Bar Restaurant, which, through the years, had turned into a sort of meeting point—a place on the beach where we ate and drank and sat for hours, as if there were not a care in the world, even when there were plenty. Like now.

18

MORPHINE AND MARGARITAS

The Sand Bar, just a short walk from the cottage, escaped Josephine's wrath, probably because the restaurant was elevated on pilings, so that the water rushed under the building and slinked back into the boundaries of the Gulf. The height of only a few feet was all it took to save it from the claws of Josephine.

The Sand Bar actually began as a real sand bar in the '50s. The floor was nothing more than a tiny island pounded hard by the drinkers who stood up to one long counter. Liquor bottles lined up along the shack wall and a refrigerator kept the beer cold. The first time I went there, I was barely taller than the barstool. My dad drank a beer and talked with his friend Cosby Bernard, a Chicago architect, who said an explosion of condominium growth was set to go off along the barrier keys, all the way from Tampa to Naples. He was concerned about the density on Longboat Key to the south of Anna Maria Island where the high-rise buildings on either side of the key were so close you could throw a baseball from a bayside condo to a Gulf-side house and break a window. As he predicted, the multi-unit buildings, many over six stories, went up on Longboat Key, and like clockwork, for three to six months, the northerners closed themselves up in their getaways of white carpet, glass-topped tables, and bamboo. Unfortunately, the only two-lane spine that ran through the island along Gulf Drive and Longboat Key couldn't keep up.

In contrast, the crowding on Anna Marie consisted of shacks and small stucco ranch homes. The two islands adjoined by a bridge were worlds apart. Anna Maria became a slightly quirky colony of northerners—many of them artists, teachers, professionals—who hung out on the fishing piers, and, of course, at the Sand Bar, and tried to preserve the feel of Old Florida.

But the Sand Bar changed. The one counter stuck in the sand grew into a beachfront destination where grouper and shrimp—blackened, broiled, boiled, or buttered—was served. Somewhere in the bones of the fancy wraparound teak counter, the original bar top still existed, and just north of that center, a wooden deck with umbrella tables now spread out to seat a hundred diners and drinkers.

Lucy and I sat at the bar and ordered margaritas, kicking them up a notch with floaters of Cuervo, while we waited for a table out on the deck. Over the years, as part of our Anna Maria ritual, we often ended up sitting out on the deck for hours. We covered the white plastic chairs with beach towels, so we wouldn't have the print of chair splats embedded on the backs of our flawless thighs. It had happened before.

That afternoon, a few regulars sat at the round white tables—Sharon and Vince from Sycamore, Keith Bailey from the bait shop at the Rod and Reel Pier, and a short, bald, loud guy I'd never seen before. He picked Lucy out right away, or rather the front middle section of Lucy, as he opened and closed his legs and yakked into a cell phone. It was clear he had the office on the line, and he was working hard to impress everyone on the deck that he had big business to attend to. He annoyed me, but Lucy was already giving him and his skimpy little Speedo the once over.

"Will you stop?" I said.

Lucy shot me a look, like she'd been caught. "He's kind of cute, don't you think?"

"He's bald."

"So?"

"He's talking loud so we'll notice him."

"And again, so? He has a hot bod."

"It looks like he thinks you do, too."

"Well, he checked you out." Lucy threw that in to mollify me, but it landed with a thud. I stared at the Gulf, where a pelican cruised and then abruptly dove after his unsuspecting prey.

I dove into the margarita. The lime bit my taste buds and the Cuervo went straight to my head. I sat back in the chair and twirled the plastic tumbler in circles.

"Lucy?"

"Huh?"

"Remember that morning?" She looked up at me as if she understood, and then, we were both back with Mom the day she died.

"I really don't want to think about it," Lucy said. "Or talk about it."

"I know. But I think about it. A lot. Did we do right?"

"What do you mean?" Lucy said. "She was crying; almost every day she was moaning and crying." Many times, Lucy cried, too, telling Mom she could go, but, for some reason, she wouldn't.

Lucy looked like she was about to cry right then. Her

flirtation forgotten, she stared sideways out at the water, a shiny bleached lock of hair over one eye. She took a long slug of her margarita.

I felt uncomfortable bringing the pain to the surface again. There hadn't been a moment's peace since Mom's demise, and then all the confusion in moving Dad seemed to propel us both to this moment.

"It was the right thing to do," I said, trying to elicit a response. We sat in silence then, each of us back in the doll-house, with the hospice nurse and Mom in the hospital bed.

"Of course it was. What else were we going to do?" she said. Instantly her expression switched. Lucy had a theatrical quality that changed the way she looked with every mood, a happy fanciful face that lit up and drew you to her. She was not exactly pretty, but neither was Scarlett O'Hara. Lucy could be silly and stupid, and sometimes I wanted to kick her, but she could be decisive without looking back. She surprised me with her decisiveness. This was where metal struck metal, and it never made us dull; it made us sharp. As the eldest, I had to believe that I was going in the right direction. It was expected. But it was important that Lucy and I agreed. I couldn't tell why that was true, but it was. We finished each other's sentences. She supported my way of thinking, even when, overtly, she didn't, because she said things that made me stop and think until it felt right. It was one of the good things about Lucy. It was one of the good things about having her as a sister.

A day or so before Mom died, it was my turn among the siblings to sleep in our parents' room and administer the morphine. Mom was in the hospital bed set up in the bay window. Dad was asleep in their king-size bed. I sat on the edge of the bed and stared at the white mound that was my mother. I set the alarm for 1:00 a.m., but I didn't need an alarm clock. I didn't sleep. What was the use, knowing I'd be buzzed out of it in less than an hour? The morphine only worked for a little while, and then the cancer had its way. Again.

I put the dropper filled with morphine inside her cheek and slowly squeezed. One drop at a time, so she didn't choke. She absorbed the drug, rather than swallowing it. Almost instantly she was quiet again.

I sat back down on the edge of the bed between my parents. I gazed at my mother a few feet away, then turned to see that my dad was lying on the far side of the bed. His eyes were wide open. I thought he'd been sleeping, but he wasn't. I couldn't speak, and neither did he. In the faint night light, I could see the glimmer of one big tear spilling from the corner of his eye. That tear felt like a boulder smashing into me.

When would this ever end?

The night was black with another morning far off—when the birds would twitter in the holly bushes outside the window. My mother lingering in this comatose state. She was there, but she wasn't—even though the hospice nurse said Mom could hear us. I hoped she heard the twittering of birds and not the squabbling of her kids, day in and day out.

Still, I sat, propped on some pillows. Hadn't it always been like that? Me. Propped between my parents, seeking affection and approval, laughing and disagreeing, but often, in it together. I didn't feel together in this. I felt miserably distant, and I could see a door closing—and wondered what would open next.

My father rested with his eyes open, but not a sound or movement came from him. I touched his wrist.

Dad let out a low grumble, and I leaned forward to listen, but then he seemed to drift away. He was half asleep, his face relaxed into soft lines, eyes now closed.

"Good night, Dad. Please, sleep...." I sang to him in a whisper: *May God bless you wherever you may go.*

These words he sang to us at night when we were little, after making finger puppets, and making half dollars disappear, and telling us stories about McGillicutty, who got into trouble and then got out of it, a character, I guess, who bore a striking resemblance to my father as a child. Good night, Dad.

Like Mom, Dad was different now, too. More asleep than lively, and in that aspect, he was in tune with Mom. I still couldn't figure out how all this had happened so fast. Where did my parents go? Dad sang songs and told stories such a short time ago. He and Mom went to China only a few years ago, and last year, we were all down at Anna Maria sitting on the deck of the Sand Bar eating grouper sandwiches and drinking margaritas, enjoying the orange sunset while it snowed in Chicago.

My night watch nearing an end, I dozed, sitting upright. Sunrise was on its way, and it was time for another dose of morphine. I hated to move her, but she was getting restless. I put my arm around the back of my mother's neck and gently bent her upright while I held the dropper ready. It was easy to do, because she was light and didn't respond when I began the slow drip into her cheek. I hummed something, and I told her I was tired and that she looked beautiful and delicate like a silver fairy queen. But in the half dark, I shuddered and looked away from her bone-white face. The skin had pulled tight on her skull. This wasn't my mother anymore. I couldn't stand to see her like this, her frail, stick arms, her belly distended, and not a single response from her except for a moan. She had always laughed so much.

I finished administering the drops and laid her back on the pillow.

She began to cough and gag, her face twisting, her eyes still closed. I struggled to right her again, but she went rigid, weakening my grip on her. Finally, I managed to sit her up, patting her back, rubbing and soothing her.

Then, like a shot with no warning, a fountain of brown liquid gushed out of her mouth, and then again. My senses shattered. Horror blotted out the dim room and the white bedclothes stained with evil. Dawn crept in slowly behind me, while Mom heaved, ready to crack. She bent over and gagged. She couldn't catch her breath. I thumped her back, wiped her mouth and chin, her gown soaked with the awful stuff. I yelled, and then I yelled again, but I couldn't hear myself. I looked at the strange liquid pooling on the bed, the light filtering in, an eery blue, and I held on.

My father was silent, not moving at all. It was terrible that my father, the Navy officer who had commanded a ship, was so out of it he couldn't do a thing to help. He didn't even speak while my mother gagged and coughed and I held her, coaxing her to relax, all the while, exploding inside. She was strangling. At that moment, I hoped it would end. Mercifully. I wanted my mother to die. To just not have to do this anymore. I didn't want to have to do this anymore. I was out of mind. Out of this world. In hell. I wanted this over with.

Now.

I didn't know what to do, and then I heard Lucy running from the back bedroom. She grabbed the aspirator, an awful little vacuum cleaner on a stand in the corner. It looked like a torture device. I drew Mom closer. Lucy flipped a switch and held the hose firmly, shifting the small carriage that wheeled on a rickety stand. She cupped Mom's jaw, working to pry it open.

"You're not going to use that thing!" I said, paralyzed. The machine had a hose that resembled the long proboscis of some sort of monster. It made a horrendous noise—the only noise in the world—while it sucked rhythmically with an awesome, steady authority. It was saving a life where there was hardly any at all.

Lucy didn't even look at me, while she took up my position next to the bed. My sister Lucy, the restaurant maven of Chicago, hanger-on of celebrities and beautiful people, who could hardly operate a blender except to make darn good eggnog, stuck the end of the hose into Mom's mouth and sucked the fluid from her throat so that the gagging and coughing stopped. My mother's bird-like neck relaxed, and I looked at my sister, who had never impressed me, not in all my life, more than she did that moment. We looked at Mom's face, now smoothed over in sleep, which showed no recognition of what had happened.

We rolled her over gently and she woke up a little, without opening her eyes—she never opened her eyes again—and then she groaned when we moved her to change the gown and sheets. It was the sound I cannot forget.

"I thought I was killing her with all that morphine," I said.

"Well, I don't think so," said Lucy. She'd flipped her gaze from the water back to me and held onto her second margarita, then neatly changed the subject. "Bali chicken or blackened grouper?"

"I don't care," I said. "Listen, I want to talk about this."

"You really know how to kill a buzz, don't you?"

I took a gulp of the margarita to chase that buzz, and so did Lucy.

"Don't you remember what the hospice nurse told us?" Lucy's question was rhetorical. Of course. I remembered every word. "After you started interrogating her like she'd just arrived from Old Salem?"

"I guess. It's one of those times I went off the chain."

Lucy threw her head back and laughed. "You! That's great. You're a regular Rottweiler, and you tell me that was one of those times." She had another good laugh, then squeezed half a lime in her drink. "The nurse told us not to let up on the morphine. She said the vomiting was part of the process. Don't you remember that? The GD process! "

The grouper sandwich and Mediterranean plate arrived. Our discussion had absolutely no effect on Lucy's appetite, while I could only shove the olives around my hummus. Lucy took a huge bite of the fish. It was so easy for her to live in the moment, taking one bite at a time. It was something I would always have to work on. I hated her for about half a second.

"Oh, yes, the process," I said. "That was good. I really did lose it when she said that."

"Yeah, and then the poor thing tried to explain to you, that things happen."

"No, shit happens! And the whole long insufferable insane journey into the unknown was all just that!"

"Well, you do know how to put your finger on it," said Lucy. "If you recall—geez, you have a short memory some-times—after that god-awful night with the choking and the aspirator and all, what did that nurse tell us?"

"That there were a lot of powerful drugs in the house, and that we should definitely not let up on the morphine."

That was when we decided. Lucy and I stepped up the doses of morphine. We didn't talk about it; we just did it. Every half hour. We did not let her have any pain. Not even for a second. We tried to stay ahead of it, although the nurse said we couldn't stay ahead of it.

"It will win," she said.

At one point, Julia appeared to say that we shouldn't give Mom too much morphine, because she would have "an adverse reaction."

Lucy and I ignored Julia.

At noon that June morning, greyer and colder than a November day, the hospice nurse found me sitting on a dining room chair with a shot of Jameson's warming to my touch through the crystal tumbler. I was numb, and I wanted to be even more numb.

"It's time," the nurse said.

We all gathered around my mother's bed. I stood at the foot, watching her. She didn't move, and we didn't say a word, except to pray. My father's white, papery fingers absently stumbled over the beads of a black rosary, while he leaned over his wife. Each breath she took seemed to be her last, until finally the breathing turned ragged and coarse—and then she relaxed, gave in. If she could have said it, she would have—"Peace." In a way she did. We felt it. It was over. Dad fell back in the chair. A shiver raced through me the instant she was gone.

I became a different person altogether then. A person without a mother. One who was expected to "grow up and get on with it, and be strong." I could hear her say it like she was standing next to me.

The waiter appeared with two frothy, green, salted margaritas, snapping me back to the present. He wore a blue Hawaiian shirt, and his greased black hair stuck up in all directions.

"You have an admirer," he said. He jerked his head in the direction of the bald hot-bod and plunked the drinks down in front of us. Baldie was right behind him.

"Mind if I join you?" he said. He must have thought the invitation was in the bag, because he was loaded up with a drink in one hand, and a cell phone and legal pad in the other.

"Yes, we do mind." Lucy whipped her head around, blond curls on fire. "We're talking about how we killed our mother."

His mouth dropped open and he started to back away. "Wow!"

"Lucy! We did not kill our mother," I hissed. I looked up at our visitor and smiled. "I'm sorry. We had a death in the family. My sister is upset."

In fact, Lucy was drunk. I leaned over and peered at her. "Are you all right?" I hadn't been able to eat or drink very much, due to my brain going around in circles. Our visitor left briskly.

"Lucy?"

"No we did not," she said, straightening up in the chair. "We did not kill our mother. We did what she wanted, in the end. She didn't want to go to Marilyn and Ben's wedding that June, and she didn't. She told me she did not want to lie around and die for weeks in a coma, and she did, and that was enough of that!"

"Yes."

"She's somewhere in heaven, watching us. You hear that?" said Lucy. She grinned and sipped her drink. "I can hear the clicking of those gorgeous apricot nails, probably on a bridge table somewhere up there."

No sooner had she said this, than behind us, a woodpecker began tapping high up in the Australian pine that shaded the deck of the Sand Bar. I looked up into the long-needled branches and spied the little redheaded fellow, and Lucy and I both laughed.

"Yes, I suppose you are right."

Lucy's birthday was washed out. Ellie and Bruce left for Chicago, roasted red after falling asleep on the beach, and hung over worse than Josephine. Lucy and Marque were due to leave the next day, but not before we took a trip to Moore's for stone crab, a true Gulf of Mexico delicacy that became available for half the year starting in October. I hated to think how the crab claws come to the table—removed from the crab that is then thrown back into the Gulf to grow some more. But I thanked them every season, with butter dripping off my chin and onto my bib.

Marque was gallant and patient. He wore a tight-fitting, black designer T-shirt of some sort with a squiggly weave, and loose, white linen pants. If I'd had a camera, I could have sent his photo off to *GQ* for a cover shot. Marque helped transport Dad into the car, up the stairs to the restaurant, and into his seat at the table, where we could see the bay through a cool, blue-grey expanse of glass. Then he bowed. Dad loved it.

"Good lord," I said under my breath, trying to catch Lucy's eye. She was busy hailing the waiter for the first round of drinks.

Marque leaned across the table, listening to Dad tell a story about the last time he and Mom were in Paris.

"We were waiting in line at the *gare*—isn't that what you call it?" Dad said. "The station? To buy train tickets, you know, and when we got up to the window, the attendant slammed his little gate down in our faces. Thank you very much!"

Marque leaned back, clicked his tongue. He often heard about the adventures of Americans in France. He was used to it, but his generation had a fresh, more global perspective on international relations—and this was not a matter of global importance. "*De rien*," he murmured, his full, usually petulant lips, turning down sympathetically.

"Re-en! Go again? My foot! Huh! I wouldn't go back in there to save myself. But, I tell ya, the look on that guy's face was something else. When a man's got to go, a man's got to go. He looked constipated as all get-out."

Marque shot up in his seat and laughed. Food, drinks, and laughs for all! I shook my head, caught a glimpse of smiles passing from one face to another, Lucy sliding one hand onto Marque's thigh. We stuffed hush puppies, cole slaw, and crab into our mouths. Dad and I sipped Manhattans, a reminder of the first drink he ever bought me on my first flight to college—when we even smoked on the airplane.

"How about that Josephine?" said Dad. He lifted his glass, and then turned to Lucy in a salute. "That was some birthday for our Lucy." He was in fine form, enjoying the small family circle, and his cocktail.

"Yes, that Lucia," Marque said. "She make her birthday, how you say, a splash?"

After dinner, Lucy came over to kiss Dad good-bye. "How do you like Marque?" she whispered.

"He has a fine set of teeth," Dad said. "I know you'll be a good mother to him."

"Dad, I'm not his mother," Lucy said, narrowing her eyes at me, because I was laughing.

"I know, I know," he said, and winked.

19

INSIDE THE EGG

We were just about settled in our new old house. The red rugs looked smashing on the freshly laid white tile floor. Somehow the contractor covered all the brown plastic paneling and replaced the drop ceiling in the family room to make the place sparkle in Snow Peek (sic) white. The kitchen cabinets weren't in as yet, but the house looked new, and white as a clean sheet of paper on which to write the latest chapter of The Adventure.

We did establish a routine, but every day brought a new twist of its own.

At 6:00 a.m., I woke up the kids, and at 6:15, Tick finally streaked to the shower. He came out five minutes later in a cloud of steam and Old Spice, his hair parted in the middle and plastered down on either side of his head where it stayed until he got to the bus stop and it turned into a haystack again. He wore shorts, low on his skinny hips, and polyester '60s shirt he picked up at Goodwill. Buying him new clothes was a waste of time. He was "old school like that," he said.

One very early morning, I checked Dad before I went to Tick's room. Dad was sitting on the side of his bed, and off in his bathroom, with steam whooshing out from under the door, I heard Tick singing these old "Walkin' Blues." The soap clunked on the tile and doors and bottles clicked loudly making the only sounds of that silent hour.

"What's going on?" I said, my tone demanding and irascible. I was more than a little irritated that Tick had woken his grandfather so early.

Dad raised one hand and looked up at me. "It's fine."

"It's not fine. You're awake, and it's way too early."

"I'm all right. You know I'll go back to sleep."

"But I don't want him in here waking you up. Tell him to use the other bathroom in the hall."

"Leave him alone. I tell you, he's fine."

I wasn't going anywhere with this argument. Besides, it was way too early for one. Tick had another bathroom he could use. He didn't have to be waking up his grandfather at six in the morning.

"I tell you, it's fine," Dad said. "This is our bathroom. We have an understanding, Tick and I. I mean it. I'm telling you to leave it alone."

I didn't want to start the day off on a bad note, but then slowly—so slowly for a non-morning person—I began to get the picture. I was thrilled, and, once again, surprised: Dad and Tick had an "understanding."

"All right," I said.

"Good," he said. "I want him to like me."

I walked over to him and kissed the top of his wispy head. "Mission accomplished." I swung his legs around onto the bed and under the covers. He crossed his hands on top of the covers and smiled. Tick's blues song was coming to a close, and I left the room quietly. Let those walkin' dogs lie, and let the shower rain forth, I said to myself.

I should have thanked Tick. The "understanding," I learned, was that Tick helped Dad into the bathroom early almost every morning, so I didn't have to deal with that business. It was a lesson taught to me by my young son—I didn't have to micro-manage everything.

Tick went to school, and later I turned on the *Today* show. Katie and Matt announced the worst news of the day, nationally speaking, before moving on to tips on how to grow moss, make and bake twenty dishes with carrots, and decorate the mantel. They interviewed the bright and the thoughtful, who answered "absolutely" to every rhetorical question posed to them during each two-minute interview. I was surprised to hear that there were so many absolutes in the world. Especially since I wasn't absolutely sure of anything anymore. But they were.

Is this the biggest test of "trusty" pots and pans in the world? Absolutely. Ivanka, at seventeen, you earn $10,000 a photo shoot. Absolutely. Do you think the Dalai Lama will return? Absolutely.

As I watched the world go by in small bites, I wanted to be there again in New York, walking amongst the crowd. Absolutely anonymous. No one depending on me, or calling me up.

The camera panned Rockefeller Center, and I saw myself walking there dressed in a green seersucker coat dress in 1967, pointed-toe shoes killing me but not caring a bit, because I was going to an interview at *Time* magazine. I also had an interview at *Look* at 488 Madison that day. Both magazines offered me jobs in the secretarial pool for the editors. I took the *Look* job because it paid five dollars more at $85 a week. I was on top of the world. I bought a coffee ice cream cone at the corner of 53rd and Sixth Avenue, then walked all the way south to Herald Square and back up Fifth Avenue. It was a bright August day, everything shining, and I was a working girl in New York City. I soon moved out of the Barbizon Hotel for Girls on East 63rd and rented a room at Mrs. Marcella Chamber's at 811 Lexington, a second floor walk-up at only sixty-four dollars a month. I felt rich.

"Never pay more than twenty-five percent of your monthly income on rent," Dad said. "Balance the old budget."

Rich, not because I was balancing my budget, but because I was in the most exciting city in the world, where David Rockefeller tipped his hat outside P.J. Clarke's after a late night hamburger, and I went dancing at Ruffles in the Pierre with an older man. Where, at the card table on the corner of Sixth Avenue and Eighth Street in the Village, protestors against the war in Vietnam collected signatures; the wealthy folk on Sutton Place near Marilyn Monroe's old place on East 57th walked their poodles and watched the river go by from the pocket park. The smell of hot dogs and chestnuts mingled with the pizza and blintzes and Chinese food. I didn't have to spend anything on food, because I worked for food editor Elizabeth Alston. We tested broccoli and pilaf with pistachios, eggs piperade, and pizzas that Peter Max drew up in a psychedelic layout for the magazine article.

In those years, I couldn't turn my head without finding another adventure. I loved New York. I love New York. My stint in Florida with Dad and the kids felt temporary, and so far away from that earlier, independent life. Everything, I decided, is temporary. Except New York.

I longed to get on a plane and go there again, and I would.

But before I made that happen, I had other things to do. For one, I had to get Little Sunshine out of bed and off to school on time. I smoothed away the gold streaks of tangled hair, and studied her freckles, and patted her legs and rubbed her back. But nothing. She slept like a rock, just like her Big Sunshine. I told her it was after eight. I heard the same old complaint: "Just five more minutes."

Fifteen minutes later, the frenzy began as the clothes, bags, and shoes whirled from room to room. She wasn't a morning person, and she didn't like to chat. She was in a twit because she couldn't get her shirt tucked in quite right over the top of her jean shorts. I watched from the sofa, with eyes half closed and my mug of sugary tea about to slip from my grasp, as she ran back and forth, changing a succession of shirts and pants until she decided on the pink T-shirt with the jeans shorts, finally all rolled, belted, and tucked into place. I could see her in the bathroom, at the sink, peering into the mirror, turning her head from side to side, applying lip gloss, wrapping her hair in a scrunchie. She pulled it out and shook her long hair, took a whiff of the inhaler for her distressed breathing, assembled the contents of her Little Kitty purse and her Jansport backpack, gathered the apple, the two dollars, the gym shorts, permission slip, homework, and trombone. I got tired watching her. She finally sat down, briefly, to eat a few orange slices and yogurt without lumps.

She gave me a kiss and was out the door before nine, a tornado of activity, and her room looked it. That afternoon she would have baseball practice—her coach said she ran "like a deer." And she was a finalist in the county speech contest with her first-hand rendition of "Queen of the Quiet Table"—where she often reigned for talking too much. She placed second among all fifth graders in the county. She was the most beautiful fifth grader in the land, and the apple of Old Sunshine's eye.

The day after her prize-winning speech, a large paper cone

arrived from the florist with her name written on a small white card. I put the package on the table next to the door, where it commanded attention throughout the day. Dad sat in his chair watching television, watching the door.

Finally, at 4:30, the front door flew open, and there she was in a flurry of sports equipment and books.

"Hi, Sunshine," she said, lunging at him for a kiss. He was a sucker for affection. She stuck her nose in his mouth and drew back, laughing. Dad let out a mock howl.

"Quit teasing," I said. "And, by the way, miss, it looks like you have a package there on the table."

She turned around and went for the card: From Your Sweetheart Sunshine.

"For me?"

"For you," said Dad.

She tore the paper off and a profusion of white gloxinia, done up with pink ribbon, exploded from the wrappings. "Oh," said Little Sunshine.

Dad grinned from ear to ear. "You like? That's for my great little speaker."

"Sunshine," she said, lunging at him this time with a hug that almost knocked his chair over. "I love it. My first flowers."

"Well, it won't be your last," he said, hugging her back.

The plant flourished on the bookshelf in her room in a sunny spot. She watered and fed it, turned it and pinched back the dead flowers, so that it grew in the sunshine.

I never did find out how that flower made it to our door.

Dad was a complicated man—a once prominent business-man and naval officer—working on a relationship with his young grandchildren, caring deeply about what they thought of him. This surprised me, and heartened me. Some good things came along all by themselves.

Dad's big contribution was getting along with the kids, but he was like an old kid himself. Mom said that children need schedules. Dad thrived on a schedule, too. He wanted to know what the plans were day to day. Sometimes I told him the day before, but that turned out to be a bad idea most of the time. He began staying awake ruminating about the upcoming events—visits from friends, family, therapists, doctor appointments, haircuts, excursions to lunch or dinner. I gradually stopped telling him the plans for the following day. He protested some, but the schedules on the USS *Barnes* (his aircraft carrier during World War II) weren't relevant, and I told him so. He slept much better.

I went in to wake him by 10:00 one morning. I opened the door quietly and found him almost dressed, sitting on the side of the bed in his pants and a bright green golf T-shirt.

"Lorin called," he said.

"Who?" It was a goofy thing to say. He didn't have a telephone, and if he did, I guessed he wouldn't know how to use it with all the buttons. In the dim light, I couldn't see his face, but I felt a fleeting dread that something was wrong.

"Who, Dad?" I said again.

"You know. Lor-in. Larry. Lorry. Lor-en."

I still didn't get it. Then he pointed to the emblem on the front of his shirt. "Ralph," he said. "He wants to play polo today." Then he laughed.

Dad usually took a shower and shaved, dressed himself, and put his teeth in, mostly on his own. I was determined that he do most of these duties himself, for as long as he could, and the longer the better. It kept him going and independent, although some days it tired him out. I stood in the doorway of the bedroom, sometimes like a cheerleader, sometimes like a cop directing traffic.

The shower was the challenge. I'd had bars installed and a shower chair for him to sit on and wash himself, but I had to help him get started, setting the water to the right temperature and putting the towels out, then stepping out of the way. It got to be a regular dance every morning, but he got the job done.

I laid out his clothes, his diaper, and golf shirt, and slid the belt through the loops of his pants. His socks and shoes together, ready for him to pull on last. Sometimes I ducked in to help him out. It took him a good hour, but at last he rolled out on his walker, with his hat and jacket on, his hair combed, and face pink from the shaver, smelling of Old Spice from the bottle he shared with Tick.

Some day—I hated to think when—he wouldn't be able to do this himself. Then what? What were we going to do then? Each day I thought about it, and each day I put the thought aside, because each day was different. Like Lucy, I was living in the moment, and giving it my best. Under the circumstances, though, I really didn't know what my best was.

He was enjoying himself, and that was the important thing. He ate a huge breakfast of grits, butter and syrup, a banana, a bowl of frosty flakes, cinnamon toast, a couple of scrambled eggs twice a week, a glass of milk, coffee, and prune juice. He read the sports section, then folded it into a ratty bundle, and stuck it under his arm. He headed toward the patio and sat in his chair under the mango tree to watch the cat that Tick named Puny, but whom Dad called Blacky. I watched Dad and the cat, and the bright green parrots, graceful egrets, pokey doves, brilliant cardinals, and the blur of hummingbirds that visited our sanctuary, all under the ever-loving vigilance of Blacky.

One day, Blacky caught a gull and leapt around the backyard with it. She shook it wildly, feathers flying, me running about and squawking in chorus with the bird. Dad sat on the patio, bouncing his cane up and down, squawking loudest of all. I didn't know if he was cheering on the bird, the cat, or me. I felt for that bird, but I gave up and retreated to the patio, after which the cat finally dropped it.

"That was quite a performance," he said, stubbing out his cigarette. "You all have the fight in you. Hey, team, fight!" He got up, slowly, heading toward Donald O'Connor on Turner Classics. Then he stopped and turned. "Just make sure that bird isn't suffering."

Three days a week we had a visit from a rehabilitative expert—a therapist—and we often went to the doctor. After which, Dad took a two-hour nap.

It was not a demanding schedule, but it needed close attention all the same. Dad was upset when breakfast was late, or he missed his cigarette, his movie, his sports section. Our day revolved around these simple things, and in between the shifts, I did humongous mounds of laundry, sweeping, and cooking. I paid the bills, fed the cat, pulled the weeds, bought the groceries, gassed and washed the car, and cleaned out the garage. The kids came home late in the afternoon, only to drop their backpacks, grab their sports equipment, and disappear until dinner.

One morning, after Dad was ensconced with Richard Widmark, I struggled toward the garage with a load of wet sheets—it didn't seem to matter how much I limited liquid intake, or how many diapers Dad wore, he still "leaked," as he called it. I had to strip his bed and wash the sheets almost every day.

In order to get to the washing machine in the garage, I had to go through Tick's room (the former laundry room). Typically, his bed wasn't made, as if he would even bother. His guitar stood ready at the foot of the bed; the built-in desk was covered with Legos, wrappers of edibles, notebook paper (balled up), a jock strap, at least a dozen books, and a baseball glove. And centered in the mess was a black and white composition book. I knew what it was. I stopped and plunked the clothes basket on the floor, curious to see what was written inside the notebook. For just a second, I weighed Tick's privacy against my curiosity. The latter won, again. I opened the notebook.

My mother brought up moving to Florida a long time ago— way over a year ago. She didn't want to stay in what she called "the armpit of America" with my father living down the street. So we left town.

At first I thought my mom was bluffing, but I was very wrong about that. My mom doesn't bluff.

This new life all started with the divorce. My dad had a mistress and then married her shortly after the divorce, right too soon to accept, if you ask me, and it makes me wonder. He moved to Lansing for a while, then got hitched and moved to Munster, which is only two minutes away from where I lived. That was good because I missed him a lot and I was lucky enough to see him and call him whenever I wanted, no matter what time it was. I still talk to him on the phone, and I see him sometimes once a month, but it really isn't the same like it used to be. I guess we all have to make the most of it.

My mom worked for the newspaper and she was paid very little. She always loved Florida and wanted to come here and start over. I guess I can't blame her. I felt obligated to go with my mom because I'm a mama's boy, and I didn't want to leave her and my little sister alone.

And then she said The Gamps was coming with us. Well, that about did it for me. Before I wasn't too happy about the idea of going to Florida, but with the Gamps, that was a whole different story. He's one of my heroes, if not my hero of all time. Gamps is cool.

My cousin Jason said I would own the island! God! Was he wrong! At first, I thought the same way he did. In my past, I was always popular and had a lot of friends. But when I came down to Florida, I should have kept to myself. Been seen and not heard. I prayed I would have fun and not be depressed and would fit in better. Surprisingly, it kinda works, most of the time. I've had my ups and downs and I've managed to acquire some friends at the local fishing pier, which is a hangout for island youth. I helped Kevin cut up that bull shark he caught on the pier right after we got down here. Now that was cool. You're not going find any eight-foot, one-inch bull shark (make a note of that) in Munster—except in your nightmares.

My expectations were wrong at first. I know that now. I'm learning lessons in life. I've got my eyes open and I try to see and let myself experience some amazing things about life, God, and people, and I'll keep trying. I've learned most importantly that nothing is ever what you expect, and nothing ever stays the same. Maybe that's a good thing, and maybe it's not. You never know.

20

ONE DAY AT A TIME

Jack drove up in a powder blue Cadillac convertible. How he ever found the car at a local rental was a mystery. Jack had his resources. But it did seem an odd choice, since he usually drove the latest black BMW, or an overloaded Buick. He wore a new leather flight jacket, and his hair was windblown. I'd always thought he resembled a young Burt Reynolds, but his eyes were wearing bags and his face looked puffy, mainly because he was back to drinking fine wines.

"Wow, some wheels you have there," I said, stepping around the holly hedge at the end of the driveway.

"The cottage is a mess," he said. I didn't see the connection, but Jack often dissembled. He used to send sympathy cards on birthdays.

"Yes. Steve's taking care of it, as you know," I said, folding my arms. Then I repeated myself. "Nice car."

"Yeah, it's snowing in Chicago," he said, and chuckled, waving vaguely in the direction of the convertible.

After our awkward hug, he went right in to see Dad, who sat out on the patio trying to coax a three-foot-tall egret into taking a hunk of salami. Dad pushed the salami in the direction of the egret with his cane, but the bird backed away, carefully and slowly, lifting its yellow feet high with each step. Dad tapped the cane again and the bird unfolded enormous white wings and soared over the hibiscus hedge.

Dad's face lit up when he saw Jack. Jack offered Dad a Marlboro.

"He can only have two a day," I said in my most authoritative voice. It was a bad thing to let my Dad continue smoking, but I rationed him two—sometimes three—cigarettes a day, or I didn't hear the end of it. He tried to wheedle another out of me, accusing me of not being able to count. But I held out.

Neither one of them looked at me. I left them sharing a cigarette, talking about lathes and railroad car parts.

I flew off to the beach with the egret.

Later that evening my brother came back and we all sat together under the mango tree on the patio. I lit votive candles on the round table, then we nibbled on chicken wings and guacamole and enjoyed the cool November evening. It was too cool for me, but not for Jack, who was glad to be out of the northern weather. The breeze swirled leaves around us in small funnels, and we listened to the wind in the trees and the roll and break of the gulf hitting the beach a few blocks away.

Dad was quiet, nodding in his chair. With the night folding around us, I didn't feel the need to talk.

"Well, you seem to have done well here," said Jack. He chuckled, not looking at me.

"Yes, we are doing well. Dad's happy. The kids are doing great."

"And you?"

"Me? Why do ask, Jack?" I almost said, Why do you even care? But I bit it off. It wasn't the right time; the moon was a rare silver piece, shining through the mango tree.

"Because. It's important." That's all he said. He drained the last of his red wine and slid the chair back. He kissed the top of Dad's head, gave my shoulder a squeeze. Jack had a tennis game in Sarasota next day with business partners. He stayed in Florida a week. He didn't come over to see Dad again for the rest of his visit.

The cottage was under construction, after getting a double whammy from Josephine, followed by a milder-mannered storm called Opal. Fortunately, the cottage was less than half destroyed—a borderline case—so it was saved from condemnation by the city fathers and mothers of Anna Maria. Our contractor gathered local, state, and federal permits to rebuild the porch and fix the rest of the house. He recommended a concrete floor on the porch, instead of the former planks. But when the inspector came by and saw the additional plans for concrete, another permit was required. One of the joys of building in Florida, especially in the flood zone, is that one permit deserves another. So, until all the permits were collected and the insurance paid off, the work on the cottage was on hold. And with that, we couldn't count on renters for the rest of that season. It was a wonder anything got done in the glossy world that is Florida.

Since the cottage wasn't available, the family didn't come to visit for the holidays. But that did not mean it was a slow time for visitors. Dad's old friends had found Florida over the years, and they stopped by. We had lunches at the Sand Bar, Moore's, and Lynch's.

Also, my two elderly aunts from Bradenton came to visit—Aunt Marian and Aunt Roma. Aunt Marian, one evening with a fresh bottle of Pinch, and donuts every Thursday. She sat with Dad while I went out on errands. A retired school-teacher and Dad's younger sister, she lived in a small condo in Bradenton, played bridge with her friends, and traveled with her son and his wife. I hoped to be like her one day—lovely, white-haired, gentle, and dignified—which was quite a stretch for me. Yet, in the spirit of that hope, it was Aunt Marian who encouraged—and mentored—my next career. After raising nine children with Uncle Ed, she went back to school to get her master's degree and then taught middle school for twelve years. I told her I was thinking of teaching, but I needed those two years of education and English credits.

"Just take one course at a time, and you'll be done before you know it," she said. "That's all there is to it."

One day at a time.

Two of the smartest people I ever knew were my Aunt Marian and Kurt Nimmergut, my co-pilot flying over Alta Loma. You'll get there, they said.

My Aunt Roma usually drove out to the island with Aunt Marian. She brought blue cheese dip, chocolate cake with mini chocolate chips, and rum-soaked pound cake. A meticulous gardener of ferns and azaleas, she loved the peace of her small white stucco house with a flourishing backyard of orange, grapefruit, and kumquat trees that she sprayed and cultivated—and we raided every winter.

Dad, Marian, and Roma sat at the long table in the family room at the back of the house overlooking the wide yard shaded with plumeria and majo trees and oleander. As the sun filtered into their warm afternoons, they chuckled over lightweight vodka tonics, chicken salad sandwiches, and butter cookies, while reminiscing about high school, poker parties at the farm, and the old days.

Dad was content, and the kids were happy and busy with school and sports and their friends. It was the making of The Adventure. If they were getting along fine, it was a good place to start—for my peace of mind. I could have put it to Jack that way, but Jack wouldn't understand. And I didn't want to open up another discussion about the availability of Polish maids in Indiana, or the necessity of providing him with financial statements. It was a regular dance with Jack—and with Julia—just to get away from them and find some peace.

I escaped to the dock to watch the clouds sweep across the sky like neon curtains. I always looked forward to the evening, and the sunset never disappointed me. It was different every time, just like Tick said. The canal was a placid, glittering ribbon of black water, reflecting streaks of bright orange sky. An occasional mullet broke the surface with a gentle splash. What a moment to savor.

Of course, it didn't last.

21

THE LEG

Along with the lovely cool days of early winter, with the hibiscus still blooming and the first oranges appearing as tiny green marbles, "The Leg"—like an obnoxious guest that refused to leave—came to visit and stay.

There was Dad, and then there was "The Leg," which abruptly took on a life of its own. For years, he'd had difficulty walking because of a bad back, and the stroke left him weak on the left side of his body. The Leg always twinged, but all of a sudden, there it was, acting up mightily and screaming for attention.

"Oh, 'The Leg,'" he said just about every time he moved, got up, walked, or rolled over. It was his constant lament, and the more I heard him complain about The Leg, the more of a pain it was, generally speaking. I was sorry that his leg hurt, but there seemed little that could be done about it. I took him to the family practitioner who prescribed over-the-counter painkillers. We were trying to avoid the side effects of fancy drugs. At first, Dad took Tylenol, which worked well for a time, and almost always put him directly to sleep.

But The Leg persisted. We went to see a neurologist who

suspected that the problem was associated with his bad back. Dad had chronic stenosis of the spine, a pinching arthritic condition of calcium deposits that put pressure on the nerves in the lower region of his back. Dad had back surgery years before, and that seemed to have alleviated much of the old back pain. But with age came the deteriorating condition. The full-blown problem of The Leg was something new.

The doctor reviewed the x-rays of the old back operation and declared it had been a complete success, marveling at the good job on Dad's back. He said it was "the best work on a four-and-five lumbar" he'd ever seen.

But the x-ray also confirmed that the pain in his leg was the result of the chronic, debilitating stenosis in the spine. Doctors had removed some of the deposit, but apparently not all of it, or enough of it. Another operation to relieve the condition was out of the question because no doctor, the neurologist said, would operate on an elderly man who had already had a back operation, along with a stroke and cancer. I had to agree, but, God knows, I'd met enough doctors without a shred of common sense in the years since my parents started to fall apart. Maybe there was one out there who would do another operation, and it might really work, by accident. I didn't know what to do. Dad was having fits with The Leg.

"If the back operation was so successful, why does he have this pain in his leg?" I asked. I thought that was a logical question after all the praise about the back operation. The doctor held the x-ray in one hand and flapped it up to the light, while Dad sat on the examining table.

"The leg is, after all, connected to his back," the doctor said.

"Well, yes." I waited for him to elaborate on this

pronouncement that didn't require a one-hour wait and ninety-five dollars for ten minutes of his time.

Dad had nothing to say on the matter, nor on the success of the back operation that left him with such pain in his right leg. But then the doctor turned to him and asked him what it felt like.

"It feels like a knife stabbing up from the bottom of my foot and my whole leg is on fire and I tell you, oh mother of God, it's killing me," said Dad.

The doctor nodded.

"Now, he has pain in a different place, and it's the result of the back business," I said, trying once more to get a handle on The Leg. "Why is he in worse pain than before the successful back operation?"

"The answer is simple," the doctor said. "You will always have a residual effect after an operation like this in the lumbar region, no matter what you do."

"But you said the back operation was successful," I said.

"Oh, yes, it was successful."

"He's in pain. Worse pain." We continued on the merry-go-round in hell.

The doctor nodded. Again.

"That's true. His leg hurts, and there are new medications we can try. Ultram, Neurontin, to name two. Let's try one of these."

Here we go again. He included all of us in the test run, but Dad was going to be the guinea pig. We were going to try more pills. My heart sank. But we had to try something.

The doctor prescribed Neurontin, a brand new miracle capsule that was supposed to work on the pain center of his brain. The cost—$1.80 a pill. Three-a-day for six weeks. And it had no effect whatsoever, except to make Dad nauseated.

He sat with a towel or a bucket nearby, because he didn't know when he might throw up.

The following month, the doctor sent him to a specialist for a cortisone injection to the spine. These had worked in the past, before the operation, but the treatments routinely wore off. He tried another anyway, but it didn't work either.

He had therapy, massages, back braces, support hose, none of which did much good, and getting him into the support hose nearly broke my back.

No matter what, we couldn't seem to get away from The Leg. The pills were merely a crutch—a quick fix—and every doctor had a favorite. Generally, Dad was getting worse. Maybe there wouldn't be any improvement. I had to face the facts that at some point nothing would work for anything. Getting old had its terminus. Still, I was impatient.

I asked the pharmacist about the effects of taking Aleve and Tylenol for a long stretch. They seemed to be the only pills that worked with a modicum of regularity and didn't upset his stomach. She didn't see a problem with that.

"But maybe his condition is getting worse," she said. "Did you ask the doctor for a stronger pill?"

Some days The Leg didn't bother him much. Mom had arthritis, which she called "Arthur," who "traveled," but always came back. There were good days and bad. As time wore on, Dad complained more and more that he couldn't walk, even with the aid of the walker. As a consequence, he didn't want to get up. So, he wet himself.

We worked out a little arrangement to give him some dignity when he needed dry pants. I stood behind him while he dropped his trousers and the wet diaper and then I stuck the dry one between his legs and he maneuvered it into place.

Sometimes in all this, reality struck out of the blue. The

situation is not going to get any better. I didn't listen. We had to keep trying.

Still, overall, he was in a better humor—I couldn't have been happier when The Leg went away and left us all in peace. Since leaving Indiana, Dad had regained weight and lost the unhealthy pallor. In Florida, he began to enjoy himself with my aunts and visitors, in private "conferences" with Tick— and even in the playful teasing with Little Sunshine. He was a regular Old Sunshine. The only regular medication that worked had been vitamins and baby aspirin, with the occasional help of Tylenol or Aleve.

But, the parade of pills never did it for him. They didn't relieve the pain in his leg, and they hadn't worked on symptoms of depression when Mom was dying. It was the crux of my general argument with Julia, and the doctor. Either the pill, or the dosage, was wrong. I could never figure it out. He didn't stay with one long enough to discover why, because they all made him so goofy or sick to his stomach.

On another visit to the neurologist, I said, "Isn't there something we can do?"

"Things of the last resort," he said. "We don't really want to try them if this new drug works."

The new drug did not work.

So, we moved on to one of the "things of the last resort." This thing turned out to be the Spinal Cord Stimulator. The stimulator was meant to intercept the pain signals from the brain to the leg. Basically, the contraption looked like a remote control attached to a wire. The wire went through the skin and was attached to the spine and the remote was hooked up to a belt on the stimulatee—a.k.a., Dad. It sounded simple enough, although I didn't like the idea of Dad operating like one of those remote control cars the kids got for Christmas and broke by the time the new year rolled around.

The doctor told Dad that he could adjust the dial on the remote to advance a tingling sensation and interrupt the pain, and for the life of him, Dad couldn't understand how tingling had anything at all to do with the knifing and stabbing from the bottom of his feet up and down his whole leg. But Dad was willing to try it.

My buzzer went off. I recalled another electronic moment with my parents that didn't work. That was the experiment with an electronic gizmo from the fast-hearing franchise of hearing aids. It was supposed to correct the problem of Dad not hearing Mom, especially when they were in the car, and at most any other time, too. She plunked down the $200 deposit, and the device arrived, never to be inserted correctly, or permanently in my father's left ear, which was all I could figure out through the yelling back and forth about the new ear. He couldn't get used to it, because, he decided, he didn't want it in his ear and he couldn't use his left side very well after the stroke. The miracle didn't fit or feel right, or work, no matter what they did. Without results there either, Mom wanted her money back.

The ear device was not really for Dad. Actually, his hearing was pretty good. The audiologist said he had selective hearing. He simply turned the thing off when he felt like it. He heard every word of Elvis, Garth Brooks, and Reba.

"Turn on my crazy music," he'd say when we were driving along. Tick couldn't stand it. He reached over the front seat of the Cadillac like a large swooping bird and switched to some nice heavy metal, while I avoided going into a ditch.

"I hate that country stuff," Tick said. "All they do is

complain—'I left my sweetheart at the country fair and she ran off with a two-headed dwarf.'"

"Tick, this is American music. You should appreciate your great heritage."

So, Dad could hear the great heritage, and he could hear me from the passenger side of the car. But he hadn't heard Mom. That drove her crazy. He wasn't going to drive me crazy, though, no matter what. I didn't think I was as strong as my mother in a lot of ways, but I was meaner. My dad acted like he couldn't hear, and so I ignored him. I got tired of repeating myself, when, in fact, most of my remarks were chitchat and didn't bear repeating. He wanted my full attention, and I gave him that when I could. That worked, without a miracle of any sort.

I hadn't been much involved in the ear experiment, but now I was willing to go along with the Spinal Cord Stimulator technology to correct the failing back and aching leg. I should have known better. Doctors often don't listen to their patients. Instead, they act like mechanics working on old cars.

We watched a video of people talking about their stimulators and how they were pain free and finally happy. Tick wanted to know if the Gampers would be in danger during a lightening strike, all wired up like that, and my daughter said Old Sunshine could learn to work the TV with a remote control for his back, as well. He was always losing the TV remote, and grew frantic when Jimmy Stewart and Gregory Peck were just about to close the deal. I didn't think the video about the stimulator's alleged benefits was too convincing. It looked like an ad. But were all these people in the video lying about their miraculous, pain free experiences? Could that be?

Dad went to the hospital to have a temporary stimulator installed for a two-day trial run. If it worked, a permanent contraption would be hooked up to his spine several weeks later. He'd have a few wires sticking out of his back. What the devil was I thinking when the doctor told me that part?

It took less than ten minutes for the neurologist to attach the thing, and then Dad went to a hospital bed for an overnight stay. He had to lie flat on his back for twenty-four hours, during which time he could play with the dial during this period. The real test was to come the next day when he stood on his knife-stabbed right leg.

The next morning the neurologist called me at home and told me to get over to the hospital. "We tested the temporary stimulator and it's great; it works. We'll put in a permanent one in a week or so. You can pick him up and take him home," he said. "But bring him back tomorrow and we'll take out the temporary, so he can heal for the permanent procedure."

I tried to get all that, but he was gone. He was probably in a great hurry to insert another miracle spinal cord stimulator.

I found my father sitting in a chair in his hospital room with a completely devastated tray of food in front of him. There was nothing wrong with his appetite.

"How's it going?" I said. "Gee, I feel like it's Christmas and you got the brand new toy."

"Well, the pain in my leg ..."

"What? The doctor said it worked fine. What do you mean?"

"Well, I can't turn it on because every time I stand up the leg hurts."

"Dad, you're supposed to turn it on when you stand up so the leg doesn't hurt."

"Well, you see, it doesn't work that way. I'm telling you, it hurts too much."

I sat down on the edge of the bed like someone pushed me. I was deflated, but at least we had the day to fiddle with the thing and maybe get Dad used to working with it.

I took him home, and he lay in the bed, moping. He turned up the dial on the remote control attached to his belt and the leg twitched, unpleasantly. He wasn't used to the sensation. He got up to go to the bathroom and was so shaky he almost fell down. Worse still, the tingling made him want to go to the bathroom more, which was already a tortuous walk. We turned down the remote so it didn't tingle so much, and then his leg hurt.

"I feel like I have St. Vitus Dance with the thing on," he said. "And when it's off, it's like a knife. It's stabbing me again."

I pulled up the back of his shirt. Under an enormous clear bandage, I saw a bloody gauze pad and wires plastered to his yellow back. My face burned with outrage. Then, I blamed myself. This was something we wanted. This was something I actually asked a doctor to do to my father.

I didn't want Dad to see it, or know what it looked like. It was bad enough he had to feel it. I tucked his shirt in. I didn't say anything. Not just then.

The next morning, Dad came out of his room, dragging the remote on its cord like a dead pet. He didn't pay any attention as the thing skittered along the ceramic tile floor behind him. I could see by the hole in the case that the battery was gone again, after I'd stuck it back in there a couple times the day before. I felt like calling Frank in Minneapolis, whose card was attached to the remote, and telling him exactly what I thought of his instrument.

We had an appointment with the neurologist, who had a smile on his face when he swept into the tiny freezing office where my father waited wearing a thin gown and I boiled for thirty-seven minutes.

"Mike, hey, how are you?" said the doctor.

"It didn't work," I said.

"What's that? It worked fine in the hospital," the doctor said. "What happened?"

My Dad bent his head over his chest, and his shoulders shook a little. I glared at the doctor.

"Obviously we need some intelligence here to operate it," he said.

"Whose intelligence?" I said. "Yours? I don't see any intelligence working here at all."

"It's a very simple machine."

"For simple minds, or intelligent minds?" I said. "Which is it? My portable radio works better than this thing. The batteries kept falling out, so it didn't work half the time if he wanted it to."

"Did you ever hear of Scotch tape?"

"Scotch tape," I said. "For a setup that probably cost $10,000?"

"Eight thousand," he said. Then he turned to Dad and shook his head. "I'm sorry, Mike."

In a blink, the curtain flapped, and the doctor was gone before I could get up and put myself in the county jail.

Then a miracle happened. And as with most miracles that come along, this one was small and almost went unnoticed. Like a star shooting across the sky, or a violet pushing up under a tree, or a thousand-and-one things I could call miracles, but take for granted. Since then, I've learned not to take any favor, insight—or miracle—for granted.

I sat in the doctor's office where I usually spent at least one or two afternoons a week with Dad. I was dejected, but probably not as much as Dad was. Then my ears perked up. The woman across from us was telling her companion about her stenosis in the spine—and her own miracle.

"Nothing but this cheap little white pill," she was saying. "But it changed my life. I have to watch out for some side effects, but I'm telling you, don'cha know, I can walk!"

I leapt across the room and plopped down beside her, startling her.

"A little white pill?" I said.

She gave me the scoop.

"Prednisone. About six dollars for a hundred," she said. A corticosteroid used to treat arthritis. And it worked for her when nothing else did, except maybe Tylenol, which we agreed didn't require a medical degree to figure out. "Arthritis," she said. "It comes and goes, and Lordie, am I glad when it goes—but this pill has given me relief."

I asked the doctor about it that afternoon, and he agreed to put Dad on a trial run of a dose pack of Prednisone, 40 milligrams the first day, with descending amounts each day after that for a week.

For the first time in months, The Leg was gone. If it returned at all, and briefly, it came with a dull knife that couldn't quite get in there and slice its way up and down The Leg.

The warning label stated that Dad might have "difficulty sleeping, encounter mood changes, nervousness, increased appetite or indigestion, swelling, black stools, vomit that looked like coffee grounds, nausea, changes in menstrual period, headache, muscle weakness, sore throat, cold or fever," which was a pretty good rundown of all the side effects of the pills he'd been taking for years.

Fortunately, he didn't have those, or any bad or lasting side effects. He always ate a lot and was nervous from time to time, but that was pretty much his normal state anyway. The doctor kept an eye out for all the signs, because cortico-steroids are hard on the organs. The only sign, though, was one of relief. He was better, and that was good. In fact, the Prednisone gave him complete relief for long periods. He was in a state of euphoria, and so was I.

So, we decided to take advantage of the new freedom and get out on the road. *Cueillez les roses de la vie*, Lucy always said. "Gather the roses of life." Today.

So, with The Leg gone, we were free to move about Florida. I decided to plan a trip to Disney World. We ate smoked turkey legs, went on Dumbo and the Tea Cups, and took many turns on It's a Small World After All (Dad's favorite). Tick managed to hoist his grandfather up onto the horse on the merry-go-round. Dad was not satisfied to sit on the bench.

"I want to go around one more time on that horse," he said. And he did.

22

IRELAND. WHY NOT?

Lucy worked as a manager at the Ritz-Carlton Hotel in Chicago, a fantastic job that had its ups and downs. She had to stand up all day—that was the downer—but she hung out with the stars. She was supposed to keep a professional distance from them, but this was difficult for Lucy. There was the afternoon she delivered cocktail napkins to the bar so she could get a peek at Mel Gibson kicking back with his brother over a few Heinekens in the Atrium. She made a point of standing near the elevator when Jerry Garcia, with his wild hair and weird entourage came swooping past. She watched Harrison Ford from the restaurant reservation stand, while he charmed the maître d' and ordered a California pinot noir. Her snooping around about the comings and goings of the stars at the Ritz caused no end of trouble with her boss. Even walking around on duty was a source of agitation. More than once, a couple came up to Lucy and offered her a hundred dollars to leave them alone in a room for twenty minutes, so they could check the suitability of a suite for an office meeting. "Do I have 'stupid' written on my forehead?" Lucy asked the drunken duo who tottered over to her desk.

Lucy generally maintained her decorum, even though a great number of the human beings she dealt with did not—including the CEO's wife who threw a fit when Lucy accidentally ordered a white limo instead of a black one for a shopping trip. "Always and ever, ever and always," the wife huffed at Lucy, biting off the words. "Black, I said blaaaaack, not white." Lucy worked hard, but sometimes, she drew the line with a huff of her own.

Lucy wasn't crazy about the stress of the job, but there were the perks. She called me to say that she and her co-workers were planning a trip to Ireland on hotel business, which was sure to involve a great deal of eating and drinking. She asked if I'd like to go.

Did I want to go? After a horrific year of losing our mother to cancer and my marriage to anger, along with the general chaos of moving, surviving a hurricane, repairing the cottage, and The Leg, yes, I thought—for a fraction of a second—yes, I'd love to go.

But how?

"I'll bet Dad would really like the trip," said Lucy. "Why don't you ask him, too?"

"What?"

"He'd love to go to Ireland. It would be a blast."

I stared out my kitchen window at a squirrel (I hoped it was a squirrel) chewing on a mango, while Lucy no doubt was standing in her blue pumps in the sumptuous offices of the Ritz.

"Lucy, Dad has trouble getting to the bathroom." But as soon as I said it, I thought about how much Dad loved Ireland. "OK, I'll ask him, but I don't know what he'll say. He's different every day."

"What's that supposed to mean?"

"Since Mom died, he's acting goofier than ever. It was terrible for him, Lucy."

"Well, don't you think I know that?!" she snapped.

"Yes, we both know that."

"Yes. Lord."

We were both thinking about the awful Year of the Dollhouse, and about how we wanted to forget the whole thing.

"Look," she said, "you know him, so talk to him."

"I will. He might just take to the idea. Some days, he seems to be doing fine, but there are the little surprises."

"Like?"

"He just has a lot of issues ... aches and pains. You know, it's a bitch to get old."

"Before we're old bitches, let's go. Let's do this," she said. "You ask him."

I agreed. On my way to the living room to talk with him, my eyes strayed to the pile of medical forms and nutrition charts, exercise routines for the elderly and insurance guidelines for this and that. Getting old was certainly one enormous pain. Staying young wasn't easy, either. I picked up the applications for the kids' soccer tryouts, bills for gymnastics and guitar lessons. Certain shoes, shirts, and shorts. Places to be—and on time. It had to get done. My plans for a teaching career were on hold; I was "the caregiver" in the sandwich between Dad and the kids.

In the meantime, a trip to Ireland seemed like a fine diversion.

Dad sat in his rocker watching John Wayne ride up on a trio of varmints. The television was turned up all the way. When Ted Turner came up with the continuous offering of old movies on Turner Classics, he had my Dad in mind. Dad could have eaten, slept, and lived in that chair with Barbara Stanwyck and Joel McCrae to keep him company, and it would have suited him fine. He was normally not a demanding person. He just wanted to have his television programs, his martini with Tom Brokaw (and me), and his two or three cigarettes. He also needed to be warm, and today, he'd chosen his outfit accordingly—several layers of shirts and a sweater, a jacket, and his tweed cap to ward off a possible, though improbable, chill.

"Oh, look at that." He slapped the arm of his chair and offered me his cheek for a kiss, not missing the posse gallop over the hill. "Always thought he should run for president. John Wayne would have made a fine president."

"Dad, Hollywood is not the practice field for becoming president of the United States." I often took this schoolmarm tone with him, and I was beginning to annoy myself.

"Well, look what happened with that fine Ronald Reagan. Great Irishman to boot."

"You're the great one," I said. I flopped onto the couch and checked out the tube. My Dad was a great Irishman, a business leader, and the life of the party. His mother was a Murninghan from County Cork, and his father was a German from the Alsace Lorraine. This mix of ancestry and his attitude adjustment throughout the day had prompted my mother to say that Dad woke up a German and went to bed an Irishman.

I waited until the film credits rolled. It was no use trying to get his "good ear" when John Wayne had his attention.

"Dad."

"Yeees?"

His voice dipped and rose, and then his blue eyes were on

me. I grabbed the opportunity to get my hands on the remote control and turn down the volume.

"Dad, how would you like to go to Ireland?"

That got his attention. He grinned and his eyebrows shot up, flashing a glimpse of a younger Dad. He'd been to Ireland many times with Mom, and in the summer of 1981, they rented a castle in Glin for a month and invited us all over there to live it up on the banks of the Shannon with the knight, Desmond Fitzgerald. Lounging in the garden, we sipped cocktails, surrounded by manicured topiary and a straight lane of pebbles bordered with pruned hedges. One evening a cow wandered onto the wide lawn, the knight dropped his gin and tonic and chased her back to the pasture. One very early morning, she escaped again and gave birth to a black-and-white calf under my bedroom window.

Dad and I, sitting in that Florida living room, were thinking the same thing: Ireland. The days at the castle began with Irish breakfasts of sausage and eggs and breads served on silver trays and blue china in the royal-red dining room. Oona, the housekeeper, stood by my mother, who was seated at the long table in a carved armchair under the paintings of old knights.

"How many for dinner, madame?"

My mother clasped her hands, the queen of the castle. She had no trouble filling that chair. "Ten, I believe" she said, smiling at Oona.

"That will be grand," Oona said.

That evening, we ate fresh salmon with homemade mayonnaise and buttered potatoes, all garnished with fresh dill—a dinner so memorable, yet so simply prepared. I've never thought of fish and potatoes again in quite the same way. She carried the impossibly large tray—a tiny, straight little lady, always dressed in a uniform of a navy cardigan sweater, wool skirt, tights, and sensible shoes. Her expression never changed much; she didn't smile a lot, but when she did, a light went on behind those clear blue eyes.

"I trust her entirely. She's the treasure of the castle," the knight told my mother. "Please, you mustn't push her too much."

I suppose we did—not on purpose—but because of our sheer, outrageous delight in spending our days there. Oona was gracious at our delight. Nothing ruffled her, not even when the number of guests topped out at fourteen. I slept in a blue satin bedroom with a four-poster bed and wide windows that overlooked a stretch of gardens. Mick Jagger had more or less occupied the very same bedroom.

"A desperate-looking fellow, he was," said Nancy, the cook. "I couldn't take my eyes off him." He'd jumped on the bed and broke it, and the knight replaced it well before my arrival.

Ireland was a place in our hearts and a place of great family memories.

"Ireland?" Dad said. Immediately, his shoulders shook up and down in anticipation of a good cry. His emotions floated so easily to the surface in bouts of tears, especially on the subject of Ireland.

I reached over and shook Dad a little. Sometimes, that brought him back to earth.

"What do you say? About going to Ireland?"

"Yes, yes, let's go, let's go." A smile broke across his face. He let out a good, loud laugh. "I'd sure like to go to the pub and belly up to the bar. At least one more time."

Little Sunshine was delighted to go, but Tick said he couldn't make it, not with soccer and guitar and "plans" on his agenda.

"What do you mean?" I said. "Just what are these plans?"

"Oh, you know, Mom, just plans. Stuff comes up. I'll be fine. I can stay at Tony Mark's."

He was pulling away from me. I could feel it again, but I also felt that I had to trust him. Trust had to start somewhere, and it was about time. Tick was just this side of fifteen years old.

"Well, I guess so. You are busy, and you'd better stay busy with school and practice." I tried to sound stern, but it was difficult with this engaging kid who had taken on a lot of adventure in just a couple of years. He always threw himself into his plans, including teaching himself to play the guitar. His instructor, George, told me that Tick had a technique more promising than B.B. King's. I didn't know much about technique, but I could hear what was going on in that tiny laundry-room-turned-bedroom. I stood outside his door sometimes and wondered: Where did that come from? Tick was full of rude and lovely surprises, and I wouldn't have had it any other way, because then I wouldn't have him at all. My Island Boy. Tick will be fine.

Little Sunshine dug right into the business of planning the trip. She did a collage for school with family pictures from Ireland—pictures of castles and pubs and gardens that we photographed years before she was even born. She twisted her long chestnut hair into a knot on top of her head and practiced her Irish dancing until she nearly tapped a hole in her hard shoes. She'd taken Irish dance lessons at the Trinity school in Chicago—and so had Tick. They'd both been in the St. Patrick's Day parade, wearing their Aran Islands sweaters, freezing to death, and glad of it. Florida was so different, a place of swimming, year-round sports, and bike riding, with not the remotest connection to their Midwestern roots. My daughter—and Tick—left a life behind, and, I hoped, were getting the most out of The Adventure.

"Girl, are you going to take that act on tour?" I said, watching her dance to the wild, repetitive strings and squeezebox of the reel. Laughing, she kicked her legs and kept her arms straight at her sides.

"Mom! Why not?"

Little Sunshine, Dad, and I planned to fly over with Lucy's team from the hotel. And then Lucy called and said she couldn't go.

An enormous amount of convention business came into the hotel all at once, and it required booking ASAP. Lucy was tied down. She said it was a great idea for me to go ahead and take Dad anyway.

"Why not?" she said. "What the hell?"

"Sounds like it to me. I don't think I can take a ten year old and an old man in a wheelchair to Ireland by myself."

"That doesn't sound like my old sister Nan," said Lucy.

I asked my other siblings if they would like to go with us. They told me I was nuts, taking a be-stroked man across the ocean on an airplane to God-knows-where once you get there, if you get there. That was the sum of their thoughts on the matter. Besides, they said, the winter weather in Ireland was always especially grim.

"It'll be too cold to play tennis," brother Jack said. The

weather also mattered to my sister, Julia. "I'd go if it were warmer."

My daughter, however, was not discouraged. "I can do it, Mom."

We could do this. Our ancestors crossed the Atlantic in the bottom of those awful ships. I didn't have a clue about hardship, about giving birth in the freezing lower deck next to the engine room, such as the case of great Aunt Margaret and cousin Timothy, who made it after all. We could do this, even if Little Sunshine and I had to wheel Dad all over Ireland and I had to prop him up at the bar for that Paddy whiskey and a glass of Harp.

Dad's doctors—the neurologist and the urologist—said Dad was able to travel to Ireland. Then we paid a visit to the family doctor. This would be the test, because if Dr. Gordon said we could go, then we could go.

Dad sat on a little metal stool with his hands folded and a smile on his face when Dr. Gordon breezed into the small office, taking up the entire room with his large, white-coated presence. He was a lively ebullient man who used his right arm to make a point.

"Ireland! Well, why not?" he said. "It might even do you all some good."

I liked him because he took care of Dad with gentility and humor, and a good dose of common sense. The more I got involved in the medicine of old age, I was seeing less and less of that.

Dr. Gordon recommended saline nasal spray and anti-nausea pills, antacids, and Tylenol for the flight. Then his jowls deflated. He looked at me out of the corner of his eye.

"Don't forget the diapers. You'll play hell getting diapers over there, and what about getting him in and out of the restrooms? What about the airplane?" He hardly made eye contact then. "Oh, mercy!"

But I'd already made up my mind.

He shook his head, gave Dad a hearty pat on the back, and waved in my direction, all the while opening the office door to escape. "Well, good luck!" He was out the door with the flip of a chart.

I wanted to make the trip as comfortable as possible. I did my research and found a driver who would pick us up at the airport and take us around, and we kept all of our prior reservations made through Lucy. The staff at the Shelbourne Hotel had a reputation for hospitality, like all the Irish. I called the agent at the hotel to discuss our situation. She cheered me on. "Oh, it will be brilliant," she said in lilting Irish laughter. "You bring your dad and the wee one and come on now. It'll be foin."

The flight was remarkably calm. We slept through most of it, except for Dad, who said he didn't sleep at all, even though he snored with his large, white head resting on the pillow and his legs tucked under a blue fleece blanket. Getting back and forth to the bathroom was a production, but we made it with relative ease—and limited liquid intake.

Our driver, John McCrory, met us in baggage claim at the airport in Dublin. He looked exactly like I thought he would: tall with silver hair and a strong jaw, and a twinkle in his eye. He held a tweed cap in one hand and wore a long black coat. He gave me a crisp nod and a big smile, and he and Dad shook hands, John bending slightly to Dad who presided in a wheelchair like arriving royalty. They became fast friends on the spot. Little Sunshine danced amid the confusion, with the luggage and tourists and the blaring of announcements.

I relaxed, but we had a long way to go.

John rolled Dad along in the wheelchair to a large black Mercedes, put Dad in the front seat, and loaded the luggage in the trunk. With dispatch, he said, "So there," and we were off to the Shelbourne. It wasn't a long ride, but it was a welcome breather to drink in the cozy rows of stucco houses that gave way to the big city of small whizzing cars driving with abandon. Dublin, on the outskirts, looked like London—or Chicago and New York—but then the city revealed its distinctive Georgian architecture of classic grey stone buildings with enormous, bright green, blue, or red doors and gleaming brass fittings. Frosted nineteenth-century street lamps festooned with seahorses and leaves. Black iron gates opening to spotless alleyways.

We pulled up to the hotel overlooking St. Stephen's Green, surrounded by Georgian townhouses with the doors of Dublin. On that February afternoon, midday walkers bundled in tweed ambled briskly around the pots of winter flowers, brilliant under a patch of silver sky shining through very tall trees. An old woman was feeding the birds.

John McGrory and Eddy, the doorman, lifted Dad out of the car and into the wheelchair. A minute later, two men arrived with an instant ramp so they could roll Dad into the hotel. Then, the helpers disappeared. I followed Little Sunshine up a few steps from the damp street into the lobby, where a fire crackled at the hearth. Little Sunshine landed on a heap of luggage piled neatly on the well-worn carpeting. More polished brass planters and vases full of flowers splashed the small lobby with deep purple, yellow, shades of red, so lush I wanted to pinch them.

"Mom! Look!" said Little Sunshine. She rubbed her hands together in front of the fire and wiggled among the suitcases. Her eyes beamed at a silver tray of tiny sandwiches and fruit and almond petits fours on a marble table off the lobby. A small woman in a black dress with starchy white cuffs and collar poured hot chocolate into china cups for a young couple seated on a small divan.

Just in time for tea. I smiled and nodded at Little Sunshine, then turned to the receptionist who slid some paperwork toward me. "We are so happy to see you." John was back and chatting with Dad, and it didn't look like I could pry them apart. But I finally got John's ear. We made tentative plans to meet some time later in the week to take a tour around Dublin.

So far so good. We've made it well into the first day.

"Oh, the gale was blowin' for days til just last night," said Eddy. He busied himself with the luggage cart. "Until ye landed, it was frightful. But now it looks like it might clear up for ye a bit."

Good weather often followed me. My luck changed through the years, due entirely to some quirk of nature, and prayer. It simply happened, and after growing up in gloomy stretches of cold, snowy weather, this could only mean a fortunate turn of events. Through the lobby doors, the sky over St. Stephen's shone with a streak of gold in the silver. It was a good omen.

"Yes, the weather," I said. "The rain is soft in Ireland. I like it very much."

"Ye do, do ye?" he said, as he finished loading the cart. "Still, we'll see if we can't order ye some proper weather for yeer holiday." I tipped him, and he tipped his hat in return.

THE LAST CADILLAC

In Ireland, holiday and vacation are the same (that is, any time off), and the Irish are adept at helping visitors experience their holiday. They tell jokes and pour Guinness. They stop whatever they are doing to take the lost and confused to wherever they are headed, even if it means giving up some precious time. And inevitably, a brief encounter with any one of our Irish hosts gets down to the question of the day: "Have ye been to see the Great Mouse at the Disney?"

Our adjoining rooms overlooked St. Stephen's Green. I pulled back the heavy blue silk drapery and stared at a wide view of treetops, carriages, and traffic six stories below. Dad and Little Sunshine were already down for a nap, but I was wide awake, poking at the damask bedcovers, stacking underwear in the polished mahogany dresser. I drifted over to the window again and looked down at the busy street and into the park where splashes of primroses, fuchsia, and alyssum bloomed everywhere. It was late February, but the soft rains and temperate climate made all of Ireland a regular garden year-round. A horse carriage clip-clopped past the hotel, and taxis and walkers crisscrossed the paths among the hedges. In my head, hours of jet engines still droned away. I needed to sleep, but I couldn't lie down and let all that life down in Dublin swirl around without me. I left a note for Little Sunshine and went down the lift for a short walk.

It was not a holiday for most Dubliners. Rushing workers were swinging briefcases, weaving in and out of Grafton Street, faces set. It was time for many of them to be getting off the job. I bustled along like one of them and mingled with trench-coated girls with short, dark hair and fresh, ruddy white faces. Clutching my long green gabardine coat around me, I wove through the crowd and reveled in the moist, temperate Irish air. They looked at me and I looked back at my kinsmen and women, knowing I was one of them, but not knowing any of them. I thought, how crazy it is to be here, and how I'd always be reminded of the brisk pace, the rough red face of an old man in the doorway, smoking and eyeing the crowd leisurely, the young man hurrying as fast as he could to the pub or home, the young mother wiping cracker crumbs tenderly from the pink face of a cherub in a stroller. The baby dropped the cracker and the mother picked it up, brushed it lightly and handed it back to the small, outstretched fingers. "Here ye be," she said, and she caught me smiling.

At dinner, Dad drank and ate everything he could get his hands on, especially the Harp and soda bread slathered in sweet butter. Little Sunshine called it "non-stop chewing," though she wasn't much different than her grandfather in that department, and neither was I. Over the course of several days, we ate in the dining room of the Shelbourne, at the Clarence Hotel tearoom (hoping to see Bono. We didn't), and at the King Sitric north of Dublin on the sea. In short order, we ate our way through heaps of bread and scones, sole and plaice, creamy vegetable soups, hot chips, baby greens, galia melons and pastry, with a river of tea, Harp, Cork gin, and hot chocolate.

One night, while Dad slept upstairs, my daughter ate chicken sandwiches and lemon cookies, and I drank an Irish coffee in the hotel lounge. Our favorite spot was a sofa near the fireplace. We listened to the piano player. We talked to the staff when it got very late and the crowd thinned out. We stared at the Waterford crystal chandelier as big as Cinderella's coach, and we wondered out loud about all the people who had been reflected a million times over in its tiny prisms. We studied the symmetrical arrangement of paintings that hung on nearly forty feet of wall as we tried out different sofas and chairs. From the windows in the lounge, we took pictures of the horses and carriages clomping by beyond the flower boxes under the hotel windows. We watched well-dressed men and women, young and old, talking with their hands, and we made up stories about what they did all day. We wrote in our journals and brought our books down to the sitting areas we appropriated, hanging out at the Shelbourne like it was the usual thing to do.

Then one evening, my daughter wore hot pink velvet overalls and a sweater to match. The young woman on the sofa across from us said, "How pink pink pink you are."

Her boyfriend said, "Your piercing blue eyes are quite lovely tonight."

Sunshine laughed and bounced onto the sofa. Mary was a shop girl who worked in a boutique on a chic Dublin alley, and she liked to rove around the city with her boyfriend, Declan.

"Alley? You work in the alley?" my daughter asked. Her eyes opened wide, imagining the beautiful Mary with white skin and short black hair toiling away in an alley.

Declan chuckled. "It's not one of your dark places, you know, where the garbage piles up for the rats and such. We call it an alley, or the mews. Years ago, the carriage drivers used these small side streets to park their horses inside the wide doors under living quarters," he said. "Now, many of these alleys are places for fancy wankers in their fancy shops and row houses."

Mary gave him a poke and laughed. "Ah, don't be callin' me a wanker."

"Not you, me love." He wrapped his arm around her and gave her a squeeze, then he kissed her on the cheek. He had the honed features and endearing, disheveled look of an artist. In fact, he was an artist, working part-time to support his habit of splashing paint on canvas in his tiny studio. I guessed they were both about twenty-five, if not younger.

"What's a wanker?" asked my daughter.

"Someone who is puttin' on airs—someone full up to here," said Declan, putting a hand over one dark eyebrow. I took another large sip of my Paddy whiskey and hot coffee, and leaned over to choose a piece of pound cake, which I needed like another thigh. I offered the platter to Mary.

"Mom, I think we're wankers."

"I hope not," I said. We all burst into laughter.

"Aye, and you're not," said Mary. "You're loooove-ly."

They left soon after that. Having such a delightful time, I didn't notice that it got to be past midnight.

"It's like being in a story, isn't it, Mom?"

"What is?"

"Being here," she said. "We're in this very exciting story, and the people are walking around and talking in it."

"And we're turning the pages, aren't we?"

"I'd sure like to know how it turns out."

I had no idea how things would turn out for us, but we had our imaginations. My daughter and I made up a fine destiny for Mary and Declan. She got out of the alley and wore a silver dress to her wedding at Waterford Castle where the green candles lit up a crystal stairway decked out in white roses, after which Declan sold his fabulous paintings to kings and museums, and the Silver Princess and the Artist lived happily ever after with one boy and one girl, who bore a striking resemblance to Tick and Little Sunshine. The girl had freckles and danced a lot, and the boy played the guitar and was a true Viking. We needed some work on the end of it, and we finally agreed—very tired by then—how very far away the adventure of our story had carried us from Florida and all around Ireland and back to the lounge at the Shelbourne under the crystal ball of a chandelier.

23

THE TUMMY BUG

My biggest fear during our trip was that Dad would get sick, or fall down and break something, or worst of all, that he'd have another stroke. But he slept soundly. Actually, I had a heck of a time getting him out of bed, until I mentioned breakfast. He loved the Irish oatmeal, marmalade, and coffee, and he was already asking me if we could pack some in our suitcase. I also worried about the flu or food poisoning, for all of us. But when Dad didn't feel well, he never suffered quietly. He was an enormous baby about it, and ordinarily, I didn't mind babying him. I just didn't want to do it in Ireland.

Aside from all my worrying, he was weathering the trip quite well, and enjoying every minute of it. His favorite part of the day seemed to be his hour of holding court in the hotel lounge, reading the Dublin newspapers, sipping a Harp near the fire, and yapping away with Eddy, or Sarah, or Billy, or any ready, willing, and available member of the friendly staff at hand. They all loved to talk; it's an Irish gene.

Then, it happened. Someone had to get sick. After all, we were in the Land of Murphy.

On the third night, Little Sunshine started throwing up. One too many hot chocolates, I thought, but then it didn't stop. She developed a fever. I wiped her face for hours, and then I got scared. I was also very tired. Neither one of us slept for more than half an hour, with the changing of towels and wringing of hands. Dad woke up once, shuffled in on his walker, and stared at Little Sunshine for an unusually long time for him. He was satisfied that she was back to sleep, and then he went off the bathroom. "You'll handle it," he said. "And she'll be fine."

I prayed he was right, wondering if anyone up there heard me, and then I wandered out into the hallway. It was the dead of dawn and no one moved about. I tried to think about what to give her, or where to go for help. I had to do something. She was becoming dehydrated.

A cart mounded over with linen was parked at the elevators, ready for the morning rounds. A door clicked softly, and then a rustling, and a small girl in a black and white uniform rounded the corner. I had the feeling she'd been hovering close by, and now she scurried toward me, leaving her cart and clasping her hands together. Her fine black brows were knit together in concern. A tiny white cap perched on a halo of coal-black curls, she turned her head first one way, then the other, worry etching her sweet face.

"Ah, I heer-d the little one arly this morning," she said.

"It's been a bad night, and now a bad morning," I said. "But she's finally sleeping."

"It's dreadful, especially for the little ones."

I froze. Now I was really worried. "What's dreadful?"

She tilted her head and held her hands against her starched dress. "Oh, m'am, it's the tummy. Now, I shall call the hotel doctor. I'll go now, m'am. I'll do it." And she was gone, flying down the hallway as quickly as she'd appeared at my door.

I sat on the bed across from my daughter who lay flat on her back, not curled into her customary ball. She was so pale, the freckles leapt off her face. A medicinal, sweet sour odor seeped from her body. No matter how many bouts of flu and viruses and colds they fought, I never got over being scared when they got sick. On top of everything, I'd brought her on yet another crazy adventure, and the more I thought of it, the more I began to panic.

Someone knocked on the door. I opened it and stepped back. There was the doctor. I guessed it was the doctor, because she gripped a black leather bag such as those traditionally carried by doctors making house calls. But the bag was the only clue. She looked less like a doctor and more like a large, furry animal. She was very tall and covered from head to ankles in a strange brown fur that gave her the appearance of a well-worn bear.

"Dr. Mary Frances O'Shaunnessy," she said, extending long, delicate fingers. I moved out of the doorway as she took wide steps and floated into the room—if a tall bear can float.

"Ah, what a beautiful child," said Dr. Mary Frances. "Look at that now, so peaceful. Loooovely."

She put the bag down. A striking face turned to me, revealing fine, silky skin and a strong aquiline nose. Her smile warmed me like the sun coming up.

The doctor took a step back and clasped her long fingers. I waited for her to make a move toward my daughter, but she hesitated, one narrow black foot pointing out from under the hem of a long, velvet skirt that peeked out from the fur.

"Thank you for coming," I said. "It's so good of you to come out this early. She's had a fever and been throwing up all night and I don't know what to do."

"Do? It looks like you've done it. Ah, she's an angel."

"Well, thank you, very much, but I'd rather she be back to her old self, alive and well, you know. Not that she's not an angel." I rambled on. All the while the doctor seemed amused. Her eyes twinkled and she tossed her head, which caused the fur topper to wobble precariously.

"Now, ye sit and rest up, and we'll have a look. This angel, I can see, should be up and running in the green and having a lovely strawberry ice. She'll be at it again in no time soon."

I took Dr. Mary's coat and sank into an armchair. The doctor peered under my daughter's eyelid and tapped her chest slightly. Then, she popped up and straightened the fur hat that I feared would fall on my daughter, who had hardly stirred.

"What's wrong with her?" I stood up and started walking back and forth at the foot of the bed, as if I could walk off the worry.

"Ah, she has a bit of the tummy bug. Quite common with the wee visitors, not accustomed to the water and such and other things that fly about." She made a vague gesture with her long thin fingers to show the general flight pattern of the tummy bugs. "It will take twenty-four hours for the bug to run its course."

Most of that time had run out. Sunshine was dehydrated, but the fever had already passed. Dr. Mary left me with a sample of the medicine, then pirouetted out the door. She predicted an end to it (nearly to the hour), and prescribed some flat Seven-Up and a few doses of Motilium from the pharmacy on Baggott Street, which I suspected had valium in it. (I considered taking a dose or two myself.) Little Sunshine slept, and so did Dad. I wondered, as I drifted off for a nap, what sort of practice Dr. Mary would have in

Florida. I couldn't imagine her anywhere but here, so elegant and cheery in her brown fur. She had many a tummy bug to chase out of Ireland.

24

"THE BEST PUB IS
THE ONE I'M IN."

The next morning, I wandered into the lobby, looking for the newspaper, and some answers. I found Eddy, the doorman, on the front steps, a silver whistle in his teeth, brass buttons done up to the neck.

"Excuse me, I know this sounds crazy, but is there a rooster over there in the park?" It was a ridiculous question, but I had to ask it. Every morning, I was sure, my alarm clock was alive and had feathers, crowing in St. Stephen's Green across the street from the hotel—in one of the largest international cities in the world.

Eddy didn't hesitate to come up with a question of his own. He tipped forward slightly, in a sort of bow, touching the brim of his hat.

"Well, now, miss, and did ya see one walking around thar? Har in the middle of Dooblin?"

"No, I didn't see one. I've heard one or two. Maybe a flock of them over there in the park."

"But ye haven't seen one struttin' about, have ye?"

"No."

He looked puzzled and thought a while with a finger

pushing up one corner of his mouth. It was unlikely I would get a straight answer. The Irish seem incapable of it, preferring the story and the enjoyment of telling it and embellishing bits of available information, rather than ending the journey of telling it. I knew this before I even asked him, because I come by it honestly.

"Well, it's curious," he said. "I don't know for sure, but then maybe thar is the odd one or two. It's not really the custom, ye know, but one never knows in the green, many a parson has seen and heard stranger things thar and abroad." Then he told me a tale of the woman whose hat flew off, and a passerby in a carriage, who leapt out into the park to catch it, with the upshot that a romance came of it.

That settled it. I could usually get an opinion of some sort from my Irish hosts, or at least a story or two. Maybe yes, and maybe no, this, that, and tuther. At any rate, Eddy didn't clear up the matter of the rooster, so I crossed over to the park and started looking for one, not really expecting to find it at all.

I tried not to make myself look like I was lost, because one of the Irish would surely ask me what I was doing and then give up his or her afternoon to help me search. The prospect of engaging some busy Dubliner in a rooster hunt was embarrassing.

The rooster was well hidden. Although I looked around in many bushes and niches, where roosters might spend their afternoons resting up for morning duty, I didn't find any. I was tired of being awakened at such an early hour by the creature—and there was little I could do about it—but I wanted to look him in the eye. When I thought about what I was doing among the pansies and fuchsia, I stopped and gave up. The existence of a rooster in the middle of Dublin was something I had to accept. If there were a rooster or two intruding on my sleep and I couldn't prove it, then that was that. I could change some things. Others I had to accept. I had no choice.

I walked back to the hotel and into the Horseshoe Bar and ordered a pint of Harp. I raised my glass. To the rooster, who brings me into the morning, bright and early each and every lovely day in Ireland. *Slainte*!

Ireland was not easily accessible to the disabled, at least not in 1997. I don't know why I brought the wheelchair, expecting to tool around Dublin without a care. The charming stone stoops and low narrow arches and steps, the sidewalks without curb cuts, the non-existent elevators, even in most of the museums and art galleries, the gentle slopes and rain-slicked cobbled walks—all of this I had forgotten about when we decided to make the trip.

Dad could walk, but with great difficulty, so we really needed that wheelchair for the times we could use it. Wheeling it around was another matter. It wasn't easy, but it was part of the adventure. He wasn't going to sit in the hotel all day, although he probably would have enjoyed it, fully ensconced at the hearth with his group of talkative, lovely Irish acquaintances.

We got up late one morning and headed off to Bewley's on Grafton Street for coffee, eggs, and sausages. The sun shone, and the street bustled with busy young people, shopping and going to work. I wheeled Dad out of the lobby and down a ramp that suddenly appeared once again at the hand of the invisible helpers, and the three of us went rolling along the narrow sidewalk. Then we reached the curb.

I stared beyond the tips of Dad's shoes. I was looking across a great canyon. I tilted the front end of the wheelchair back to ease him over the lip of the curb. Dad yelped that I was going to kill him.

Little Sunshine said, "No, she's not killing you, but I think she will, Sunshine, if you don't stop yelling in the middle of Dublin."

I froze on the brink with the yelping father and the scampering daughter, who was beginning to see a good opportunity to tease her grandfather. It could only get worse.

Then, out of nowhere, four strong arms appeared. They picked up the wheelchair, carried Dad across the street and set him down in the pedestrian walkway. Before I could say, thank you very much, the arms were gone. That's the way we negotiated Dublin. When we came to a curb, Dad-on-wheels was lifted off the ground and into the air by his Irish hosts, who didn't seem to think a thing of it. They only tipped their hats and smiled, while I went on and on with all my thank you's.

After a week of wheeling around, eating and drinking and talking, we only had a couple of days left. So, it was time to go on a special last round of adventures.

That night, Robert picked us up from the hotel for a ride in his horse carriage. We clip-clopped past Georgian buildings shining in the gold light, and along the River Liffey that reflected nighttime Dublin like a black diamond necklace. We passed through Temple Bar's narrow alleys, past the polished, old buildings and warehouses turned into hip hotels and restaurants, around the large, modern, imposing U.S. Embassy. Finally, we wandered out onto a wide street, around a couple of brand new hotels with huge shiny windows. It was cold, so we huddled under the blankets, while Robert in his top hat and cape told us about how he and his horse, Champ, and the carriage were extras in *Braveheart* with Mel Gibson. "A regular, fine sort of fellow who sat down to dinner with everyone on the set—with the whole Irish movie army and all."

The next morning, as promised, John McGrory arrived early at the hotel to pick us up for the drive. I had the map spread out on the linen cloth in the dining room, along with my notes and books. The adventurous spirit of the last day seized me, and I looked away from the guidebooks and my lists of sights to see. John had lived in every part of Ireland, so I asked him where we should go.

"Most Americans have cooked up ideas of what they want to see," he said.

"Surprise us," I said. "Show us your Ireland."

"That'll be fine."

"John, one thing. I made a promise to Dad that we would go to the pub. He says he wants to 'belly up' to the bar one more time in Ireland."

"Then he shall do it."

"Do you have one in mind? A very good one? The best one."

"Ah, and that I do. But the best pub is the one I'm in."

On that silvery morning, John drove us north of Dublin to Malahide Castle, where my daughter ran through the dining room—where the Talbots sat down to breakfast one horrible day, hundreds of years before, and then all of them went off to die in battle. Built in 1175, the castle is mostly a Georgian creation of small medieval rooms, throughout which portraits of the noble family Talbot hang against the backdrop of the famous Malahide orange.

Dad and John wandered into the tearoom to smoke, eat currant scones, and talk. Little Sunshine and I went out to the winter garden where some 4,000 species of rare and exotic shrubs flourish on the grounds, mostly May through October. It was lush, even in the first days of March. Against all that green, the tall, spindly, black, leafless trees in the desmesne reached to the silver sky, and everywhere I looked, I thought, if trees could talk, what things I would hear from those branches and from the Irish ghosts that whispered through them: the Talbots, the druids, and Vikings, my ancestors? My daughter ran through the grounds, a pink dot of happiness, zigzagging across the wide expanse—her laughter a friendly welcome, even in this most ghostly place.

Later that afternoon, we headed off the highway on to narrow roads south of Dublin to the fishing village of An Rinn, a rare Irish-speaking part of southeast Ireland. It was no coincidence that the secluded area had been a hotbed for the Irish Republican Army. But time passed, and it was not a crime to speak Gaelic anymore. "We'll thank the Brits for backing off," John said.

The roads got narrower until John finally brought us down a boreen, a cow path rutted by cartwheels, and through a tunnel of fuchsia hedge to a clearing on a small bay in Dungarvan. It was a remote area, on the edge of the world, and I began to grow uneasy, again aware of the responsibility I had for my father and daughter, brought here because I had another great idea for an adventure. But the moment passed. John stopped the car at the Seanachai, a pub and inn with a thatched roof and freshly white-washed stucco walls. We were plunked down on the edge of nowhere, with not a soul in sight, but I felt comfort at the sight of the inn.

Mrs. Gowan, our hostess and innkeeper, peeked at us over

the spindly geraniums in the window as we got out of John's car. The weather was cool and soft with a misty sky lingering over the village.

My daughter and I jumped out of the backseat with our camera, and left the men to diddle with the walker and their cigarettes. We ambled toward the back of the inn, where we found a courtyard laid over with plywood sheets set up for the thwacking of the hard shoe in a jig or reel. My girl climbed up there and clattered away with her legs flying like she was taught in Irish dance class, back in Chicago, such a long, long way from this fishing village. Mrs. Gowan opened a window and started clapping. My little dancer froze in midair. She'd thought she had the place to herself.

I waved and Little Sunshine fled the stage, racing around the inn to the front entrance like an elf, while I followed, wrapping my long coat close, picking my way over the uneven sod. Inside the pub, the deep-set windows in the stone walls were filled with pots and vases of cut daisies and ferns, and crocks of flowers in all stages of bloom and death. Weak sunlight gilded the old wooden tables and chairs. Dad sat on a bench at the fireplace, its opening taller than a man standing. He was staring into the glowing peat fire, talking with John and Mr. Gowan, the innkeeper. I couldn't see Dad's face very well, but I could tell the lines were soft, his eyes distant and bright. He was remembering good times, and they were listening and sharing theirs with him.

"Ah, here they are now," said John.

Dad smiled. "Shall we?" John was already on his feet, lifting Dad to his walker. They both concentrated on heading toward the bar. John pushed the stools aside, and when Dad was settled, John carefully lifted one of Dad's legs so it rested on the brass railing that ran along the floor. He thought of everything.

Mr. Gowan stood behind the long dark wood bar, slowly pouring a Guinness from the tap, on and off, slicing off the foam, until the glass was ready. But Dad ordered a Paddy whiskey and a glass of Harp, a lethal combination if anyone should venture too far beyond the one shot and a beer. I drank a Harp, while Little Sunshine finished the dance in a corner with Mrs. Gowan and a large shaggy mastiff named Shep. Mrs. Gowan clutched her skirt in both hands and shared a step or two of her own. Little Sunshine followed her, heel and toe, kick! The dog got up and moved to the door.

Dad tasted the whiskey, then belted it down.

"Drown the shamrock," said John, chuckling, while he sipped his Guinness.

"*Slan abatable*," Mr. Gowan said. "Goodbye, safe home. And will ye have another, Mike, for a fare-thee-well?"

Lord, he'll have a stroke and die right here, and then we'll be in a fine mess.

But he didn't have a stroke, and he didn't have another whiskey. He lifted his Harp and took a long drink of it, setting it carefully and squarely on the coaster. He wore his Irish hat and the cane rested against the bar. He looked quite content, bellying up to the bar.

"Thanks, John, for bringing us here," Dad said.

"Ah, but the thanks is to you and your lovely family for this grand visit. Thanks a million." He turned and winked at me.

"You're a fine driver," Dad said, tapping his glass of Harp gently on the coaster. He reached for me with his other hand. "And I have a great driver here, my Nancy. Let's go. Let's go home now."

25

TICK IN THE FIGHT

"Gamps, I gotta tell you something," said Tick.

I spied the two of them through the kitchen window, seated at the round table on the patio under the blue corrugated awning. The sun shining through the rippled cover cast a watery hue on their faces. Tick grimaced. Dad turned his head.

"Lad?" My father leaned forward in his chair, and Tick fidgeted with his baseball cap.

"I got in a fight at school."

"Well, how did you do?"

I was about to go over the sink and right through the window, but my urge to eavesdrop glued me to the floor.

"It wasn't really much of a fight," said Tick. "It was over pretty fast, with a lot of pushing going on."

Dad chuckled, tapped his cane a few times on the concrete. "Of course, of course. But you need to know how to hold your own. Guard yourself, don't square off and open yourself up." Dad lifted his dukes and shifted his shoulders.

Great. Now this.

"Keep your left up and jab with your right."

"Yeah." Tick offered his grandfather a Marlboro, then lit it for him. Where was Tick getting cigarettes? And that made three that day so far for Dad.

"What happened?" Dad asked. The tapping started up again and his head was cocked at Tick. "Why'd you get in a fight?"

"I was acting too flamboyant."

"Well, what's the matter with that?" Dad drew on the cigarette. His hat was pulled down, so I couldn't see his smile, but I heard it in his voice. I saw it in the way he leaned into their conversation.

"I guess nothing. But I've never been picked on," said Tick. "I was always top dog in school, so I'm kind of used to being in the spotlight."

I closed my eyes and saw Tick at age four, standing on the piano bench in a navy coat and red bow tie, announcing that he was a "forty year old in a four-year-old body." Tick had been president of the school in fifth grade—not just his grade, but the whole school, kindergarten through five. He was the lead Christmas tree in the school play and a star catcher at baseball, and now, after all that star power, I'd brought him here.

I gripped the edge of the sink, straining to hear every word. It was all I could do to stay put. The fighting. And the cigarettes.

"I thought I'd own the island," Tick added.

"There's still time," said Dad. "Just lay low. Let them all do the talking for a while, and keep your ear to the ground."

"Huh?"

"That's just an expression. Listen for the rumbling and then act on it."

Tick was silent while Dad pulled luxuriously on his

cigarette and blew the smoke over his hat brim. "Remember when we rode the merry-go-round at Disney?" he said. "Used to be, you grabbed the brass ring and you were in luck then. They don't do that anymore, but you can still grab the brass ring, so to speak."

"Gamps, did you always have good luck?"

"I'm here with you, and your Mom and your sister, aren't I? But really, don't believe too much in luck. Make your own."

"Cool."

Tick didn't talk much in the morning, but he was always in a good mood. His expression was never that of a "cow shite on a frosty morn," which is the description his Irish great-grandmother reserved for the irascible members of the family. I appreciated this more than Tick could ever know, and I hardly every showed it. He never complained that he was sleeping in the old laundry room—while Little Sunshine got her own room, painted coral with a new rose-splashed bedspread to match.

I reminded myself of Tick's nature as I tapped him gently on the head, pulling back the covers from his shoulders to let the air conditioning nudge him from deep, cozy sleep. It was still dark out, and every school day I loathed the idea of waking him up so early. Sometimes I wanted to let him stay in bed because I knew how tired he was. The urge lasted a second and then lingered, because I knew he was having a hard time at school. Going to high school was tough no matter how you looked at it. The thought of it flashed like scenes from a miserable flaming purgatory. Tick had to be in his first class at 7:35, a barbaric time of day for kids to be "learning." It's probably why Tick told me years later he "just wasn't into the whole high school thing." He ended up spending a great deal of high school at the 7-Eleven, smoking and drinking Dr. Pepper with his friends.

But I didn't know that then.

Each morning, Tick studied the half a kiwi before he scooped it out with a grapefruit spoon. He sniffed the black current tea loaded with sugar. I was long past trying to get him to eat an egg before leaving the house.

"Tick."

"Yeah Mom?" It sounded like one word—the evolution of a response for the million times I called to him.

"Is everything all right? At school, I mean?"

"Sure. It's cool." He scooped the rest of the kiwi and plopped it into his mouth.

"Don't worry about me, Mom." He grabbed his book bag, then stopped and kissed the top of my head and took me by the shoulders. "Really. I'm OK. You've got to stop worrying about me." He looked me directly in the eye, and I couldn't look away. But as surely as he held on to me, when he let go, I felt like something had broken. Maybe it was the strength of his fingers I couldn't feel anymore, or the nearly imperceptible firm shake he gave me, this hard, brief stare from my son, no longer a baby, but far from being a man. I had to believe him, and I had to let him go, to school and to life, to his problems and to his way of fixing them.

I would not bring up the cigarette issue, or the fighting, for now. I probably should have, but I would not. I would not meddle. The timing didn't seem right. I had time. Besides, I could hear Lucy: "You're right and the world's all wrong." Well, I would just have to jump on that world and like it for damn well once.

I clamped my mouth shut and watched him stuff a

notebook into his bag, check his hair in the mirror by the front door. "See ya." The door slammed; there was never a soft click of an exit. He took long strides, finally leaping over the hedge—with the book bag—and he was gone. I was unwilling to interfere just now—afraid that would simply tear a hole, maybe only a small one, but one nevertheless, in the net that held our new, little family together. We needed to get along, and I had taken it for granted, rather blithely, that we would when I brought Dad to Florida to live with us. What if they hadn't gotten along? We never would have gotten this far. I had to thank all of them for the bonds they were making that strengthened the walls of our house. Dad seemed to fill the place, taking up the living room with his old movies and his bellowing, but Tick and Little Sunshine were far more accepting of the unusual situation than I expected. They were busy with their own schedules, which also included their own private alliances with their grandfather.

I sat on the sofa watching Storm Team Meteorologist, John Winter, tell his television audience about another glorious Florida day. And I thought of Tick going off on the bus, and for the rest of the day facing two thousand peers and a hundred teachers.

Tick said not to worry. Of course, I would worry. None of what any of us did was easy, and the older we all got, the more I worried.

26

"HAIRS" TO OUR HAPPY HOME

I hid out on the dock at the canal to think. It had been more than six months since we came back from Ireland, about a year since Dad came to Florida. We were doing all right, although some disasters—ranging from hurricanes to Dad's health problems—always managed to mix things up. At least the new hurricane season was cooperating. So far. It was early fall, still in the high eighties, and the Gulf remained relatively calm.

My chair tipped back against a stand of mangroves. It was the lazy time of day for birds and fish feeding on the canal, the last of the sun, low and golden, at five o'clock. The surface of the water dazzled, reflecting pinpoints of light off the shiny fat leaves of the mangroves; more light shimmered like fire on the concrete sea wall rising above the water line and on the bottom of the blue boat that swayed above me on davits.

The day didn't quite want to give up to the dark just yet. I hoped no one would find me. I put my feet on the railing, trying not to tip over into the ropey jungle growing out of the water up the bank. Sometimes the chair's plastic legs ended up sticking out of the roots of mangroves after a gale blew up the canal and swept every loose thing along with it. The wind had its way of picking up fishing poles and buckets and other chairs and leaving them bobbing in the backyard canal of my neighbors, whose stucco ranch houses leading to Bimini Bay were just like mine. But the Gulf wind was good. It swept away the cobwebs in my brain. On the dock, away from the turmoil in the house, I could think and plan. To keep writing. Dig into those notebooks full of half-written stories. Maybe earn some money, become a teacher. I'd called the board of education to find out about the certification procedure. It would take two years of night classes to get the education credits. I could hear Aunt Marian in my head, cheering me on, "Just take that one, and you're done before you know it."

The gulls flew over, dipping in wide lazy loops, and the mullet broke the surface of the canal, making long, flat arches as they digested their food. The leaping fish left widening circles that shooed away two ducks skimming the rivulets. Only the cat grew restless, sitting under my chair with a taut neck and wide eyes fixed on the birds and fish. Her white-tipped black tail flicked back and forth on the boards of the dock with a light swick. Somehow all these creatures got along just fine, in this pattern of feeding, leaping, and swooping, even after the hurricanes came through and upset their nests.

I couldn't hide out there for long, with idle musings. None of my neighbors appeared, except for a woman across the canal. She was trying to get fruit out of a high limb with a long stick and a little net attached to the end of it. She couldn't reach it, but she kept hopping up and down on stiff legs until she gave up and went in and left the canal to me.

I wasn't going to give up. It didn't matter how much hopping I had to do.

I stole a few more minutes, took another sip of wine, but then I got up and started walking back. It was feeding time inside the house. A casserole was bubbling in the oven, and there were pills and homework to dispense. I needed to make a trip to the drugstore, to the IGA for milk, and I had to deal with the dishes, the clothes, and answer the phone. I wanted harmony in the house, and sometimes, inevitably, I dealt with chaos. As I stepped on each of the pavers across the backyard, it dawned on me that some changes had to be made. I needed to think of my future. And now, I especially needed help in the house. These thoughts nagged at me. Despite moments of peace, I constantly felt the nagging in the back of mind, like I'd forgotten something and didn't know where I put it.

Dad sat in the rocker in the living room, and Little Sunshine stood behind him. The entire top of his head was covered in strange, little white knobs.

"What's going on?" I shrieked.

My daughter and my father looked up at me, and they laughed. On the coffee table was an array of hairbrushes, hair bands, bobby pins, clips and sprays of all sorts.

"Sunshine needs a hairdo," said my daughter, pausing in midair with a comb and a fist full of hair bands.

"The kid's not bad," Dad said. But he didn't have a mirror. His fluffy white hair had been tamed into dozens of little bun-knots. I wondered how on earth I'd ever get them out, if I ever got them out. I stepped closer to see that no permanent damage had been done. I'd stayed out on the dock way too long, and this was payment.

"Girl, how are we going to get those out?"

"Why?"

"Do you want your grandfather going around like that? He'll get arrested; they'll arrest me." But I had to laugh. Dad's pink scalp gleamed through the bumps, which were pulled so tight it nearly gave him a facelift. I made a mental note to try this myself. "Dad, doesn't it bother you?"

"No, not really. It feels good." He loved to have his hair washed because of the scalp massage. Little Sunshine was hairdresser for a day.

I put that on the list: Dad needs a haircut.

I left the two of them finishing their hairdressing session and turned to the business of getting dinner on the table. The noodles and hamburger were done, the lettuce was chilled, and I was just about to slice into a tomato when I heard a scream.

I dropped the tomato and raced to the living room. Little Sunshine had a pair of scissors in her hand and fluffs of white hair were piled up like feathers all around Dad's chair.

"Sunshine, it's a little uneven on this side, so I'll just take some off here," she said. "At your ear."

"Nooooooo."

I could have heard the shrieking if I were standing in Tampa.

"Good lord," I said. "What are you doing?"

"I'm cutting his hair. Don't you think I can cut it better than Virginia?"

Virginia, formerly of Rhode Island, and owner of Cut And Color Without A Care Creations in the Sand Dollar Plaza was a buxom bleach-blond who wielded the scissors like a machete, and I reluctantly took Dad to her for a trim once a month. She fussed over him, and he adored it, even though he looked like a pruned poodle when he left there.

Every time, I sadly thought, It'll grow back. I loved my Dad's white hair that curled slightly at the neck, like it did when I was six and his hair was black. The Florida humidity gave it extra volume that he liked to tame by plopping a khaki hat on top of that cloud.

Little Sunshine had managed to get the knobs under control, unfortunately, by cutting some of them off. The haircut, though lopsided, wasn't much better than Virginia's, I had to admit. But enough was enough.

"Give her something. She needs something," Dad said.

"I know what I'd like to give her," I scolded, hands on my hips. My daughter opened and closed the scissors and nudged a pile of the white fluff with her toe.

Little Sunshine's playful nature was just short of some serious teasing. She put the scissors carefully on the table and flounced on to the couch. "Well, all right. Next time I'll get it wet and comb it first."

"No, I don't think so. There isn't going to be a next time," I said. "Look, I know you want to help, but this was not a good idea."

She sat there with her arms crossed and her lip out.

"Are you teasing Gampy?"

"Yes," she said, and grinned. "But he said I could."

"Could what? Tease him? Make him look like that?" We both looked at Dad, who looked back at us, all too calmly, I thought. He liked attention of any sort. He sat quietly with his hands folded, waiting to be rescued. It was a good thing he loved his khaki hat.

"You shouldn't get him upset," I said. Her grin remained in place, but she wouldn't look at me. "Do you want him to get sick? He's old. We're all going to be old. How would you like someone to do that to you?"

She was thinking now.

"Do you want him to have another stroke?" That did it. The grin flopped, and a light went on behind those freckles.

"No!" She jumped up and threw her arms around her grandfather and kissed his cheek. "Gamps, I'm sorry if you don't like it."

"I think Virginia's job is safe," he said, looking up at me, patting Little Sunshine's arm. Then he chuckled.

Virginia had her work cut out for her the next day.

27

THANK HEAVEN FOR GUARDIAN ANGELS

Carol Sebastian, my good, true Indiana friend, called me once every week or so to check on me. She told me to watch my health and eat regularly. She was all about eating, and that was how we forged our friendship, especially after my divorce. We'd been part-timers together at the *Calumet Press* where one of my duties was writing up restaurant reviews. Carol and I went out once a week to eat our way through a six-page menu under the ferns, in dark wood restaurants with stained glass windows and booths, which all had pretty much the same offering throughout our Northwest Indiana beat. We dipped into tomato sauce, and gravy, and chocolate sauce, and scarfed down burgers and chops and chicken of every sort. The food landscape was pretty boring, but we managed to spice it up with some laughs and a little gossip. We were a satisfying diversion for each other.

Carol was a real food pusher. "Eat, eat. Try the artichoke dip. It has mayo and Parmesan, and I think BACON. Divine," she said. "Put something on those bones of yours." We ate and ate, or at least she did. The food didn't interest me much. Nothing did right after the divorce, but Carol did her best to try and snap me out of it. She wouldn't leave me alone, with her jokes and eating and everlasting goodwill until I came around, which I finally did, thanks in large part to Carol.

Carol was Irish and Serbian, tall, with short, wiry, dark gold hair, cut close to her head. When she called me up, I could picture her standing in her living room full of white and crystal lamps, jingling her bracelets, standing very straight while she walked briskly around the house with the phone.

"What are you doing with yourself? Where have you been?" she said.

"I live in Florida."

"Very funny. I know that, but we haven't talked in a while. Are you OK?"

"Oh, I guess."

"Tell me."

Not many people wanted to hear it, but Carol did. She drew it out of me, drilling like a dentist without Novocain, but I felt better afterwards. I needed that, although I never thought so at the time.

"It's pretty crazy sometimes," I said.

"Well, that doesn't surprise me with the set up you got yourself into."

"I know."

"You need to get some time for yourself, girl, and not be running a nursery and a nursing home at the same time," she said. "What's that philandering ex-gigolo of a husband doing to help?" Carol was not a fan of the Ex. She had blistering words for any husband who played around, especially one who had kids at home.

"He calls. My son and daughter see him, either down here, or he flies them up there for a weekend. They're not happy about the arrangement, but it works for now. I guess."

"Oh, kid," she said. "You know I love ya. How are you, and I mean *you*."

I told her I was fine. But I was not fine about the insidious decline I saw in my father and the increasingly furious schedule. "It's been quite a year, and I think it's catching up with me."

"Of course it is. And it can't go on forever, without stopping, without you taking some time for yourself. I know how you are," she said. "That's why I'm calling. You need to hear it. You need to get someone in there to help you, every day, if necessary. He can afford it. Get out there for a weekend and go soak up some of that sun you're sitting in the middle of and probably haven't even seen, except to go to the grocery store, or to the doctor, or to drive the kids around."

"Oh, Saints in Heaven."

"No, I'm no saint. I'm your guardian angel. And if I have to come down there and perch on your shoulder, well, maybe I'll do it."

"Alleluia."

She was a friend, even when I didn't see her for months, or talk to her that often. This was how I treated my friends, and as a result, I didn't have many. But I had Carol, and she was right. I needed to ask for help, but I'd been reluctant to go out and get it.

I grabbed a glass of wine and went out to the patio. It was late afternoon when the craziness stopped for an hour or so.

Carol reminded me that I wasn't who I thought I was. I couldn't do it all. Draining the glass, I looked up through the branches of the mango tree. Puffs of clouds flew over. Not a single answer happened by, except to say that I knew going down this road alone, nothing would be solved.

"There's no future in it," my grandmother had said. She'd meant gambling, and I'd gambled on The Adventure.

Finally, I really needed help on this one.

But I didn't want someone coming in and taking over. I really didn't want to share my space. It was already crowded. And I didn't want a chatty person around who might steal things, or abuse Dad. Maybe Dad wouldn't like him, or her. I was ready to defeat the idea even before we got started.

With some reluctance, I called the local HomeAid Agency that Dad's doctor recommended several times, and I at once ignored. Now, short of yelling, "Help!" into the phone, I first decided to describe the situation. The home health aide listened. That was surprising, and welcome, so I continued. I told her we needed a "self starter." Even though I didn't know exactly what I meant by that, I knew I didn't want to lead someone by the hand through each day. We needed a helper with common sense, to get along and care for funny, sweet Dad, to do some cleaning and make a meal or two. To start, that's what it boiled down to, and then we would see how it all turned out. I told the aide at the agency that Dad was a big guy, so they had better send someone who was strong enough to hustle him in and out of the shower, up out of his chair to the walker, and God forbid, should he fall down, someone who could pick him up. So far, we had lucked out, except that I thought I might be working on a hernia as a result of all the necessary tugging and lifting to get Dad around.

The agency sent Marilyn, a trim grandmother just a shade under five feet tall with short blond hair. I saw her walking up the driveway, and I thought for a second she was selling

Girl Scout cookies. But then I saw her small face, like a walnut with a wide smile. She was bouncing along in her sturdy white shoes and carrying a large blue bag that read "Manatee HomeAid Agency."

I began to form the polite words in my head to get rid of her, but then she was in the door, dropping her bag, and smiling up at me.

"Hi," she said. Marilyn looked me straight in the eye and stuck out her hand. We bonded instantly. She had fingers like twigs, and then she flew past me across the living room and looked around. There was a bird-like quality about her, but she was all hawk, not sparrow, even for such a small woman. Dad was engrossed in an old World War II movie, guns blazing, Audie Murphy shouting in the background. He didn't even look up until I took the remote out of his hand and turned down the volume. Then he fixed his baby blues on me, then on Marilyn.

"Commander Nau," he said, offering a hand toward her. He attempted to get out of his chair, but Marilyn gently pushed him back into it.

"Stay, Commando," she said.

"That's Commander," he said. "Forty years of active and reserve duty in the U.S. Navy."

She nodded, and ignored the order. To Marilyn, he was always "Commando," and Dad got used to it. Fast.

Marilyn was top gun, totally in command, and from 9:30a to 1:00p, four days a week, I turned Dad and the house over to her. She sang out—loudly—to him in the morning to get him up. He groaned, resisting the call, but then she went to work on him until he shined like a new recruit. Gradually, he went along with her instructions. But then he fully cooperated because she could get him to the breakfast table in half the time, and he was a hungry man in the morning.

I couldn't have been happier. She gave him his "showa" (Marilyn was originally from Boston) and a "head wash." She shaved him, helped him dress, and arranged his three-course breakfast, his vitamins, his ice water, his newspaper, his hat and jacket, which he needed for his trip to the patio to wait for Harvey the Egret. They rounded out their morning routine with an old movie, and Marilyn liked to watch old movies, too, fortunately. More importantly, she liked Dad and they got along fine together.

Marilyn smoked, so Dad had a smoking buddy, though I told her he was strictly rationed to two, maybe three, a day. She pushed that a little, and sometimes I turned my head when they were out on the patio chatting up a storm and creating little clouds from her Virginia Slims.

While Marilyn scuttled back and forth from the dish-washer to the washing machine, I went out to do errands, and when I came back I found that she had done as good a job as I could do, which was a total surprise. I wasn't used to delegating authority and I wasn't used to the help, so I didn't know it was possible for someone else to do loads of dishes and wash and remove all the remains and spots and spills and do it so efficiently. Marilyn took over the kitchen, laundry, and bathrooms with unerring aptitude. I didn't have to walk her through myriad details of running a household. She'd had plenty of practice, and we got the benefits of that practice.

I got so used to Marilyn and our routine that I quickly became covetous of her time when the agency called and wanted to add to her hours in other households, because the word about Marilyn had spread. Home care of the elderly was becoming big business, especially in Florida. I paid the agency $14.25 an hour of which Marilyn received ten dollars. I wanted to pay her more, and keep her all to ourselves, but she had a contract and she didn't want to lose it. Marilyn went strictly by the book. So, we coasted along, and when she told me the agency asked her to work another weekend for someone else, or that she had worked twelve days straight, I shuddered to think she might burn out, or get on a plane back to Boston. But Marilyn seemed possessed of that common sense I saw in her from the start. After one particularly long stretch, she said, "I'm not working this weekend. If they want me to, I'll tell them to go shit in their hat."

Four days a week, when I heard the front door click around nine o'clock, I sank back into my pillow, dropped the newspaper, drained my tea, and closed my eyes. It was Marilyn to the rescue.

I held my breath through the good days, but I had my eye on Tick. He seemed to be doing all right in school, bringing home a few A's in language, but F's in algebra.

"What's the point, Ma? If I ever see a hypotenuse in my whole life, I'll walk right by it." I silently agreed, but then I suggested a tutor. "I'll ask Erin," he said, dropping the matter and getting out the door with inimitable speed.

"Erin?" I said, but my only answer was the sharp click of the door.

Then I met Erin.

It was a short time after Tick and Dad's conversation on the patio—about the fight at school—when I came home from the grocery store to find Tick in the backyard with three boys and one girl—a lovely girl, tall and too thin, reminding me of a calla lily, if people are flowers. She was smiling at

Tick, and Tick was laughing, his hat pushed up as he leaned back in the patio chair.

"Hi," I said.

"Hi, Mom," Tick said. The chair clunked upright as he got up and pointed to the boys: "Pecker, I mean, sorry, Jake Becker, Jared Romeo, and Tony Mark." I already knew Tony Mark, a quiet, sweet kid whom one of Little Sunshine's friends named "Eggplant" for his ability to just sit there and not move—like the eggplant she'd spied on the kitchen counter.

"Hi," they said, a chorus of cracking voices, high and low.

"And this is Erin," said Tick. The girl named Erin came around the table and offered a slim hand.

"Hello," she said. Her voice was high and as thin as she was. I suspected she would fly off if I let go of her hand. She had clear, green eyes and wore a tight blue top and jeans that skimmed her hips. She seemed a little out of place, but relaxed, and maybe even older than these goofy boys who hovered around fifteen.

I went off to rescue the groceries before they cooked themselves in the hot car parked in the driveway. Back in the kitchen, I peeked at the bunch of them sitting on the patio. They were all laughing, but soon they peeled off and I heard, "Later, Dude."

Tick bounded into the kitchen, sweaty but happy. It was a good time to talk. Erin had offered her hand to me, and I would use her, unmercifully.

"What a nice bunch," I said. "And that girl is darling."

"Yeah," he said, leaning against the counter and reaching into a bag of potato chips.

"What's she doing hanging out with you guys?" Then I quickly added, "Not that you're not darling, too."

"Yeah, Mom, we're darling," he said, grinning. "Erin's cool."

"They're all cool. I'm glad to see you're having a good time," I said, and then I ventured forth. "It's been tough, hasn't it?"

"Yeah, kinda. But Erin's helped me a lot. She's older, but she kind of introduced me around, and she stuck with me in the cafeteria. We just hang out."

"I'm so glad." I stopped moving from appliance to counter to cupboard and looked at Tick. He was intent on getting the last crumbs out of the bag, but then he looked up at me, and smiled, and I saw the sweet boy in there.

"And she's smart. She even knows some algebra—hypotenuses and stuff," he said. "She's wonderful."

No one could ask for better than that.

28

OOOOOOOOO LADY

Along with The Leg and the stenosis, the residue of the stroke that made his left side weak and his brain confused, Dad had been diagnosed with prostate cancer several years earlier. But the condition didn't seem to concern the doctors as much as the possibility that he might have another stroke.

"A stroke will probably get him before the cancer does," the urologist told me during one our trips to the doctors. "The prostate cancer is not a big worry, especially because it grows more slowly in the elderly."

I relayed part of that message to Dad—about the prostate cancer being slow growing, avoiding mention of the stroke business—but Dad seemed unconvinced.

"That makes me leery, when you say not to worry," he said.

He was plenty worried about things that were happening to him, things he couldn't understand or control.

We sat in the doctor's office one afternoon waiting to get the results of Dad's latest Prostate Specific Antigen (PSA) test, which the doctors used to monitor factors in the blood for clues on the activity of the cancer. His PSA had been low, but it had to be checked routinely.

The waiting room was packed with old men with whom I avoided eye contact. I sat with my nose in an ancient *People* magazine so I wouldn't have to look at them and imagine their tortured genital areas. I usually didn't have to feign interest in my reading material for long because this doctor was prompt about inviting us into his white and steel parlor—an unusual circumstance. Since bringing Dad to Florida, we had been coming to see Dr. Ranken infrequently for checkups for more than a year. I liked him. He got to the point, was thorough, and he explained the situation in plain English.

The doctor came into the room and hoisted himself up on a tall metal stool. I knew he was a busy urologist, because there were always a lot of problems out there in his waiting room. I had no idea how much trouble men could have with their equipment until my father started to fall apart, and I started reading about prostates in the news and on the Internet.

"You doubled it, that old PSA," the doctor said. "We have to talk about that."

His PSA count had shot up from nineteen to forty-six in three months. Any count over twenty indicated abnormal activity, and in Dad's case, the cancer was probably on the move. The news was not good.

Dad started crying. "They cut off my Dad's balls, and it didn't do any good. I'm not going to let that happen. They won't take my balls. I'll go to my grave with my balls on."

I was at a loss for words. I turned to the doctor. Let him say something comforting, or change the diagnosis—and the subject—altogether. He was busy with the chart, so I reached over to pat Dad's arm, which I noticed was dotted with dark red spots from the Prednisone for The Leg. We had arrived at a balancing act of managing one problem against the other, trying to put one condition down at a time while dealing with another.

"Dad, they won't do that," I said. "That's not going to happen." I didn't care if it were true or not; Dad was distraught.

"Right, right," the doctor said. "We don't want surgery. You're not a good candidate for it anyway. And it's not the right thing to do at your age, in your condition. But we should talk about hormone manipulation in another way. We could give you a shot that cuts down on the production of testosterone."

"What's the theory of the hormone thing?" Dad said. I was glad he'd stopped crying into a fistful of Kleenex.

"We can take the air out of the fire," said the doctor.

"Sort of dance around it?" Dad said.

"Yes, exactly; that's good. The cancer does abate with the therapy, but it may come back. It's worth a try."

Dad was remarkably lucid at the news. He was so relieved to know that he could get a shot and not have to lose his parts.

"Dad, why don't you go ahead and try the hormone therapy?"

"I might as well. If it's going to hamper my sex life, that's no problem."

I'd heard enough about prostates and balls and testosterone, the most dangerous hormone in the world, and I wanted to get on with it and get out of there. The doctor made sense, and he had settled our health concern of the day.

The doctor gave Dad a shot of Leupron (at a cost of $1,800), which cut the production of testosterone. It was a type of chemical castration, but we did not refer to it as such, since the term seemed to carry the connotation of sexual deviation for perverts. I tried not to think of it in those terms either, or not to think of it at all, but the shot worked. He didn't have to have the surgery that was once routinely pre-scribed for prostate cancer, because Dad's PSA shot down to five and stayed there. He had none of the possible side effects, which included hot flashes and dizziness. He got a reprieve, of sorts. But the reprieve didn't last long.

The next thing I knew, Dad got an infection that brought about some unexpected benefits.

As if the prostate cancer, The Leg, and the stroke situa-tion weren't enough, Dad also had been laid low with a scary bout of throat cancer at the age of seventy. It amazed me that he kept on going, despite the list of debilitating diseases and conditions he came up with, and once they started, they didn't seem to stop. When the doctor found the throat cancer, he recommended that Dad's larynx be excised, which would have left him belching out his words through an electronic implant. My mother went into a frantic spin trying to find alternate treatment, and she found it. One doctor was willing to give Dad a series of chemo and radiation treatments that proved so successful they left his throat smooth and clear of cancer to the degree the doctor couldn't even detect Dad had had cancer.

Five years after this full recovery, at the age of seventy-six, Dad took up smoking cigars and the occasional cigarette. He said he didn't inhale, but I knew what that meant. To think that any of us went along with this, let alone gave him tobacco, gives me shivers to this day. His doctors knew he was smoking. "What's the use," they said, "at that age, a cigar or a few cigarettes a day can't hurt."

The trouble happened when it got to be more than a few a

day, as is usually the case. He sweet-talked family and friends into giving him cigarettes, and he bummed them at parties and from visitors. He even got a cigarette off a passerby in the parking lot when I left him in the car to run into Walgreens. He was worse than a kid who couldn't stay out of the cookie jar. And the worst was that I went along with it. We all did. I was a wimp for not putting my foot down. I assuaged my guilt daily when I gave him a lecture along with his ration of up to three cigarettes.

But it caught up with him. Finally, I reached the point of declaring that there would be no more rationing of cigarettes, and no more smoking. Period. Dad came down with a full-blown respiratory infection, which he apparently got from Little Sunshine, and then he made himself worse with the smoking. He needed to go to the emergency room, and just before we were ready to leave, I found him plopped in a chair wearing his hat and coat, his cane ready, and he was lighting a cigarette. The wheezing and the puffing all at once were alarming. This infection definitely was bringing about the end of his smoking career, and I was glad of it.

I picked up the squishy pack of Marlboro Lights and waved them at him. "That is your last one," I said.

He ignored me, because obviously he was enjoying his last cigarette, despite the fact he coughed between puffs. I was pretty sure he didn't believe me anyway, that I would take away his cigarettes. He really had learned to live in the moment, and he enjoyed those moments. But I was exasperated with the dumb smoking. I'd quit, but I'd let him have his ration. Now, it seemed, it would be the death of him. I got lax with Marilyn around. And Tick, Tick was smoking, and it didn't matter what lengths I took to dissuade him from it. He smoked, and he was in cahoots with his grandfather when I wasn't looking. It was an awful, vicious curse.

Dad puffed his way to the end, and then he tried to get me to relent. I was adamant "No, that was it—your last cigarette."

"What do you mean? I practically gave you your first cigarette. And now you're going to take them away from your own father?"

"For God sakes, Dad. Whatever are you talking about? You NEVER gave me a cigarette."

"That's what you say."

He never gave me cigarettes. Beginning at age twelve, I stole them from the drawer in his nightstand. My siblings and I went through a fancy charade for years to disguise the fact that we were all smoking Mom and Dad's cigarettes, as well as buying Kents at the drugstore after school for twenty-five cents a pack. We chewed gum, aired out the house, and drove the car with all the windows open, even on the worst winter days. When I developed a terrible hacking cough at sixteen, and my mother took me to get a chest x-ray, she couldn't wait to announce the results: "Your lungs are black as tar."

But short of tying us up in our rooms, we kept smoking, all of us. It was years and years before I quit.

"You should understand how I need them," Dad said. "It's in my life blood. I'll probably die of nicotine withdrawal."

"No, it's the other way around. You're going to die with it. The smoking is killing you faster than anything else you have," I said. "Just listen to yourself. Look in the mirror."

His breathing was wispy and labored and his face was pasty. But he was resolute, all the way to the emergency room. Under that slouchy hat, his lips were pursed tightly.

It gave me all the more resolve. He wanted to take a pack of cigarettes with him to the hospital, and he grabbed my purse where I'd stashed the last of the Marlboros.

"They don't treat a condemned man so badly. Have a little class (*wheeze*). Let a man down easy. Just one more; come on (*wheeze*)."

I threw my purse in the back seat and hoped he didn't lunge for it as I pulled into the drive of the hospital. He didn't. He sat still and pouted. The front of his jacket was dotted with holes from cigarette sparks. I was glad he wouldn't ever be so close to lighting himself on fire again.

He made one last wheedling plea as he got out of the car and into a wheelchair at the emergency room door. He quieted down while we waited for the doctor, and waited, and then finally, when the doctor was standing in front of him with a clipboard, about to listen to his chest and admit him with an acute respiratory infection, Dad said, "Mind if I take a break, doctor? I'd like to just step outside with my daughter." He had a wistful look in his eyes.

"Oh, Dad, that'll be fine. I'm sure you can speak freely in front of the doctor."

The doctor looked from me to Dad, and his eyebrows went up. He appeared to be confused, but I wasn't. Dad wanted a cigarette, and I wasn't having it. I didn't want to embarrass Dad, but I was close to getting there. I shook my head and put two fingers to my lips, like I was smoking. The doctor chuckled.

"If you don't let me step outside there—just there," Dad said, waving in the direction of the exit. "Just to have one. If you don't, I might have another stroke from nicotine withdrawal."

"That's not likely," said the doctor. "Be glad you quit."

"But I haven't quit," he said.

"Yes, you have." We said it together.

Dad slept in the hospital bed. Two pillows and an inclining bed propped him up, and he continued to saw logs heartily with his mouth open. I knew he'd wake up and say he hadn't slept at all. Most of his sleep was deep, short, and fitful, so most of the time, he woke up short of feeling well rested. But at least he slept some. I stood watching him, his breathing regular, coming in soft whiffs. He turned his large, white head on the pillow, and slept on. I sat down and peered up at the soap opera on the suspended television high up in a corner of the room. No one was watching the characters act out their problems with orange and green faces. It was a peculiar picture, and the actors appeared to need hospital care.

Dad's roommate, George, stared at the wall. I hadn't seen him utter a word in two days, but then he blinked and moved his head to indicate that he was alive. The day before, Dad said, "I'm bound and determined to keep George going, keep the poor man alive with some cheering up." Poor George needed it in good measure. He looked to be on his last legs, but Dad continued to push. "Man needs a boost," Dad said, in an Irish whisper the nurses could hear down the hall.

But Dad made little impression on George, who seemed unresponsive to any kind of encouragement. I asked Dad why he kept trying to turn George around. "A man's got to do what a man's got to do," Dad said. But, still, I hadn't heard a word from George's shrunken mouth, his yellow-gray skin frightening. The top of his speckled head had only a tuft of hair left on it, and that little bit came to a point. He looked less like a man and more like an infant without the cherubic fat and cheer.

I wondered if I could do anything for him, or if it mattered. He began to rock forward like he was going after something, then he sank back on the pillow. I didn't know what was wrong with him, but it looked like a general breakdown of everything. His arms were sticks and he hardly breathed at all.

Everything appeared to be wrong with George, but mostly he looked like he was "crumbling," which is how Dr. Gibson, one of Dad's doctor, often described the aging process. The doctor himself was far from that predicament at age forty or so. He was a jolly, young, a vital sort of doctor who loved to talk about gardening, and when he entered the hospital room he seemed to bounce from bed to bed like a huge white beach ball. He took me aside at one point and said Dad was stable, but frankly, "You know he's declining. Some old people just go out with a heart attack or stroke. Sometimes it's more merciful that way. And others just crumble away." He loved to use that word, crumble, which made me think of old cookies, the Coliseum, and winter streets. But it didn't remind me of Dad.

Dad wasn't crumbling, exactly. He lumbered and lolled like a doomed and quaking building. He seemed fine one day, and the next day he was a mess. My brother said Dad's stuck blood was causing his life force to actually dry up in his veins. It was another sad image to consider. Dad moved slowly with painful deliberation and maddening hesitation. Sometimes his brain electricity dribbled down to a trickle, or he would stop in mid-sentence and tune out altogether.

His leg hurt constantly because he had to take a rest from the Prednisone. So, the doctor gave him a super-duper painkiller. Dad threw it up immediately. They tried more "miracle" drugs, but none of them worked, either, so we stopped before we got on that same insane merry-go-round of medication that did nothing. My father was immune, or at the very least, not in tune, with most of the medication. He was compelled to put an unexpected spin on everything, even on crumbling.

Dad got off the hospital bed to go to the bathroom, complaining that the trip was a waste of time because he was sure nothing would come out, and in the methodical way he went about it, transferring from walker to cane, moving tortuously slowly, he finally got the job done, in about thirty minutes. I offered to help, only to get a booming response, because he was intent on doing his business at his own pace. And I could see he was babying The Leg. "NOOOO," he said. "I've got all day."

He made it back into bed and settled into the pillow, his feet touching the cold metal bars of the bed frame. It was no use trying to move him without calling the nurse. He was exhausted from the effort of going to the bathroom. I covered him up as best I could. He fell asleep, then woke up with a start, mumbled, then he shook and cried, sputtered and exploded a response to the orange reporter on CNN.

I felt useless, but at last Dad seemed comfortable. He dozed in the bed, and every once in a while I looked over at George, alternately perched upright or flat on his back, but still staring at the wall. His hospital gown covered his front, and a sheet lay over his skinny knees. George's eyes opened and closed slowly, while he remained taut and ossified as an old bone.

I decided to speak to him. "George, do you need anything? Do you want me to call the nurse?"

He just turned his head that teetered on a stick of a neck. He looked at me through round, blackened eyes like twin peepholes to the grave.

I adjusted the obnoxious fluorescent light overhead that made everything and everybody look even more ghastly than they were, except for the orange-tinted reporters on the television, who were beyond help. "That better, George?"

Why would he care? I was not reaching George. Nothing came from his lips.

This is pathetic. Just shoot me when I get like this. Just shoot me.

Really, Dad and George didn't seem to care whether I was there or not. A nurse came in with red Jello and beige cookies on a tray. I busied myself arranging the goodies for the two men, but one slept on and one went back to staring at the wall.

What were they thinking, waking up in fits, half sleeping through the rest of life? I looked up at Bill Clinton explaining away the machinations of some problem he'd gotten himself into, and all of a sudden Dad sprang awake.

"It seems when that guy gets into trouble, he goes across the ocean instead of across the street."

"What's that, Dad?" What could he be talking about now? I wondered.

"Bill—Bill and that nice Tony Blair. Clinton went to London. Now Tony's in Washington, isn't he? He and the president are great friends," Dad said. "We should have them over for dinner."

"And Hillary and Monica and Gennifer Flowers?"

"No. Who cares about flowers. Let's have tenderloin and shrimp cocktail, and some of those nice tasty eatin' things."

A "tasty eatin' thing" was an apple pie from Burger King, which for Dad was the main reason to eat lunch or dinner.

Dad turned to check on his roommate. "George, how you doin' over there?"

"Who dat? Oh, Mike, how you?"

"Fine, fine. This is my daughter, George. Did you meet my daughter?"

"Oh. Lady." His mouth formed a third black hole like each of his eyes, and now I heard his voice, which came from old, worn out, rubbery vocal cords, vibrating from the dark well of him. My dad, with his huge white face, ample stomach, and head of snowy hair looked as lively as Santa Claus next to George. Clearly, Dad was trying to pump some vitality across the room to George, who needed a lift.

"Come on! Let's get out of here and find some live music. And I could sure use a good stiff drink. What about you, George? The liquor they serve here is worse than bathtub gin," Dad said. He leaned away from the slant of his bed and the pillow fell behind his shoulder blades. "Get my blue shoes," waving his hand at me. "That's an order."

I did not feel like playing Navy or hostess to my father and George's fantasies. "Dad, Dr. Gibson said you can't get out of here until Thursday. This is only Tuesday, honey. Won't be long now."

"Let's go, let's go, let's go," Dad said, ignoring me. "I have to get out of here today."

"Don't tink I'll be going with you, Mike," said George, finally. He made a valiant effort to turn his head to Dad and me. Something wrenched inside me at seeing his pain.

"But, say, Mike," George said, flopping back on his pillow. "Don't do anyting (sic) I wouldn't do."

The Prednisone, which worked miracles on The Leg,

also lowered Dad's immune system. He had been taking a month-long break from it, and for reasons only known to modern medical science, the doctor tripled Dad's dose of Prednisone in the hospital—all the better to open his lungs. The result of that treatment was that my father developed a diabetic condition. Another lung opener, the drug Vomax, cured the wheezing, but it raised his blood pressure to 190 over 96 and wound him up tighter than a carnival barker. He was taking pills to counteract pills. I tried to get him off the pills, but it seemed we couldn't get away from them. Pills were part of the juggling act of old age, and it was hard to keep all these tiny balls in the air. They plinked and skittered into every corner of our lives, the useless little things.

"Does he really need all these pills?" I asked Dr. Gibson.

"Well, yes, he does. We're trying to make him comfortable."

"Do you think the medication is working?"

"It's hard to tell, isn't it? Especially with your father. He's a special case."

"I guess they're all special cases," I said. "But for Dad, the pills don't seem to make him any better."

But, by then, Dr. Gibson was looking at his pager, and with clipboard in hand, he whirled away and down the hall before I could say Vomax and Prednisone. I wanted to be a mind reader and see the future, or better yet, have a medical degree myself so I could call some of the shots, but since none of that was feasible, I sat down on the side of Dad's hospital bed and opened a packet of saltines to go with the tepid vegetable beef soup. Dad was more interested in his lunch—which appeared to be tan in color, with a sprig of lettuce—than anything the doctor had to say.

"Will you open this, too?" He handed over the small box of apple juice.

"Sure," I said.

It was a good moment, and I decided we would enjoy it together. One moment at a time.

Dad was about to reach his limit of pills and IV's and other tests under Medicare. After that, he would have to leave the hospital and "recuperate under supervised care." I was pondering what that meant, but I hadn't gotten an answer from Dr. Gibson. He talked about putting Dad in "an interim rest facility for recovery," but I didn't like the sound of it.

"You just won't be able to manage him alone for a while," the doctor said. "He needs the constant therapy and staff to watch him round the clock."

Marilyn was waiting in the wings, but she was not a therapist. While Dad recovered, the hospital staff, doctors included, maintained a wait-and-see attitude toward what he would need when he got out. Nobody knew what would happen with Dad, so we lived pretty much day-to-day. The hospital nurtured the aspect that it was a place of rest and recovery; it was not a place to die or be terminal—not even for poor George.

A visitor told me that George was riddled with cancer from the waist down. He moaned when he was lying down or sitting up, which pretty much excluded any possible position of comfort. The only time he seemed rested was during the brief episodes when he received pain medication. After Dad broke the ice between George and me, George often looked over at me and said, "Oh. Lady."

His greeting wasn't social. He was in pain. His eyes

grew deeper and blacker, and while he half sat up because he couldn't lie down, sometimes he said, "Ooooooooo lllllaaaady."

I left my father to look for George's nurse, and when I found her, I got straight to the point. "Would you give George in Room 402 some pain medication? He seems to be very uncomfortable."

"He just had a shot of morphine," she said, busying herself behind a Formica counter stacked with sheets of paper in varying sizes and colors, all with unintelligible writing on them. "He can't have anymore, unless the doctor prescribes it."

"Why don't you call the doctor? Ask him to prescribe more, maybe even a lot."

She looked at me, or through me, as if I made no sense at all. "Excuse me. Are you a member of the family?"

A blank wall of hot anger rose inside me. I saw my mother's face. But I kept my voice level, like they did.

"No, I am not. I'm a concerned person who has been watching George writhe around in agony, periodically, for almost two weeks," I said. All of a sudden, I felt a pang of guilt. I had waited so long to say something, all the while his condition got worse. "You can hardly stay ahead of this thing, whatever it is he's got. You need to step up the pain medicine for someone so obviously terminally ill." In my head, I heard my mother's hospice nurse saying those very words, like it was yesterday.

The nurse decided to take a different tack. "You know," she said, "he's not in here as a 'terminal'."

I had a fleeting vision of buses and planes running in and out with various destinations. She spoke of George as she would a cold concrete junction of some sort.

"He's not a terminal? Really?"

"No, he's not." She moved down the counter, sat down on a wheeled chair, whirled around until I faced her back, and she began opening drawers and shutting them in a series of claps.

"Well, then what? Is he ready for the prom?"

She ignored me. I was overstepping my bounds and I didn't care. I was going to push this as far along as I could. I just couldn't go back in there and look at George without trying. Down the course of my Dad's decline, I'd met my share of meatheads who ostensibly meant well but weren't doing any good. Hardly anyone came to see George, but I'd heard he had a son somewhere.

The next day, I ran into George's sole visitor, a neighbor who had come to see him once. I asked her to call George's son about getting the doctor to prescribe more pain medication. Maybe I didn't know what I was talking about, but I had spent nearly two weeks with George and I saw he needed relief. What were they afraid of? That George would become an addict in the short time he had left on earth? That was my prayer for George, that he would become an addict.

George's visitor, a puffy, harried woman seemed put out about being asked to deliver news to the son. Where was the son? She said she would call him, an engineer who lived in Memphis and was very busy at the time. "You can hardly get ahead of it. The pain," I said, remembering the days with my mother. "Please, call him."

On the last day of my dad's stay in the hospital, we said goodbye to George. I felt I knew him well by then, after listening to him and sitting around with him in his half-dressed, half-aware condition on the edge of the world. I touched his hand that was like a shriveled leaf. He tried to lift it, to raise himself up in the bed, moaning all the while. I patted his dry, dead arm. I tried to smile.

Dad sat in his wheelchair, with his hat on and his lap piled over with his belongings, and waved, like he was on the back of a train running for office. "Keep the faith, George."

"All right, Mike. You, too."

"It'll be OK now, George," I said, lying. "They're coming with the medicine."

"Ooooo. Lady."

29

BONKERS OVER THE BATH LADIES

Dad was able to come home from the hospital, but Marilyn wasn't there to help. She was off in California visiting her daughter—so I panicked. I recovered immediately when I found out the hospital staff was way ahead of me. Upon Dad's release from the hospital, he became eligible for daily home health care under Medicare, which is truly a good show of government dollars at work. For a prescribed length of time under the Medicare program, the doctor was able to assign different types of therapists and bath ladies to get him going and "unstick his blood," as my brother said. They helped change Dad's life, and mine, and they also ended up being his unexpected pleasure.

The morning I picked him up to take him home, he was very tired, more tired than I'd ever seen him. On the way into the house he leaned on the walker, laboring over the flagstones up to the front door. Finally, I got him into his room where he sat down on the side of the bed. He threw up.

Heart lurching, I studied him, bent over and pale. There was no reason for him to throw up. He had just completed every kind of test and therapy known to mankind and was declared well. In the hospital, he tolerated the antibiotics, and he ate heartily on a careful diet for two weeks. He didn't wheeze anymore, and, thankfully, he hadn't begged for the cigarettes. What's more, he wasn't going to have any more cigarettes. A potential problem brewed there, which I had to head off with Tick and Marilyn, but they would understand, and cooperate.

I got him as comfortable as I could in his cool, dark room, under the covers, tucked in, just like he'd done for us about forty-some years previously. I gave him a peck on the forehead, but he was already near the snoring stage. Dad would come around. He always did. I figured with George's moaning all night, and every other interruption the hospital had to offer, Dad hadn't slept well for two weeks. He needed to readjust after all the drugs. Too many drugs. He would sleep it off. Later, I'd make him a dinner of rice, lean hamburger patty, applesauce, and a roll. That would make him all better. At least I hoped it would make him better.

And he was. He slept all afternoon, and then went back to sleep after the sensible dinner that he gobbled down. He slept on and off for two days, with minimal interruption. I thought it a good idea to head off the exercise until he recovered from being in the hospital, so I asked the doctor for a temporary reprieve from the therapy. Dad rested up.

But soon the bath ladies and therapists began in earnest, and Dad took to them like he was off on a new adventure. Their daily visits were pure entertainment for him, and he was the entertainer as well. These women—mostly young women of every style and background—fussed over him, took over his bedroom, and led him out and about for short walks after his nap.

"If I'd known they were coming, I'd have gotten sicker a whole lot sooner," he said. "That little one, what's her name, Carol, we could be an item."

Each morning a different bath lady from the agency appeared at the door: Laverne, with a cap of gleaming, wavy hair, blue nails, and skin the color of fine chocolate; Jackie, who looked like Tammy Wynnette, but didn't sing; the other Jackie, who looked like Diana Ross and did sing; Carol, the former Navy petty officer, who gave Dad a good cry when she started talking about her days on the ship; Henrietta, the blond Amazon with braids on top of her head, whom Dad insisted on calling "Heidi." I saw her lift Dad off the bed like he was a toddler.

The bath lady of the day showered and dressed him, changed his bed every day, and straightened his room. He always invited her for a sort of "date" over coffee, but she was always bound for the next client—sometimes up to eight a day. Before she left, however, she sat with Dad for a few minutes to quiz him and determine how sharp he was. She recorded his bowel movements, appetite, and intake of medication. In under an hour, she was out the door like a small tornado, leaving Dad freshly combed and outfitted and smelling good, poised in front of the newspaper and ready to pounce on his Mueslix with banana, poached egg on toast, juice, fruit, and coffee, all of which he ate to the last crumb.

He was fond of his bath ladies, especially Carol. But the real love of his life was Noelle, the physical therapist, his "little sweetie," the blond mother of two with the full lips and long eyelashes, who "cued" him on how to get up and sit down properly, ride a portable bicycle, walk without dragging his left foot, keep his back straight up to the walker, and then practice walking up and down the driveway. They talked and laughed, and he flirted shamelessly.

I wondered what went on in that be-stroked brain of his—my dad, the puritan who had never played around with other women and never even allowed an off-color joke in the presence of women. He'd once dragged my mother, my sisters, and me out of *Hair* on Broadway when the actors rolled the humongous penis out on to the stage. But that Dad was surely gone. The stroke had affected that part of the brain that deals with emotions and the ability to make subtle judgments, the doctor said. So, he flirted and made off-the-wall, even slightly lewd comments sometimes.

I began to understand what my mother told me years before when he suffered his first big stroke. He had become a different man. The one she had married was gone. She'd been so sad, but I hadn't understood. I thought it was all right, because we still had Dad. The different Dad was a simpler version, a little goofier and sweeter, and fortunately for all of us and for him, he hadn't lost his sense of humor and his proclivity for the one-liner. I felt badly for caretakers who were left with the brittle shells of loved ones who turned into mean, dry, demanding people. That wasn't Dad. I was so lucky for that. There was some silver lining in the cloud that hung over his head, as his mother used to say.

Even so, it was embarrassing that sometimes he was outspoken in his love for the ladies. He told Henrietta he liked her "little panties," to which she simply smiled and put his hat on his head with a firm pat. Then, one day, he told me he had to cool it with Noelle. "I found out she wants to have another baby," he said.

Laura, the occupational therapist, looked just a tiny bit like Elizabeth Taylor, but she had the unglamorous job of trying to get him to care for himself on the toilet and dress himself. When she said she was going to teach him to make a light meal, I had to laugh out loud. The only thing he'd ever cooked in his life was a pot of oatmeal, but Laura seemed undaunted. They all seemed that way—crisp, professional, friendly to a fault—Dad's bevy of women.

Then one day, Noelle said Dad was about to graduate to a restorative therapist. I knew what that meant—Noelle was about to leave him. We decided not to bring it up to him, just yet. She said he had gained strength. I couldn't see much progress, except the he seemed to have more endurance when on his feet, and he was definitely a happier man.

After she was gone, he moped a little, like a puppy who misses the one who cuddles him and gives him treats. I wasn't worried about the situation, because Dad lived so much in the present, dependent on comforts and routine. Getting old seemed to be more and more a job of simply managing each section of the day in as practical and comfortable a manner as possible. He was freshest in the morning and then spent his energy and memory throughout the day. Forget the past, and the future, as well. Gather the roses. Today. I could hear Lucy, like she was standing there, waving a glass of Veuve Clicquot at me. But Dad kept asking about Noelle, so I ended up calling the agency that had sent her to us. They sidestepped my inquiry. Noelle had many clients, the nurse-official said. It was best for Dad to learn to adapt without one particular therapist. I couldn't quite agree, mostly because I didn't like seeing my dad so down in the dumps. All it would take would be a visit, or a phone call. I felt like he needed weaning.

I finally got hold of Noelle on the phone. I asked her to stop over for coffee. She declined, nicely, but with a firm "no" nonetheless. Some weeks later, I saw her in the bakery aisle at the grocery store with her two little blond daughters. All three of them were arguing over the pros and cons of purchasing a bag of chocolate chip cookies. Noelle was so harried, she didn't even look up and see me, and I didn't feel like interrupting her small drama and bringing her back into ours. She clearly had other situations to deal with closer to home, and Dad had been such a small corner of her world. I checked out and walked away.

Dad continued to have occasional therapy, and I could see some improvement, mostly because I wanted to see it. And then, thankfully, Marilyn came back. I'd forgotten how much I'd come to rely on her spirit—her strength and humor, her ability to inspire Commando to get up-and-at 'em, like they did on the USS *Barnes*.

We got into the swing of our good days and bad ones, and then there was the day he surprised us all. Again.

30

GOING FOR A SPIN

I got up around seven one morning and shuffled toward the front door to unlock it for Marilyn. She wasn't due until nine, but I couldn't sleep. I wanted to enjoy the day before it broke into chunks of business I had to manage, or else. There was a wicker dresser on the porch, and each drawer was full of paperwork—one drawer for me and my education applications, divorce proceedings, transcripts and certificates and the like, and then the kids had theirs: sports, school, lessons, letters, applications, permission slips. Dad had several drawers. The health insurance companies were driving me nuts with their reams of reports (one aspirin cost $1.75 in the hospital). And then there were the forms, because Dad had Blue Cross on top of Medicare. Somebody had to deal with this stuff, and that somebody would be me. I was lucky to have the time; I didn't know how anybody could deal with it part-time—but most people did.

The house was so tranquil, I hated to wake it up. The sun streamed into the porch throwing blocks of light across the long oak table and onto the tile floor. A white poinsettia still thrived after months of humid temperature. It was early winter, a good year and a half into The Adventure, and we were all thriving and surviving, especially in the peaceful moments. A gecko skittered along the jalousie windows, and the only other sound was the soft crackle of palm fronds in the backyard. I simply did not want to move from my spot at the table to mess up the day when it was so new and clean, except that I needed coffee.

I fished around in the basket for the key to unlock the door for Marilyn, but I couldn't find it, and then I saw that I didn't need it, because the door was open. I knew I'd locked it the night before, and not because I was afraid someone would get in. Most people on the island didn't lock their doors. I kept our door locked mostly because I was afraid Dad would get out. The nurses had warned me about night dementia, which my father seemed to experience. We started to notice it when Mom got sick, when he'd get up and get himself dressed, down to hat and coat. My mother couldn't sleep in peace, because Dad sometimes would start stirring at 3:00 a.m.

I half turned toward Dad's bedroom to check on him. And then I froze. The front door slowly yawned open, and the cat scurried in, curling around my legs, purring for her breakfast. Then I saw a trail of Kleenex wads dotting the flagstone walkway.

Dad left them wherever he went, usually in his pockets where they got a good shredding in the washer and dryer, but they were his unmistakable calling cards where he walked, sat, ate.

My eye followed the trail of tissues down the walk and hit the driveway. Something was not right, and for half-a-second, I couldn't tell what it was. And then I saw what was wrong with the front of the house.

The Cadillac was gone.

I raced out to the driveway and looked up and down the street. The car had not rolled away, nor were there any signs of a disturbance. The street was empty and quiet, except for the birds and the sun and breeze gently rippling through the morning. It did nothing to soothe me.

I ran back into the house and frantically raked through all the keys in the basket, looking for the ring with a large crest that held the keys to the Cadillac. Gone. I ran for my purse, to the kitchen counter, drawers, anywhere I might have put the keys, including the refrigerator and the waste-basket (where I'd found them on two occasions). I was making no sense of it. The car was gone, and a key would do no good. But the adrenalin kept pushing me, so I ran around looking until I ran out of places to look. Whoever took the car also took the keys, I was sure of it. I thought of Tick, but Tick was in Orlando at a soccer game.

I hoped that Tick had come back and taken the car out. I even hoped that Little Sunshine had decided on an outing, and all the while these crazy fantasies went through my head, I knew none of that had happened. I walked through the house toward Dad's room and pushed the door open slowly and the hump of pillows in his bed gave me a start of relief. I poked at the mound of linen on the bed.

Of course, I came up empty.

I checked the bathroom. Nothing. The house was empty, except for Little Sunshine snoring away in her burrow. She would have heard nothing.

The sinking feeling took over. I ran around the house, calling for Dad. Dad wasn't there. The neighbors probably could've heard me up and down the canal. The canal! For years I worried about the kids falling in the pool, or drowning in the Gulf, and now I ran out the back door to see if my father was floating in the canal. Two ducks rode the breezy rills on the surface, and they flapped away when they heard me clunking over the dock. He could still be in there, I thought. But I would surely have heard a two-hundred-pound man fall into the canal. My bedroom was thirty feet away. The older I got, the more exacerbated became my fears about everything, but I simply told myself he was not in the canal.

My mind went back to the trail of Kleenex on the walkway, and the missing car. I couldn't shake the clues.

I called the police and told them to be on the lookout for a late-model Cadillac. Then I said the unthinkable: "Be sure to look for a white-haired man driving it."

"Ma'am, do you know that's about every other driver, in every other car on the road, hereabouts?" said the dispatcher.

"Yes, I know, but you don't understand. He doesn't have any idea where he's going."

"None of 'em do, ma'am. I notice they seem to be driving around helpless."

"Please. Just look. He's got white hair, his name is Mike, and the car's mocha."

After I hung up, I realized he probably had his khaki hat on, and that car wasn't mocha—mocha was coffee brown, not purplish-gray. This was not turning out well.

I kept searching the house. No windows or doors were open or broken. He could have been kidnapped, but that would be a stretch, wrestling my hefty Dad out the door. It would have been like lifting a whale from a tank.

The fact was, he was gone.

I can't find my father!

He was alone somewhere, and at some point, he would be

confused, crying, and helpless, which is exactly where I was headed, too.

I stood on the porch, my arms folded around me, and looked out at the black surface of the canal, thinking horrible thoughts. But it did no good to sit there, making up even worse scenarios: of Dad and the Cadillac wrapped around a fence or telephone pole, of Dad running over a young biker or racing off the road and into a playground full of kids practicing baseball.

And it would be all my fault. Not his. I so blithely asked for this responsibility, and now look at what I've done.

I got up and paced around the kitchen. I could hear ball practice start up, and it wasn't even nine yet. I should call the police again. The possibilities of this whimsical adventure seemed endless, and I began to get angry, except that he couldn't possibly know the consequences of what he was doing. Would he know enough to come home? Here? In Florida? In his mind, he was probably back in Hammond, Indiana, on his way to United Boiler Heating and Foundry for a day's work in his office and with the men in the plant. He hardly ever found himself in the present. He loved his life and all the times and people that had been; the present was too painful, and the future was something he didn't like to talk about.

I went out the front door again, and this time I paid close attention to the Kleenex on the walk. They hadn't blown away, but it was a still morning. The cat brushed up against me again, agitated and meowing loudly. What about the cat? Yes, the cat had been outside when I opened the door. She was a house cat, and she'd not gone far. She never stayed out long, and she had not been at the window mewing to come in, which was her usual way of getting our attention almost as soon as she went out the door. If Dad had taken the car, he had probably let the cat out when he left. It had to have been recently.

I started walking down Willow Avenue toward Gulf Drive, more out of nervous energy than anything else. Then I picked up the pace, sandals flapping loudly on the broken shell that skittered over the asphalt. Not a soul, nor a car was on the street, and not a sound, except for the doves cooing in the bushes. I had three blocks to go to get to the main drive, and then I saw something, a dot turning off Gulf Drive toward me. I stopped and peered down the street. The dot was definitely a shade of mocha, moving slowly and growing larger and larger, the sunlight beaming off glass. I started to run. I ran fast toward the dot, as fast as my flip-flops would take me.

I ran all the way down Willow Avenue. When I was within ten feet of the Cadillac, I screamed, "Stop!"

But the driver was already stopped, right in the middle of the street.

Dad was hunched far down in the driver's seat, his white knuckles gripping the wheel and his hat pulled down so low I couldn't see his face. I yanked the door open and grabbed him around the neck with joy and relief. He was stiff as a tree trunk. He didn't even turn to look at me; he just stared straight ahead.

"Ow," he said, flinching inside the circle of my arms.

I remembered the bad neck and the arthritis, so I let him go, reluctantly.

"You're killing me," he yelped.

"I'd like to." But I was laughing. "Dad, where have you been?"

"Oh, I don't know. Just down to see Leonard at the shop. Had a feeling things weren't going too well down there."

"Dad, Leonard's in Indiana." This information had no effect on him whatsoever. He was lost in another world. He hadn't seen Leonard, his beloved foreman and right-hand man, since he retired and left town for Florida. I thanked God he hadn't been looking for Leonard in south Chicago traffic on a Saturday morning. The traffic on Anna Maria Island was thin and slow, and when a car went by, it was clocking about twenty. It was still no place for my father to be driving around. He could hardly manage his two-hundred-pound frame, much less a two-thousand-pound car.

Dad looked back down the road and kept his hands on the wheel.

"Dad, I've been worried to death about you. Please, don't do this again."

"Do what again?"

He looked up at me, the confusion deep and impenetrable in those sea-blue eyes. It wouldn't do any good to try and untangle the morning's crazy adventure. His senility was like water rushing through my fingers; I couldn't grab hold of it, understand it, manage it at all. Some days were just like that, most of the time now. No one had told me the depth and breadth of that senility and—especially—how it could come and go. I would get frustrated when he couldn't remember something, but in that moment, he couldn't. Later on, on another day, he could. It was the progression of the disease; the dementia came and went without an itinerary. We just had to follow along and do the best we could. That would have been the pill to die for, one that leveled out and rebuilt or, at least, stabilized the senile brain, one that gave comfort to the demented—and, as a result, to the supposedly sane.

It wouldn't do any good to ask him where he'd gone, because he usually didn't remember details. Details were confusing, unless they happened fifty years ago. Standing in the street, sizing him up, it looked to me like he'd already spent what lucidity he woke up with. I had no idea how long he'd been up, but it had to have been a strenuous, tiring morning for him. I had to deal with The Now to get through to him and figure out a way to budge him away from the wheel, permanently.

With the car door open, we took up the width of the road, and thankfully, the place was deserted. I put my hand on his arm, afraid he would resist, but he stayed rooted to the wheel. Sometimes he was docile as a child, and other times, he grunted and rumbled like an old bull. I'd never been able to manage if he started flailing around or became violent. It was still something to watch for. The therapists and nurses warned me about that, too, but I was getting used to Dad's change of moods, from confused to lucid, but mostly cooperative. Every day I had a different dad.

"Dad, why don't you scoot over and let me drive for a bit?" I tried for a light tone, like I was offering him a bowl of spumoni, his favorite ice cream.

He began to give it up. His fingers relaxed slightly on the steering wheel, and he slumped a little in the seat. Then the moment froze and clicked into my brain, to stay there forever in memory, of Dad and me and the Cadillac, in the middle of a sunny bright morning with a single bird looping overhead. The air was so full of promise for a day of boating and picnics, sunbathing and walking on the beach, but instead I felt that other events were ahead for us. I was going to another level of taking care of Dad, of protecting him from himself, and I was scared.

His grip tightened.

I waited, and then I ran my hand up and down his arm, gently, but he didn't move. He kept holding on to the steering wheel like it was the only tangible thing in a permanent state of fog. He acted the same way when I drove him around, or when he got into the shower, or entered a stairwell, or into any situation where he didn't have control anymore. He hung on to the handlebars for dear life. He was afraid, too.

At least we were in it together.

He looked away, and I couldn't see his eyes except for the straight white lashes under the brim of that hat. I waited for him to mentally get his bearings. He'd gone out for a spin, not really knowing what he was doing, and now, he'd finally come back to us, and we were all safe. I was just glad he was safe.

We were at a crossing where the tie between us was about to pull tighter, and for once, I waited patiently for him to respond. I had to move slowly to get through this, to build whatever understanding we could—even if the reality was that he might forget the whole thing in a minute. I didn't want to think about that. I always held on to the belief that some of my dad was always in there somewhere, and would stay in there until the end of him. We needed a new understanding, mostly for safety's sake, and I didn't want to reach out and take it, so I waited for Dad.

"Dad?"

"Yes?" He lifted his face and he fixed his eyes steadily, surely, without taking them off me, and I let that gaze be a strong link between us. His expression changed from a blank stare to one of sweetness and peace, and I saw a lot of the old dad come back.

"I'm so tired. Let's go home," he said. "You drive. It's your turn."

I hadn't yelled at him. I'd waited patiently for him to get a grip on the moment and respond. In the words of my grandmother, he was a poor soulie lamb. And he admitted that he was tired.

He was slipping further and further away. Into dementia.

I hated that word. Dementia. It was a black hole; it was taking my dad, the smartest and strongest man in the world, a fact I had to accept even as I watched, and hoped for good days, while his mind drifted away.

We made it step by step back into the house. I steered him to the breakfast table, half coaxing, half dragging, and when I fixed him a bowl of frosty flakes with a banana on top, he perked up. He started to put globs of sugar on the cereal before I caught him, and then he began wolfing it down. Sometimes I let him get after the sugar bowl; it wouldn't kill him, like the booze and cigarettes. I kept a parental eye on him and the kids. But I had definitely let my guard down this morning, I thought, staring out at the canal. I needed to tighten the controls, lock the doors and hide the keys, because I couldn't afford to slack off. Dad finished the last lick of milk, like the cat.

Just then, Marilyn's car crunched over the shells in the drive, and two seconds later, she appeared in the doorway. "The Commando's already up?" she said, as she plopped a large canvas bag on the kitchen floor. I was wiping up the counter, and Dad was talking to the cat at the breakfast table.

"The Commando's been up and out already," I said. I told her how we started out our day. Both hands went up to her cheeks so fast I thought she'd lift herself off the ground.

"He what?"

She skipped out of the kitchen and over to his side at the table in the family room. She began poking around at his back and arms. He looked up at her, with a blank, tired expression. I noticed for the first time what a good job he'd done of dressing himself. He'd managed to get his nightshirt tucked into his khakis, his jacket on, and his boat-shoes— sans socks—on to his feet, but he looked mighty tired.

"Commando? You out driving your tank this morning?" Marilyn squeaked. "You leave that to the generals, you hear?"

"Sure, sure." He was agreeable when attention was lathered on. "But, you know, I'm awfully tired. I think I'll take a little nap."

We tucked him into bed and stood in the bedroom doorway, shaking our heads at him. Dad was already snoring. "He'll get a 'showa' and good head wash when he gets up," she said. She ran off to the laundry room, talking to herself and getting into a lather about the misadventures of The Commando.

I went out to the patio and sat at the table drinking coffee, in a daze of relief that we had survived until 10:00a.

Then Marilyn stopped midway between the kitchen and the laundry and shouted at me through the kitchen window.

"Where in heaven's name did he go?"

"I have no idea. I tried to get it out of him, but he was too confused, and too tired. If the sheriff shows up, we'll know. But so far, so good."

I was hoping he hadn't stuck up the Circle K for a pack of smokes, or run over a jogger. He may have had a mission, besides going off to see Leonard, but I would never know. I was still amazed he'd driven more than three blocks away and back—which was all the evidence I had—and I was relieved more than I could say that he was back safe and sound.

A heron alighted on the dock and picked along carefully, and then it took off over the canal. The danger was outside, and inside, and this was one of the things I didn't consider when Dad so innocently made his announcement, sitting on the patio at the dollhouse up North: "I'm going with you."

The phone rang and cut through the morning silence. I almost didn't answer it. I didn't want to talk to anyone after the hunt for Dad. I just wanted to re-group and maybe mop the floor for the tenth time that week, a therapeutic exercise that seemed to let my demonic energy flow out through the squeegee. I especially didn't want to talk on the phone. I'd have gotten Caller ID if I weren't so cheap—and call waiting, if I were ruder.

No question about it, during that particular stretch of time in my life, I was isolating myself and becoming dangerously anti-social, but this was something I didn't see, nor would I admit, if asked.

I let it ring six times. Unfortunately, I picked it up.

It was my sister the nurse. "How are you?" she said, in an official tone.

"Do you really want to know?"

31

THE PLUME

"I'm fine," I said. I lied. "We're all fine."

My impulse was to cut the conversation short. It was too bad that it had come to this. I didn't want anything to do with my sister the nurse.

I tried to speak in a friendly tone, but the sound of my voice stiffened with each the syllable. We always started off in a fairly civil manner, but I knew where it would end, with a plume of annoyance rising up inside me. She always wanted something, but she never asked for it directly. She led me along and we inevitably ended up in a free for all. Our relationship was a disaster. I regretted how far we'd come from the days when she wore an eyelet bonnet, when I had just turned seven and she was barely seven months, and I was so happy to take care of her! We had grown apart as sisters, and the further apart we grew, the less agreement we had on the best way to care for Dad. In fact, we never agreed on anything.

"How are you doing with Dad? Do you have help, and some time to yourself?"

"Oh, yes," I said brightly. "We're a little family down here."

"He has a family up here, too, you know," she said.

I didn't answer.

Finally she said, "Don't you think you should get on with your life, instead of babysitting Dad?"

"Excuse me? I'm not babysitting Dad."

"Well, maybe not exactly. But that's what I'd call it," she huffed.

"Well, I don't. He lets me know what he wants, and I can usually figure out what he needs. He's getting along fine. We all are."

"I think I should take over. I have a better handle on what he needs, you know, as far as the meds and therapy and such."

"We have doctors and drugstores down here."

"That isn't what I mean and you know it."

"No, I don't know it. And, goddamit, what do you mean?"

If she told me she was the "professional" one more time, I was going to throw the phone in the canal. But she was the nurse, and she wanted control of Dad. I had the control. Before we left for Florida, Dad designated me his health care representative. My sister the nurse didn't say a word to me at the time, and I hadn't given the matter much thought. It was a piece of paper, a simple piece of paper that just made sense because he was coming to live with me. His family doctor and Joe, the accountant, pointed this out. I didn't even have the presence of mind to think of it—with all my lists and plans to move out of there as fast as I could. But the issue of the health care authorization remained at low boil in the relationship with my sister the nurse. She didn't throw it in my face exactly. Instead, she needled and annoyed, called me with insistent, off-the-wall demands that made no sense at all.

I felt that plume of annoyance puffing out as big as a hot air balloon.

"Look, he likes it down here, and he's doing just fine," I said. I didn't mention that he nagged me for martinis, as he reached out to grope his therapist's rear end. I also left out the part about his early-morning spin around the island. I wondered where he went, but it was the last thing I'd ever mention to her. I couldn't level with her. She was still telling everyone that I had kidnapped Dad, according to one cousin. That hurt. I hadn't tied him up and hustled him out of Northwest Indiana; he wanted to go.

I couldn't be honest with her, and God forbid, let on that I wasn't in control of the situation with Dad. I'd just have to keep all the doors shut and locked, along with my mouth.

"Why don't you visit him?" I asked, trying to wind up the call and diffuse the plume that was ready to burst into flame. "I'll get you a plane ticket."

"You'll get me a plane ticket. That's nice of you," she said. The sound of her voice froze our connection in one unbending, brittle line, from North to South. "I just can't fly off like that."

"Oh, now you can't just fly off. That's interesting. How about that magic umbrella of yours, Nurse Poppins? You've never missed a party, and you came to see Mom all the time. Now you can't come down and see Dad once in a while, even if I get you a ticket."

There was dead silence on the line as I stood in my kitchen and bit my lip, and she adjusted her nurse's cap.

"I don't want you to get me a ticket," she said. "I don't want to visit him. I want him to come back up here and live near us. And, by the way, what puts you in a position to buy ME a ticket?"

"Ah, there's the rub, isn't it. That I would buy you a ticket with his American Express card, which he has asked me to do. For all of you."

"Really."

"Really," I said, quietly, not letting the plume take over and smother me. "And I would, if you'd let me."

I didn't give a flying fig if she came down to Florida to visit or not. I was sick of her needling and hoped she'd leave me alone. No, leave us alone. Maybe the hostility would evaporate and we could get along, even make some sense of it all.

Who was I kidding?

I hung up. My hand was still cramped from gripping the phone in a strangle-hold when it rang again. Now I was definitely not going to answer it, but I did. It was Lucy.

"You've done everything, and if I can give you a break, I'd like to do it so you can get your life back on track."

"Huh? Who have you been talking to?"

"Why?"

"Because I just had an unpleasant conversation with our sister, and I don't feel like having another one with you."

"Oh, stop it. Why do you get so defensive? And why do you let her bother you? She's just trying to do her job. She's a nurse, for God's sake, and you're the oldest. Never the twain shall meet."

"Well, you got that right. But she gives me a fat pain."

"Forget it. You're doing a great job. He loves it down there. I know he does, and she knows it, too. So what the fuck?"

"You have such a nice way of putting it."

"I'm trying to help you over here," she said. "Jesus almighty, you must be burned out."

"I'm doing all right."

"Just all right? Is all right good enough?" she said. "Come on. What do you think?"

"What do I think? No one's asked me that. Ever."

"Well, I'm asking you now. What do you think about taking a break?"

Until she said it, it never occurred to me to think about taking a break. If I did, I would have to think about how off-track life had gone. Our mother was dead, our father was in Florida, and the family was tattered beyond repair, it seemed. It was a good time to think, for once.

"We have to look at all this. We aren't a family anymore. It goes beyond where Dad happens to be living," she said.

"I suppose so. But what's important now is taking care of him, and I'll keep doing that for now, the best I can."

I tried to focus.

"All right," Lucy said. "I just want you to know. I'm here. You can call me. Just to talk, that's all."

"Just to talk. Thanks. That's good. That's very, very good."

I walked out across the backyard, picking my way through the weeds over the stepping stones, and with each step, I saw more clearly.

For now, it wasn't just about me. It was about all of us as a family, but in that particular moment, the spotlight was on Dad. I hadn't really thought about my siblings in the decision to take Dad to Florida. Dad hadn't either. I'd taken it for granted that they'd go along with the plan to take care of Dad, once it was on the table and they saw how much he wanted to go. But it hadn't turned out like that. We didn't feel like a family together.

That was only part of it. Deep down, I had to admit that I wasn't Daddy's little girl anymore, and that was the part I kept holding on to. I just didn't want to give that up at all. I didn't want to give up my dad.

As such, I would continue to cherish the relationship I had with my father, and I would be his caretaker. And I must take care of my kids, those kids that grew and grew. They were learning a lot from Dad, and from me, and The Adventure. The kids were growing, but I kept returning to that strange reversal of roles with Dad. Dad wasn't taking care of me anymore. I was taking care of him, and I didn't weigh this as much as I just went ahead and did what I had to do. He needed the care. He needed me now.

I had to think about the future. I wasn't going to be able to stay in this house on the canal, with the increasing taxes and flood insurance, if I didn't start thinking seriously about a job. The freelancing began to run out after we landed in Florida, although I continued to write some articles for the newspaper and others in the early months. We were well into our second year together in Florida, Dad paying rent, the Ex sending support, and I still had some savings from the house and furnishings. I hated to think of it, the temporary life of caring for Dad. But it always got back to that in my mind. After Dad, what? The world would shift again. So, I needed to put a serious spin on it. Dad was fast approaching eighty, and he was still dodging one health scare after another. I could not deny the fact, even as much as I tried to tell myself how resilient he was, how he leapt from one crisis to another. Time was running out.

What I wanted to do was to be a teacher—not a news writer with weekend and holiday shifts, because I needed to be with the kids. I needed to start doing something about getting my certification, beyond shuffling papers and making phone calls. I had to get off my ass, instead of filling the late afternoons with wallowing and resentment toward my siblings. Some day, after this hiatus as caretaker was finished, I'd have to start over. Really start over. Again.

I walked into the kitchen and looked at the clock. It was four, and Dad was down for a late nap before his martini and the news with Tom and me. The kids were hanging out at the community center. My daughter had taken to cheerleading, a perfect occupation for her, and Tick was playing soccer. And me? What was I up to? It was time for a chardonnay. I poured it into the glass and I put the frosty globe of wine, like a piece of cool fruit, up against my forehead.

Ah, relief!

The wine felt good going down, and the tile under my feet felt soothing. I stared out the kitchen window at the mango tree with a canopy that spread over nearly half the backyard. Before I called the school board, I would get out there and rake up the pesky brown gravel and the ripened fruit that fell off the tree, which the squirrels attacked and left teeming with ants. The cleanup was a major yard chore, but it was worth it. The Kent mangos were stringless and juicy, and tasted sweeter than peaches. I thought about picking some to go with chicken. The mango would give it an exotic flavor, but I would probably be the only one who liked it. My daughter wanted chicken nuggets every night, and Dad had a craving for grilled peanut-butter-and-ham sandwiches. It was his favorite treat, because that was the treat he shared with Mom at the malt shop when he was courting her, when he suavely ordered a soda with two straws and one straw went up his nose. It was their first date. "I guess I really impressed her," he said. His shoulders shook when he told the story, remembering it, and I patted him, and then I went into the kitchen and made him another peanut-butter-and-ham sandwich. We all ate sandwiches for dinner a lot. Tick would eat anything, if I could get him to sit still long enough. He didn't really care what I fixed; eating was boring, he said.

But Tick liked mangos. When they were almost gone in the late fall, he'd climb to the top of the tree giving me fits. Higher than the squirrels he went to get the last of the sweetest mangos that had baked in the sunshine. He had gone up on his second harrowing trip to the top of the tree—we had long passed our October anniversary in the house—and the last of the mangos sat on the windowsill.

It was still a strange, beastly time of the year, when summer would not give up and the hurricanes threatened in the last days of November, when the breeze in midday hardly moved at all, except for the wild bursts of tropical weather. I stood at the sink and I didn't feel like doing much of anything. I should have been out there raking, but instead, I watched the great, long, leafy branches sway and scrape the window.

The rain was coming. The weather moved with the sudden whip of the branches, and it told me that we were going to get more than our daily tropical shower. The wind clacked through the palm trees, and the cloud's shadows scurried across the backyard. Sometimes, it was frightening to see the weather change so fast, from blue to grey, roaring in from out of nowhere across a calm sky.

The still day began to billow up in our faces. Hurricane Earl was headed north through the Gulf on its way to the panhandle. I'd heard it on the news and then forgotten about it, and now, here he was, as advertised. I didn't believe all I heard from the forecasters, but they were getting better about predicting the location and strength of hurricanes, once they'd formed. Predicting landfall was another matter. We would probably have a good ten hours to get out if one were due to land. But not to worry with Earl, the forecasters said. Earl promised to buzz right by us, but not without brushing us with his ragged edge of wind and rain. I could see him getting stronger in the limbs of the mango tree, whipping branches back and forth against the house. The gusts sent the last of the ripe fruit plonking to the ground by the dozen. One crashed on to the window sill and startled me out of a daydream.

I took a sip of wine. It was already 4:30 and I hadn't done anything all day. I would wait this one out and hope for the best. I was getting used to hurricanes.

32

IT WAS AN AWFUL RAIN

Earl came and went, as pesky as a visit from a long-winded, sloppy relative. He made himself at home, littering the yard with branches and lids of garbage cans from far down the street. In his wake, puddles became breeding grounds for mosquitoes, and sewer lines overflowed, making the Gulf inhospitable to swimmers and fish alike. I viewed the paper bags, newspapers, and half a bicycle in the front yard. I wondered if Earl had emptied the recycling bin and all my wine bottles had rolled down the street. I feared that I was turning into a drunk, paralyzed, staring at trees, waiting for the rain, waiting for something. There was no sense waiting; no one was going to tap me on the head with a magic wand.

I needed a nap, just a short one to block out reality. Just for an hour.

I flopped on my bed, readjusted the pillows under my head. I looked out the sliding glass doors. A squirrel whipped down the plumeria in a great flurry of leaves and scattered the last of the pink blossoms. The hurricane had caused little damage to the yard, except for the huge branch of the majo tree that cracked loudly and crashed down in the middle of the night, at which time I rolled over. I hadn't bothered to look because I didn't want to deal with the yard.

Billy, my neighbor, knocked on my door to tell me that my tree had taken out the fence between us. That wasn't a good thing, considering Billy. I silently hoped he would forgive the damage of my crashing branches, as I forgave his barking German shepherd. Billy offered to work on the fence separating our two yards and help out any way he could.

"Free of charge, darlin'," he said. A leer curled up on his fat lips holding the toothpick that stuck out of his upper dentures, and I chose not to comment on his lascivious attitude, or on his hideous dog. It wouldn't have been neighborly.

"Thanks, Billy. Talk to you later," I said, a bit rudely, but I was tired. I didn't want to deal with Billy. I fled to my retreat and curled up in the comforter.

I was all of ten minutes into the nap when the front door slammed. Tick was back, probably with a vengeance from the sound of it. More and more these days, doors and windows and cabinets did not whoosh or click shut quietly under his hand. They crashed behind him. Having a teenage son and knowing what to do with him were getting tricky. Sometimes I felt like I was walking on eggshells around him. I turned over and buried my face in the pillow.

At some point in the past few months—how fast it happened—he had changed, or I had, or we all had. Nothing stayed the same. But Tick was growing up. Many times, I thought that I'd given him too much freedom. He was not surly or rude, but he was often distant. That was expected of a teen-ager, but it was the abyss that I feared, that distant space where things just happen, without control or forethought. I'd had plenty of experience not fore-thinking, and I was afraid of the consequences of that pattern where Tick was concerned. I tried to give him privacy, but at the same time, I was worried I was giving him too much. I needed to know what he was doing with himself all those long hours he wasn't in the house eating Cheez-its, playing the guitar, and sneaking a cigarette with his grandfather—although, to Tick's credit, he stopped the latter.

I didn't look forward to a confrontation as I burrowed into my comforter, but then I knew there wouldn't be one, since I'd been nagging him to get home at a decent hour for dinner, and here he was. I suspected that he was smoking pot, although he refused to admit it. He shut down tight when I brought it up. I finally brought it up once again—that and the smoking of all cigarettes—in a short, economical burst of questioning, and then he was gone. His eyes were often bloodshot slits, with a silly fixed grin on his face that was the mirror of attitude adjustment through chemistry. I looked in the mirror at my own reflection, and I saw the same expression of disaster staring back at me. Yet, I expected him to listen to me, his mother, in my demanding tone with a chardonnay in one hand and a fermented look on my face.

He stood outlined in the doorway of the bedroom. God, he'd gotten tall, and I hadn't noticed that about him. I'd mostly noticed the marijuana-induced grins and the back of him when I started to question him about where he was going and with whom. I couldn't see his face until he leaned forward, and then I saw the hollow expression, a cross between fear and anguish, and at once I knew something was wrong. I was suddenly afraid; it washed over me like dirty water. His hair was plastered to his forehead, and he was breathing hard, like he'd been running. He just stood there in the doorway, looking at me while I sat on the edge of the bed.

"What's wrong?"

"Erin's dead."

Neither one of us moved for a horrible second, both of us spinning through the awful realization of those final words. It couldn't be true that his beautiful little neighbor and school chum, someone so young and good, was gone, irrevocably gone and not ever coming back—the long white hair that flew when she turned her head quickly, the girl who spoke in that high, clear voice, "Is Tick home?"

"How do you know?" I said, demanding that he prove himself wrong. Somehow, bad news made me angry. It was a dangerous flood inside that threatened to drown me and everyone around me. I just didn't want to cope. Maybe it was a rumor, I thought; maybe he didn't know for sure. Not confirming the dreadful news would avoid the possibility it was true and keep it from becoming reality.

But he was staring past me, into realms of disbelief.

"I just saw her at the pier this morning. And now she's gone, just like that." He collapsed in the doorframe, his expression fixed in shock, or resignation. I couldn't tell.

"How? Who told you? How do you know that?"

Something snapped. His eyes, mouth tightened. He had to deal with me, and he was frustrated that he'd even come to tell me. The impatience of the young was cutting, and a reminder that I was getting older by the minute and less useful in his life. Now I was of no use at all.

"I went over there after practice. Her father came to the door and he told me. He just stood there and said it." Tick put his head in his hands.

Finally, I said, "How?"

He looked up at me then, and waited until it settled over him. "She went into town with Jared. They were in his truck, and someone hit them. On her side."

He delivered the news in a remarkable staccato, punching the air with the awful pieces of information. I got the picture immediately: an outing, stolen from the day, gone bad. Still, I sat on the edge of the bed, and the only thing that went through my mind, the selfish thought that flit from one brain cell to the next, was that Tick had not been with them.

"What about Jared?"

"He's fine. He walked away."

Tick's face changed from the shock to one of awful loss. His cheeks burned red, and he dropped his head to his knees. I went over to him and touched his hair. He was crying, and there was nothing I could do, except sit there with him and share his grief, as if I could take some away, or cut it in half.

It had been an awful wreck. The kids had taken a left turn in front of a fully loaded truck weighted down with lumber. It smashed into Erin's side of the car, killing her instantly. The fact that Jared walked away from the accident was both terrible and lucky. He had driven his friend to her death, and he had to live with that. All of his friends were grief stricken, blaming him and themselves for all the stupid things they had gotten away with.

Tick had never been able to thank Erin for helping him. I told him he could repay her by doing the same for others, an idea he liked, but it wasn't going to bring her back.

The funeral was supposed to heal a wound, but it opened many. In the church, a huge poster-size school picture of Erin was propped next to her urn so that she appeared larger than life. It made a cruel impression during a service when even the pastor broke down.

Her parents, long divorced and grieving horribly, later fought over who would get their daughter's ashes. The fight ended when they divided her, spreading some of Erin over the Gulf of Mexico and scattering the rest of her ashes off Chicago's Oak Street beach on Lake Michigan.

It drove Tick crazy—this Solomon's curse of sorts—not knowing where the last of his friend was, and no amount of Christian preaching at the service, or from me and Dad and his dad, that she would be one with everyone in heaven, in the world, one in his heart and mind forever, made it better. He could not be consoled.

Tick was mostly angry with Erin's parents, who had split her in two. "How could they do this?" he demanded. "How could her parents do this?"

"Parents do crazy things," I said, knowing perfectly well that I was talking about myself.

33

"I WANT A MARTINI."

The fallen trees left by Hurricane Earl caused more than superficial damage to Billy's fence, and a branch from my majo tree involved more than a few sticks. It was more like a tree trunk that extended its long torso through Billy's yard and left its leafy tip hanging over the seawall into the canal. Finally, I had to face him over the repairs. I stood in the backyard, looking into a deep hole where the enormous tree trunk had fallen. It made quite an impression, on Billy and me.

"Didn't you hear it, darlin'? Oooo, you must be some sleeper," Billy said.

Ooooo, I wished he wouldn't call me 'darlin.' He made me feel greasy when he said it. And I didn't want to discuss my sleeping habits with him, either. He stood a safe eight feet away, but soon he was inching closer, until I got a whiff of tobacco, beer, and testosterone that nearly knocked me over. It didn't help that his aura was cooking in the hot afternoon that hovered at 100 degrees, even in the shade of the mangled majo tree. The canal glinted with late afternoon sun, and birds cawed and dipped for mullet. I didn't want to deal with the hole in my yard, and I especially did not want to deal with Billy.

"Yes, ma'am. That was some strike."

"What strike? What are you talking about?"

"Why the lightnin' strike that took out this here little old tree and made this hoo-mon-gus hole in our yards." Now he was drawing us together as one, in the wake of Earl. I was about to turn and run into the house.

"Billy, I don't remember any lightening strike the night Earl came through."

"Well, 'course not. Yee-all must sleep like a little old she bear in winter." Then he cackled so I could see the large black hole where teeth should have been.

I didn't know where he got his theories, or what part of the god- forsaken earth he'd crawled from. He looked and smelled like the dregs of a wilderness camp, and he didn't make any sense. I didn't remember any lightning strike exactly. But searching my brain, I did come up with a flash of memory, of one nightmarish crack in the hellacious storm: a very loud shrieking sound like the earth was breaking apart and it was protesting, and here it was, the result, in my backyard, and Billy's.

Alltreecare, the best tree-trimming business in the area, was on the way to clean up the mess. They came out of St. Louis, run by a guy named Felix McLoughlin, but they were all over the southeast after a hurricane ripped through. I was going to pay to get the stuff hauled away, and I was thankful that the tree trunk had fallen away from the house, cutting a path across our yards and into the canal.

Felix came up behind me with a chain saw, and with hardly a nod, he got to work cutting up some fallen branches. "Mighty busy since Earl," he said, bending over with an arm-wresting pull on the starter. He had long, tangled hair and ropey arms as strong as Popeye's, and Irish songs fueled his energy, which was considerable.

Billy lounged on the broken fence, discussing the aspect of my property on top of his property when Tick hollered from the patio. I couldn't hear him with the chain saw in my ear, and I was distracted with Billy's breath in my face, so I went over to where my son fidgeted with his hands in his back pockets. He showed no interest in coming closer, and I couldn't say I blamed him.

"Goin' to Erin's," he said. My heart stopped when he said it, because he was going to her house, and that was all.

"Wait, I have a chicken and some potato salad I want to take over there. Will you wait a minute? I'll drive you."

Tick looked over at Billy, who appeared to be telling Felix what to do. Felix waved his left hand at him like he was swatting a mosquito.

"Looks like you're busy. I gotta go, Mom. Can't wait."

I started to go after him, when the decibel went up on Billy's directions. I turned around to deal with the cleanup, annoyed at Billy and Felix and Earl, and that Tick wouldn't wait one minute to go with me to deliver the food. He just wasn't going to go along with almost anything I suggested. I had to get over it, but I had to keep trying to communicate with my son. It just wasn't at the top of my agenda that afternoon.

Tick had his hand on the door when he stopped and yelled back at me. "You better check Gamps, Mom. He's being funny again."

Oh, God. I'd forgotten about Dad.

He was due to get up from his nap, and my daughter was just back from the community center where she was making posters for the Fun Fair. I was getting far behind in my after-noon of rounds. I looked over at Felix, who had a great deal of chopping and clearing ahead, which I quickly estimated would run into the hundreds of dollars to finish. At least he'd gotten rid of Billy, who was ambling over the torn hibiscus bushes and broken fence, probably to grab another beer. Felix had not turned off the chain saw for a beat, which ef-fectively ended the one-way conversation with Billy. I'd have to remember that one and buy a chain saw.

I spun toward the house, sprinting across the patio and into the porch. Dad cruised past me on his walker with Little Sunshine right behind him. This couldn't be good. My daughter was teasing her grandfather lately, and most of the time Dad took it. In fact, most of the time, he acted like he liked it. He made little quips that set my girl off. Her wild bursts of laughter must have entertained him, because he kept egging her on. The two of them were like children. She had a small, stuffed pink pig they tossed back and forth between them. Little Sunshine had now taken to braiding his hair—I forbade the scissors—so that Dad ended up with little springs all over his head, sometimes with bows, as they watched MTV together. Dad loved Madonna, and that "Irish bald one." He seemed to lose seventy years when he goofed off with his granddaughter, when he and my girl called their own special club to order. I was not a member of that club. I cheerfully stepped aside. This was a club in which age was less a factor than the antics of its members.

I stood on the porch and watched them for a minute, wondering what to do next, whether to intervene or just yell, "Stop!" The two of them were speeding around like two planets in orbit. I was fixed on the circular pattern they were making, round and round past me and through the kitchen, out the far door and back around past me again.

"Hi," I said. But they ignored me.

Dad had his hat on and his khaki jacket, which he wore no matter the weather or the occasion, and he leaned on his wheeled walker and scooted by, back through the kitchen. My daughter caught up with him and held on to him, pushing and cheering, dangerously so.

"Dad, when did you get up?"

"I don't know," he shouted over his shoulder.

"What are you two doing?"

"Playing," said Little Sunshine.

"Where's my martini?" Dad said. It was obvious they were not only different planets, they were on different orbits altogether. They'd passed through the kitchen and they were coming back around, and now I could see his face, and it wasn't good. He was plainly tired, but he didn't stop. He was in pursuit, and he wasn't getting anywhere.

"Stop!"

They both came to a halt and looked at me, startled. I guess I yelled, but I was alarmed to see Dad cutting this manic path, and my daughter racing behind him. Little Sunshine peeled off and ran to her bedroom, obviously bored with the play. She'd stirred up enough for one afternoon.

"How was it at the center? Did you get the posters finished?" I yelled after her. It seemed I was doing a lot of yelling lately.

Dad was gone again, scooting back through the kitchen, due to make the turn past the breakfast table, cutting close to the piano and coming up to face me where I still stood in the doorway to the porch.

"Dad! Stop! Go on over to the rocker."

Nothing. He kept going, now hunched over the walker

281

and gripping the sidebars with white knuckles. He didn't seem to hear me at all. He was on automatic.

I tried again. "Dad, please, stop. The rocker. Go."

"Where?" He glanced at me as he wheeled past. He didn't even slow down.

"Where what? Where's your rocker?" I tried to "cue" him, in the language of the therapists. But it didn't make any impression.

"Yes, I know it's here. I'm going. Go, go, go." But he didn't go to the rocker. He kept going toward the kitchen.

My patience was gone. I'd make him remember where his rocker was, and I'd will him to calm down.

"Dad, come on. Stop now, and go sit down." I came closer to him, hands on my hips.

"Hi, my little sweetie," he said, as if he'd just realized I was standing there. He had some eighty pounds on me, and I couldn't force him into the rocker, nor was that a very good idea. My face grew hot with annoyance and frustration. I didn't feel like little sweetie; I felt like the Daughter from Hell.

"Go sit down. Now." He stopped then and looked at me. His face crumpled like paper, and he started to shake with dry sobs.

"Oh, Dad." My hands rested on the front of his walker and I looked into his blue eyes, trying to find him in there. My daughter had given him a wintergreen Life Saver, his favorite. His breath smelled like the leafy-green jelly candies he bought for us when we were kids, and now he stared at me like he was lost.

"Dad, go sit in your rocker and I'll get you some ice water."

He loved ice water and breaking up ice cubes with his remarkable chompers, which was not a good thing, but it was better than downing Absolut. He preferred the ice with vodka and some "fresh squoze" orange juice. This was his

Sunday brunch treat, and every day, he asked me if it was Sunday, because sometimes the week had more than one Sunday in it.

"I don't want any water. I want a martini."

"Dad, it isn't time yet. Tom Brokaw isn't on until 6:30." Tom lifted Dad's social barometer, and the news show never failed to get Dad out of bed from a nap or ground him to the schedule.

"Oh, all right. Then give me a cigarette." He wasn't going to get a cigarette, so this was the time I had to distract him. It was then I saw the large wet stain on his pants leg. He'd have to be changed, and Marilyn was gone for the day. I hated this part. But he had to be dry.

"Dad, first we have to go change. And then we're going to think about what day it is. I think it's Sunday." I gave him a little poke in the arm, and he chuckled.

He didn't say a word, but let me steer him toward his bathroom where we did this little dance. He stood with his back to me and dropped his trousers and the diaper he wore, and then I guided him into a fresh one. I shut out the humiliation with brisk movements and odd bits of encouragement.

"Grab the other side, Dad. That's it. Now let me tape you up." I peeled away the covering on the tape and wrapped him in the clean white diaper, one leg at a time, then got him into dry pants. He must have hated it, but he didn't say anything, which gave me the luxury of skipping around this bit of caretaking with little notice.

We both found the rocker together out on the patio in the sun, and I pretended it was Sunday. I gave him a screwdriver, mostly orange juice with a cap full of vodka floating on top. I settled for ice water and a breather. Felix and Billy were gone. The afternoon was waning, and for the moment, peace reigned.

34

EAT YOUR CHEEZ-ITS

I looked over at Dad, tentatively taking a sip of his "juice." I was trying to take care of him, make him comfortable and happy, while my girl was dancing around to her own tune and Tick was moving away into his own world. The kids were both getting older; they were supposed to grow up. I hoped that did not mean Tick had to grow away from me. But something else was happening. He didn't seem to be as happy and he'd become more secretive, especially with Erin's death. We'd always talked openly together when he was younger, and now we'd nearly stopped. I hardly noticed it until it was upon me, and that was not good.

We all took a step back with Erin's death. I was grateful that Tick stuck closer to home through that second winter of The Adventure, forging an even tighter bond with Dad. The two of them watched old World War II documentaries on PBS, and I caught Tick passing a Marlboro to Dad, secretively, like two old war buddies in a ditch. All right. I turned away. I had so much to nag about, I decided it best to pick my battles, those that I had a small chance of winning.

I don't know how the argument started, but it got full

blown before I knew it. It began with the beer bottles I found in the garbage can, and the yelling that ensued. I shouted, and he slammed things. Back-and-forth we went with accusations, criticism, and responsibility, and the consequences of drinking. I was right, and he was wrong, and we were going nowhere.

"I hate you! I hate Dad! I'm sick of listening to both of you. I'm getting out of here, and I never want to see either of you again!"

I stared at him—not really angry, not hurt, just bewildered and surprised. He hardly saw his dad, maybe once every month or so, although they did talk on the phone. A new feeling with ragged edges—like a huge tear in our universe—made me stop. I didn't answer him. What Tick said really didn't surprise me all that much, because I'd felt the outburst building for some time. The beer bottles had just brought all of it to a head.

Tick settled down on the side of his bed and looked up at me. He changed the subject, of course, because if we went on in that vein it clearly was a dead end.

"Be reasonable, Mom," he said. "Think how Dad feels, not having us around." He blamed his parents—me especially—for further wrenching the family apart. Of course, I didn't call this failure. I called it something else. It was The Adventure.

I didn't know what to say to him. So I said nothing. I stood there while he got up and took several loping steps back and forth across the kitchen, grabbing things, a glass, a can of Mountain Dew, a box of Cheez-its, all nestled in the fold of a long arm. A few ice cubes went sliding and clinking across the kitchen floor like spent bullets. Well, at least he was eating, I thought. All functions had not stopped.

In another second, he was out of the kitchen and slamming the door to his room, retreating, getting away from me. But I was not going to leave him, and the words he said stuck in my heart. I thought I was doing good, but if he felt that way, I had failed him somehow. Tick's world had been broken because his parents couldn't get along. How could I think the divorce would not matter so much to the kids, that it would just go away with time and that it was just between his father and me? It didn't go away, not only when it happened, but for years later, in ways I never thought would happen. Like a death the divorce was done, but it was always there with all of its consequences and considerations and what-ifs. I thought it was over, but it would never be over for the children; they were still living through it in ways different than how their parents coped, the old people who wanted to bury the bad and get on with the new. The Adventure.

In the midst of it, hanging over Tick, was Erin's death, and the bitterness and loss and reaction that came of it. Tick had a thing about the "marred fascism" of parenthood—a tidbit I overheard from my perch at the kitchen sink one afternoon. He was growing up and he wanted to call some of the shots; he didn't want choices taken away from him, and, of course, I didn't want that either. It was a point we could agree on.

I had to start somewhere and I would start now. Go slowly. Breathe. Deeply. And listen. I knew what I should do. I needed to make my emotions and mouth follow directions from my head. Put one foot in front of the other and start. Go to door. Knock. Talk.

"Tick, can I come in?"

"What."

"Tick?"

"COME IN."

He sat on the edge of the bed, and I could tell he'd been crying, but he kept his head down, hunching his broad shoulders. He looked all angles there, with his elbows crooked on his knees and his hands and feet too large. The Cheez-its and Mountain Dew were left untouched on the floor. How could someone so big look so vulnerable? How did he get so big so fast? Where was I when that happened? What have I been doing all this time?

I hesitated in the doorway.

"Well?" he said.

"Tick …"

"WHAT."

"Please."

"Whatever."

This was the way most of our conversations went. One-word sentences that reminded me with an ache of the last words I had with his Dad, one word at a time for fear we'd inflict worse than we'd already done.

I plopped down on a bar stool he used for practicing the guitar, and I looked at him. I was always rushing ahead. Now I would not do that anymore. My kids were teaching me how to act in this crazy circle I found myself running in, from parent to children to me.

"Are we going to have this conversation one word at a time?" I said, hardly speaking above a whisper.

"What's wrong with that?"

"Nothing, I guess. At least we're being careful, and we might not say too much at once, too much stuff that's bad that we can't take back."

He looked up at me then, and I saw a frustration I'd never seen before, or maybe, I didn't want to see it before. I think it was often there, but I had never seen it so clearly, the tension that hovered around his beautiful, green-hazel eyes. His pupils were dark and ferocious, his eyebrows like fractures. And now I looked, and I finally saw that look for what it was.

"It's awful. I know it is."

"You don't know," he said. His jaw angled sharply, and he set his teeth.

"You think you're the only person who's been sixteen? I was sixteen. Your father was sixteen. Millions of people have been, and are, sixteen! You're not alone, for God's sake." My voice was rising, and the more I tried to push it down, it boiled up. "You're not the only one!"

"Tell me about it."

And I did, starting with high school. Tick hated high school, and I did, too, because Dad made me go to the new Catholic school in North Hammond, instead of letting me go to the new public high school in town where all my buddies from eighth grade were going. Tick and I both understood that same feeling of disconnect at the time of our lives when every minute of every young day was the very end of the world.

Somehow the conversation landed on that morning I found his dad's car in the alley at four in the morning, that searing, ripping feeling of when I found him at that woman's house. I had screamed and railed, and Tick had heard all of it, including my rage following the call from Mrs. Minkie-wicz—about another tryst. That morning in the kitchen should have been a wake up call for me, but it wasn't. I let things spiral away, until Tick and I found ourselves at the edge of a discussion that was a long time coming. Tick, so young, had already gone through searing, ripping feelings of his own.

"What I said—it's you, it's Dad. It's Erin. I can't stand it."

"You're talking around it. What exactly is it?"

"All of it. It's just too … too confusing. It's just all of it."

"What? Like we're all just bouncing off walls, making a bunch of noise?"

"Something like that. I guess I feel like things are broken," he said.

And then I knew what he meant.

"Mom, we're not together. We're just a bunch of parts and we're not a family. Is this a family?"

"Yes, Tick, this is our family. And family can get weird sometimes."

Tick grinned then, and he laughed like a man. Yet, I saw the face of my young son when he was four years old and he danced on the piano bench, singing, all the words to "Memory" from *Cats*.

"I feel weird a lot," he said. "Really out of place and time."

"What do you mean?" Of course, I'd dragged him out of childhood to Florida. Who wouldn't be confused? He was always serious, putting Legos and toy ships together, playing the guitar and listening to music. He did all of these things with such concentration and intent, while the rest of the world went by.

"I mean, I've never felt young."

"Is that good, Tick? Or bad?"

"It's good," he said. "I look at the Gampers, and I see myself sometimes."

"And?"

"That's good, Ma. That's real good."

35

THE LONG DRIVE

The yellow Mustang wouldn't move out of the way. We were behind it in the ambulance, with the siren blaring, and it still wouldn't move. It stayed in front of us, weaving side-to-side, until I thought I'd scream.

The siren on top of the ambulance didn't seem very loud from inside, but it must have burned a hole in the eardrum of the driver in front of us. At least I hoped it did.

I would just ride out this nightmare, if I could. Actually, I had no choice. I would never wake up from it anyway, never forget the whole miserable day, and if I ever caught up with the driver of that yellow mustang, I would forgive myself for what I did to him. One beefy, hairy arm hung out the window and his fat head rose out of a blob of shoulders. I had murder in my heart. But the obstinate, pockmarked roof of the car ahead just stared back at me, as other cars parted the way and moved to the shoulder of the road.

"Can't you do something?" I shouted at the ambulance driver. I made a mental note to get the Mustang driver's license plate number, which I promptly forgot.

The young crew-cut driver next to me clenched his jaw

and looked over the wheel before glancing at me briefly. He was cool and appropriately calm, all the while he had a crazy person in the shotgun seat. But there was not a thing I could do, and I was beside myself, because I couldn't do anything to get rid of the jerk that lingered in our path to the hospital.

"All right now, ma'am," the driver said. "We'll be there, yes, we will. You just stay peaceful-like." It must have been part of the job training, and he was doing well. He had an immediate calming effect on me.

But it didn't last more than a second. I tried again, frantically. "Please. Can't you rev up this siren or something? Do you have a gun?"

He looked at me sideways. "Ma'am that will be puttin' more trouble on top of your troubles."

"I'm sorry. I know. Does this happen often?"

"Happens almost every day. World is full of jerks, except for the dead ones. Sorry, ma'am." He turned red then.

I stared forward, unthinking.

"Ma'am, I'm sorry about this, but there's not much we can do." He bounced the heel of his hand off the steering wheel for emphasis. "Never fails. But I'd sure like to get a-holt of one of these dopes. Just once. They'd need an ambulance they-selves."

"Why don't you honk?"

"Ma'am, he don't pay 'tention to the siren. How he gonna hear that horn? Or give a hoot?"

Someone was making sense. I wasn't. But the jerk in the yellow Mustang still didn't move.

The ambulance driver gripped the steering wheel and pushed the cab forward a few more feet, so that he nearly rode up on the rusted bumper of the Mustang. He raised his elbows slightly, and I had the feeling we were going to fly over the yellow hunk of junk in front of us.

The driver gritted his teeth. "Let's make up some time now."

But in that moment, I knew we didn't need time. Time was up.

I had the sick feeling it didn't matter anyway. We could have crawled to the hospital. My father was dead. I was sure of it, although they hadn't pronounced him dead. The words could not be said over him in his bedroom, while he was lying on the floor and the technicians worked over him. That was for the doctor to pronounce, and that meant the never-ending trip to the emergency room.

Marilyn had been part of the goodbye, and it was hard for her, although she'd had a lot of goodbyes in her time, she told me.

"Oh, Miss, it's hard sometimes, especially with ones like the Commando. But there aren't many of those; I should say, there aren't any." Hiring her had been one of the sterling decisions of my life. She made Dad laugh, and she made him comfortable. She knew her job, and she did it well and with a sense of humor.

She wasn't there at the end. But, many times, she had gone the extra mile. She had told me firmly, stating the obvious, "You need help, Miss." I knew that her administrator didn't approve of the extra days Marilyn worked. So I always wanted to make sure she didn't get into trouble. But that didn't stand in the way. I never saw her in action at the agency, but I imagined tiny Marilyn facing her boss, giving it all-hell.

"Oh, I'll do what I want," she said. "I'm too old not to."

I could only guess where she got her strength. She was one of those rare ones who has the built-in ability not to stop. Not to give up. She had wiry, blond hair and tobacco-stained teeth, and the most patience I'd seen since Mother Teresa. Marilyn continued to smoke, but she didn't smoke with the Commando anymore, not after the hospital episode. Instead, she went out on the dock and puffed away and then hurried back, her polyester jacket with blue bears rustling as she pumped her arms to return quickly to duty. Dad told Marilyn that her place would be "higher in the kingdom of heaven" for all her help.

"Well, I don't know about any high place in heaven," she said. "And frankly, I'd prefer a hillbilly heaven, don'cha know, if there ever is such a thing. Oh, just let me at that Billy Ray Cyrus."

I cringed at the thought. But there had to be a place in heaven for Marilyn. She certainly went through difficult times on earth, lugging around old people and cleaning up after them, all with a good dose of loving care. She was supposed to be giving me some time off, but I usually stuck around to make sure they came out all right in their travels from the bathroom, to the family room, and down for a movie. Marilyn had all the angles and holds and methods to maneuver Dad up and down, and around.

One morning, not long before he died, she said, "Oh, lookee, now the Commando is bobbing away again. He gets so tired, don't he? I believe it's about time for that nap."

"Marilyn, he just got up."

"I know. I know. It don't hurt to humor him. He sure likes that pillow."

The morning Dad died, he was sparkling clean, powdered and Old-Spiced, and freshly dressed up in new khakis. He was shining top-to-toe, and even his cheeks had a smooth pink glow about them. He carried his slouch hat with the pins from places he'd traveled and presidents he'd voted for (Republican). His hair was fluffy from his "head wash." When he came lurching out of his bedroom on the walker, he stopped for me to appreciate the spectacle, and he gave me a cheek to sniff and peck at. I loved the smell of Old Spice, and he knew it.

I fixed him a peanut butter-and-ham sandwich for breakfast. He had insisted. I reminded him that it was breakfast, and it was poached-egg day.

"What the hell. It's Saturday," I said.

I came to sit at the table with Dad in the sunny family room. All the windows were cranked out, letting in a perfect, early spring breeze. When he picked up the grilled sandwich, dripping with peanut butter, he told me again about his first date with his beautiful wife. I heard all about it, sitting at the table while he finished off the sandwich and glass of milk, afterward picking at a bowl of melon. I was planning to make sure Dad was clean and dry and wrapped into bed for his nap by 3:00 p.m.

Dad was still hunched over his plate. All of a sudden, he looked so tired. I figured it was the ordeal of showering and getting dressed, especially putting the dress socks over his swollen feet and into his slip-on boat shoes. He loved the idea that he wore deck shoes, although he hadn't commanded a deck in sixty years.

Dad was eighty-one and one week. When I looked at him, I was struck at how much he'd aged—and just recently, it seemed. The effects of his refreshing shower had begun to sag, the skin hanging on his cheeks, and lately he'd had an unusual grey pallor.

Leave it to my brother—not long before Dad died—to remind me that Dad was not looking well. It was around the holidays, and Jack made an appearance in a rented convertible.

"He doesn't look so hot," my brother said.

"I wonder how you'll look when you're eighty," I said. My brother had no concept of ever being eighty. Life was one long round of tennis.

As usual, the conversation took another unpleasant turn from there. We were in the kitchen, each of us leaning against our respective counters for support. He was wearing a cream, fine-cotton knit argyle with a V-neck.

"New Irish sweater? From Glin or Dingle or some other playground?" I said.

"Scotland," he said. His lip stuck out. He was too old for pouting.

He was drinking a glass of some French red wine he'd bought for fifty dollars at Island Liquors, which catered to the elite who didn't buy at Publix. I didn't drink it. Red wine gave me a headache. He said he wanted to talk. I fortified myself with a Publix pinot grigio and braced myself. It was no fun talking to any of them anymore.

"I want to see all the bills from Dad's charge accounts and other expenses," he said.

"Excuse me?"

"Yeah, you heard me." He had a sort of light, offhand tone in his voice, like he was ordering the janitor to sweep his office.

"I think we've had this conversation before."

"Well, we're having it again."

"And since when do I need to answer to you?"

"Since now, and I think I'm speaking for the other members of this family, as well."

"Really."

"Really."

"What is your point?"

"Well, I want to see what you're spending his money on. He has a pension, and credit cards. I want to know."

I looked around at the kitchen. What could he possibly be talking about? I'd bought a frying pan, some stainless steel flatware, and a bunch of linens to replace those Dad had burned a hole through, and wet the bed on every night. His diapers alone were approaching the weekly food ration.

I stood up straight and stared at him. I wanted him to look at me, but he was studying the tip of one of his Cole Haans.

"I think you are way out of line," I said.

"No, I am not. Where are those bills?" He looked toward the other room, as if to make off for every drawer in the house. I couldn't believe what I was hearing and seeing from this spoiled brat of a millionaire, who played tennis and swilled fine wine and wore expensive sweaters from all over the world, and who had been to see his father twice this year. All I could think was: I made you chocolate chip cookies and sent them to you at camp. I felt cold inside, although it was eighty-six degrees outside.

"He has one charge card. I closed all the rest, and you know that. I do not answer to you. I answer to Dad's accountant and his lawyer, and it is none of your business how I run this household."

I put my glass on the counter with an authoritative clink and left him standing there, along with his insults hanging in the air.

My brother had dutifully visited Dad for his birthday on March 24, making an appearance the day before and the day after, and then he'd disappeared to the Naples Country Club. He dropped in another holiday or two over the years, and I wondered how different it would have been had Dad stayed in the dollhouse up North.

But my brother was right about one thing. It was true Dad didn't look well. The doctor had made the prognosis that he would experience a sort of deterioration involving mini-strokes until a massive stroke ended his life, a condition that killed his mother. Dr. Parks said this as gently as possible when I asked about Dad's health.

"We don't know much. We're just looking at history and your father's records to make an assumption."

He also reminded me that Dad's condition was a genetic pre-disposition that affected alternating generations by gender, as he wagged a finger at me and told me to exercise and never take up smoking again. I gave my sisters the news, and they acted like it was my idea they'd all catch mini-strokes.

The doctor said to keep Dad comfortable and on a schedule of sorts, including the physical therapy that was hardly exercise at all. He moved around as little as possible. He mostly sat and cooed and ogled the pretty home health aide who bent over him for forty-five minutes every Tuesday and Thursday afternoon. She made him lift an arm at a time, or a leg, while she asked him a few questions, and he usually commented on her lipstick or hair-do. He missed his nap for her visits. Whereas, normally, he barely had the energy to stay awake an entire afternoon.

That last day, we headed toward the television for a brief look at the TCM channel before his nap. But he moved slowly, dragging his leg more than usual. He was barely able to stand upright.

"Are you OK there?" I asked, knowing how perfectly useless that question was.

"I have to lie down, oh, I'm so tired," he said.

Then, in the next instant, it happened. I held a plate in one hand and an empty glass in the other. I stood rooted to the tile floor as I watched my father slowly teeter sideways, like falling off a horse.

In fact, it was odd, that decades before I had seen him do just that—on a bright Sunday afternoon, fall off that big, black, shiny horse named Pat, without a scratch.

I moved quickly in front of him, trying to break his fall, and all I could think was that he would squash me. I didn't know where to grab him. I dropped the plate and it shattered as the walker rolled away toward the front door like it wanted to leave. Dad hit the upholstered arm of the couch and glanced off the corner of the TV table before coming to rest on his side. He cut himself on the tray table. A small squiggle of blood appear on his forehead.

"Oh, Oh, Oh."

It was the only sound after the thudding, the shattering. Somehow, I managed to hold onto him, and indeed, break his fall, or at least slow it down. I was no help at all, only adding to the confusion and the mess with broken glass all over the floor.

I righted him, and now he was almost dead weight. But somehow, I got him in the bedroom.

He was lying on his back in bed. I called 911. "Get over here now. Yes, it's an emergency … I think he's dying." I could barely speak, my voice shook so, as did the rest of me. I was cold all over. I focused on the phone in my hand. "What do I do?"

"Is he breathing?" the assistant asked.

"I don't know. Yes, I think so." His eyes were open but glazed, and more prominent than usual, almost as if the destruction going on in his head was reflected in his gaze. He made little puffing sounds, in and out through his lips, and I noticed some peanut butter in the corner of his mouth. He had not gotten sick, nor made a sound since telling me he was tired before the fall.

"Give him mouth-to-mouth resuscitation. Now, until we get there. We're on the way."

"But I don't know how." How stupid of me. I'd never taken a CPR course, and I had an elderly parent living with me for all that time. The thought of it annoyed me. I should know how to do this, but I didn't. And I was so afraid.

"I don't know what I'm doing," I said. "Will I hurt him?"

"No, you won't. There's no such thing as a bad effort. It's all good."

Then she told me to close off his nose and breathe in through his mouth in a regular pattern. She stayed on the phone while I tried it.

I pinched his nose shut. He had no cartilage left from his days as a boxer, and it was like touching a fold of tough skin. I couldn't remember ever touching his nose. I leaned closer and I could smell the peanut butter. His lips were dry and I breathed in slowly, then regularly. The puffing had stopped and I looked into his eyes. He didn't see me at all when I called to him.

Then he lifted his head and looked toward the corner of the room. He started talking.

"Dad, who's there? What are you saying?"

He tried to tell me, but it was useless. He stared across the room, talking, talking, talking, like it was the most normal day of his life, like he had something to say, so deliberately, and he wouldn't lie back until he said it, whatever it was. I couldn't understand a word. Then he fell back on his pillow. His eyes were still open, seeing only what he could see, and his breathing was so shallow I could hardly sense it.

I heard the truck, and then the metallic sound of doors slamming and men talking and yelling to hurry. Two technicians appeared in the bedroom with a stretcher. They dropped it to the floor and loaded Dad on to it in one sweep.

They stretched him out on the bedroom floor to work him over. I finally had to ask the question I was dreading. "Is he gone?"

The technician was soft spoken, courteous, young, but so knowing for that age, as he handled the gear and pointed the way to get moving. "It's not for us to say, ma'am," he said. "We'll meet the doctor in the emergency."

They did things I never thought to do. They loosened his shirt and his belt, and checked his mouth for obstruction, and took off his shoes. They tried to resuscitate him with paddles. And I didn't have the presence of mind to tell them Dad had a DNR—Do Not Resuscitate—order in his medical records. All I could think about, all I could fear, was that he was already dead.

He'd met someone in the corner of that room, someone standing in the sunshine, who helped him along. I hoped it was like that. He had to be with them.

I didn't care what these medical people said, because they

didn't know him and what my dad, the strongest man in the world, was capable of. But it didn't seem he was with me anymore. I didn't want to believe it, watching them load Dad into the back of the ambulance, chasing after them out the door, jumping into the front seat.

Dad rode in the back of the ambulance, and I turned to look at him, clutching his toes in a grip, talking to him. But there was no response. His eyes were closed, and I didn't know if he had closed them, or they had been closed for him. And what did it matter? His eyes were closed.

They seemed to know that they couldn't do anything further. He didn't have an IV, like they do in the movies. It was clear to me that he wasn't breathing anymore. Somewhere along the way, he had stopped doing the most automatic thing we do to stay on this earth. I never knew the exact second he stopped, but I know he had last words to say to someone standing in the corner of the bedroom. I had looked over that way, and I saw nothing. But he did.

I didn't want to admit he was gone. I was beyond crying and in another zone that made me numb. I wanted to go back, re-trace and figure out how I'd gotten to this place. But there was no going back, only forward.

Conditions were clear as we sped along the road on the way to the hospital. The driver glanced in the rear view mirror, but he kept a steady pace behind the yellow Mustang in front of us. It was a thirty-minute drive, and after frantically venting myself on the driver to make some magic and get us there, I slumped down in my seat, tired and sick at heart. I'd known this would come one day, but there was no way to prepare for it. I had no idea loss could feel so bottomless.

I looked behind me into the back of the ambulance. The cover was pulled up to his chin, and I could see his face. I watched for a faint hint of life in him. I couldn't see anything.

I swung around to the road again, and the rusty car the color of bile was still in front, even while the ambulance driver inched forward and then back, pressing the Mustang to move over. And then with a cocky swerve, the driver in front of us dropped sideways into the right lane. I looked down into the driver's seat and saw a young man with a fat, leering face. A cigarette dangled from his lips. He righted himself in the lane and craned up at me, and as the ambulance lunged for the open road, the freak in the Mustang rolled his window down and shot us the middle finger.

"Well, at least we know what we're dealing with," said the ambulance driver. "In this business, it's always best to know what you're dealing with—here, we have it, a perfect A-number-one asshole."

I gave him a half-smile.

He grinned. "Sorry, ma'am."

"I hear you," I said.

When they wheeled Dad into the emergency room, the doctor was waiting there—the first time I'd ever seen a doctor waiting for him! And he was dead, so he couldn't appreciate it. So I appreciated it for both of us.

But, this time, the doctor hardly looked at him. The medics, the notes, the summary, I guessed, had filled him in. It was just a matter of signing the papers.

"How did he die?" The strange sound of my words seemed to come from another place, from within the tile walls and stainless-steel fixtures and shelving, bouncing off the cold, hard surface of the place where my father lay dead.

"Your father most likely had a stroke," the doctor said. "A massive one before he even fell."

"How do you know that? Are you sure?"

"Nothing is sure. You say he fell?"

"Yes, he sort of drifted off to his side, and just fell sideways."

"That's good," he said. "What I mean is, that it was very fast."

"All I remember is the strange breathing—like little desperate puffs—and his eyes. They weren't his eyes any more."

"Yes, you are right. Everything is in the eyes."

"But, I don't think he could see anything anymore. He was in another world."

"Yes, he was." Our sentences dissolved into smaller and smaller pieces that hung in the air, but I didn't want to let go.

Fortunately, the doctor was a good one.

"We'll leave you now, to have a moment ..."

I stood next to Dad in the middle of an open section of the emergency room in the hospital. Not a soul was there, except Dad and I, our last meeting in this cold place. All I could think was how he hated to be cold. But he was cold, and his face, when I touched it, had no resiliency and warmth, no one-liners and jokes, no more crinkles around those pale blue eyes.

He'd made it into spring, and he didn't see 9/11 and the horrors that followed. If he had, that would have killed him alone. If I'd done an inventory, I could have said there were some reasons that Dad was at peace.

I lingered over him, tucking the sheet around his chin and stroking his white hair that was still unruly, untamed, no matter how much I smoothed it and combed it with my fingers. Some things do not change. It was a strange hour on a late Friday afternoon, before the overdoses, abuses, and accidents rolled in. No one was there that day, except for us. Dad was at peace. I touched his forehead, wishing for the old warmth to come back, but it was gone. I said goodbye, in an instant that will live forever in my head until the day I die.

36

THE STRONGEST MAN
IN THE WORLD

I went back to the house a couple of years after I sold it. I drove past it slowly, down to the cul-de-sac and back again. The day was hot and silent except for the invisible doves and crackling palms and distant tumble of waves. I rolled down the window and the heavy island air whooshed in and hit me with all its usual mighty force. I slowed the car almost to a stop to look at the house, to will back a good memory or two, and mixed feelings rushed over me. When I looked back on it all, it was hard. Would I do it again? Not the same way. But I would do it. The only problem was that there would be no second chance. We had to go with what we were handed.

The new owners of the house made the best of it. The stucco had been white from its roof to the ground; now it was a deep buttery yellow and the barrel tile roof was painted brick red. My bright red French door was just as I'd left it. A tiny American flag was draped on a grapevine wreath at the door. Dad would have liked that—a touch I never thought of. The loud greetings and laughter, going in and out of that door, were only memories but I could hear them, drowning out the slamming and sneaking about and the escape, as Dad had done, scaring the daylights out of me.

I drove on slowly. The holly that lined the driveway had grown up, round and bushy, and the silver palm by the door was a huge sphere of waving fronds. The white stone yard was completely free of the weeds I'd chased and sprayed relentlessly, and, of course, the glass chunks of unmade bluebirds of happiness were long gone. Someone living there must be happy, I thought, people who cared about the house, and I was glad for that. It was a sad sight, and happy at the same time, because The Adventure of our lives had taken us up and down so many times.

Tick went to the University of Illinois–Chicago. He said he wanted to become an international lawyer, and in the meantime, he was playing lead guitar and singing in two bands, or solo, all over the city. My daughter was president of the National Honor Society, a cheerleader, and a juggler of meetings, parties, and life in high school. Then she went to New York for a couple of years to Fordham University, finally studying medical technology near Chicago. She's going to be a nurse and take care of me when I'm old, she said. "Whenever that is, and not anytime soon. Then I'll braid your hair every day."

How I admire those two for all they've done, and are doing.

Me, I became an English teacher, thanks to Aunt Marian and to finally getting off my duff. It worked out well. And I made a sort of truce with my brother the tennis whiz, my sister the restaurateur/saleswoman extraordinaire, and my sister the nurse. None of them apologized for the hurtful accusations and the backbiting; I haven't, either. But we are talking, civilly, infrequently—but at least civilly—remembering that we are still a family, however fractured it has become.

I drove away from the house, remembering the time I'd raced down the street toward Dad. He had turned the driving over to me. I was sad, yes, and foggy in a flood of remembering all of it. And, no, I wasn't sorry. It was The Adventure. I kept driving. I was free. The street looked the same, and Dad was in heaven with Mom, and all was right with the world, inside and out, I thought, slowly accelerating the last Cadillac and driving away.

Tick, on Then, Now, and Ever After

As the surviving male family member of our Anna Maria Island branch, I just want to say one last thing. It was a great time. And it was weird. I'm in college now, after getting kicked out of two high schools. Mom doesn't like to remember it exactly that way, but that's the way it was. I hated high school, and so we parted ways, twice.

My sister is a woman, and I can't believe that, and my mom is happy now, I think. She wasn't for a long time, with every-thing happening so fast. Nothing ever stayed the same for her ,or for us, and I regretted that, while at the same time liking it. I guess that's life. In the end, there was nothing and no one my mom could really count on, not even me and my sister, or the Gampers, for that matter, but I know we all tried. We had to because we're a family. We lost a lot, but in the end we gained a lot, too.

I lost Erin. Everybody lost Erin, but no one lost her the way I did. Every person means something special to each and every single person differently. Erin was like an angel to me. She looked me right in the eye and listened to me, and I listened to every word she ever said. I felt lonely that first day of school, walking through those halls with 2,000 students, not knowing anyone, except Erin. Tall, blond, soft, beautiful Erin. Heaven is lucky. It has Erin.

Everything changed after Erin's death, and it was so stupid, the way she died. Jared walked away from the accident, and they tried to make him go to the hospital for a checkup, but you can't fix what happened to Jared. I don't blame him, really. He's just a knucklehead, born and raised up one, like most of us. He just had a bad run of luck, and Gampers always said, you make your own luck. After Erin died, she made Jared get off the beer and pot and shit. I know she did, because he's a straight dude now. At least that's one good thing that came of losing Erin, although there really isn't anything good in it. It's hard for me to say.

Erin's ashes are scattered in the water. I always thought sunsets were the bomb, but now when I look at them, I see Erin, in all the colors and in the clouds flying over the Gulf, or the lake. Crazy. In the end, I guess that's OK. I know Erin would be cool with it, even about her ashes and all. Erin's mom is an island mom, like my mom, real different, kind of passionate and stubborn about some things. They both do what they think is right, and it turns out all right. You have to do what you think is right, even if you doubt yourself. You just have to, and then maybe adjust the situation.

Gampers would say that. He's gone, and I miss him so much. I think about him all the time. He'd agree, and stand by me, like he did my mom and my sister.

My teacher asked us to write about our proudest moment. I didn't have to think about that one for very long. I wrote about the day my grandfather fell down, and I picked him up by myself, and he was all right, not hurt at all, and he thanked me. "You're a strong, strong lad," he said. "A good man." I guess something happened to me the minute he said that. I could have lifted him up to the roof.

I've had some crazy friends, and some awful good ones, too, but, in the end, he is probably the best one I ever had. We talked for hours sometimes. He didn't remember later all of what we talked about. I could tell because I had to remind him a lot, and I sort of quizzed him without getting him mad at me. Maybe he didn't remember right then, but I remember. I'll always remember, and I'll tell my kid one day, about their great grandfather, the strongest man in the world.

~ THE END ~

ACKNOWLEDGEMENTS

My family gave me inspiration—and perspiration—in the making of this story. A family has a way of doing that. A little laughing, some crying, and a whole lot of growing up, apart, and back together again. Whew! That's good.

Thanks to Donald Nicholas "Mike" Nau and Patricia McLoughlin Nau, my parents, for their endless sense of adventure and bottomless love.

And to my sibs—I have three brothers and three sisters; however, only three of them were involved in the personal drama of *The Last Cadillac*. In addition—full disclosure—I have five children. Only the two younger ones made the move to Florida with me and Dad. I thank all of them for their humor, kindness, and intelligence.

I was blessed to have Frances Ella Pike McLoughlin Nau Sullivan and Miles Henry Sullivan along for The Adventure. They made The Adventure, and they taught me a thing or two about the resilience, strength, and love of children, as did their older brothers, James Patrick, Donald Nicholas "Mick," and Amos Wiley. Thank you to their dad for his love and care of all of them.

Thanks to Charles J. Nau, for the typewriter, and his support, love, and suggestions, and to Catherine Adams, who read the story and had so many good ideas to improve the manuscript. To Mary Ann Johnson, David Armand, Karol Jackowski, and Kris Mauk—more than words can say—Thank you! And to Jennifer Whaley and Jeff Everett, for their polished technical expertise, humor, and for lending a hand when their hands were full.

And, thank you, especially, to Donna Essner, Kristina Blank Makansi, and Lisa Miller of Amphorae Publishing Group for their prodigious talent, warm acceptance, wise words and choices, and support.

ABOUT THE AUTHOR

NANCY NAU SULLIVAN has worked as a newspaper journalist, teacher, and most recently, as a university English Specialist in the Peace Corps in Mexico. She has taught English in Chicago, Argentina, and at a boys' prison in Florida. In her later years, she earned her master's degree in journalism from Marquette University. Her stories have appeared in *Akashic Books*, *The Blotter*, *The Atherton Review*, and *skirt!magazine*. Her story, "Once I Had a Bunch of Thyme," won honors at the Carnegie Center in Lexington, KY. *The Last Cadillac* is her first book.

CPSIA information can be obtained at www.ICGtesting.com
Printed in the USA
LVOW07s0200240316

480415LV00003B/4/P